Educating Entrepreneurial Citizens

Educating Entrepreneurial Citizens examines the multiple and contradictory purposes and effects of entrepreneurship education aimed at addressing youth unemployment and alleviating poverty in Tanzania.

Governments in sub-Saharan Africa face increasing pressure to educate young people through secondary school, supposedly equipping them with knowledge and skills for employment and their future. At the same time, many youths do not complete their education and there are insufficient jobs to employ graduates. The development community sees entrepreneurship education as one viable solution to the double edged problem of inadequate education and few jobs. But while entrepreneurship education is aligned with a governing rationality of neoliberalism that requires individuals to create their own livelihoods without government social supports, the two NGO programs discussed in this book draw on a rights-based discourse that seeks to educate those not served by government schools, providing them with educational and social supports to be included in society. The chapters explore the tensions that occur when international organizations and NGOs draw on both neoliberal and liberal human rights discourses to address the problems of poverty, unemployment and poor quality education. Furthermore, when these neo/liberal perspectives meet local ideas of reciprocity and solidarity, they create friction and alter the programs and effects they have on youth.

The book introduces the concept of *entrepreneurial citizens*—those who utilize their innovative skills and behaviors to claim both economic and social rights from which they had been previously excluded. The programs taught youths how to develop their own enterprises, to earn profits, and to save for their own futures; but youths used their education, skills and labor to provide for basic needs, to be included in society, and to support their and their families' well-being. By showing the contradictory effects of entrepreneurship education programs, the book asks international agencies and governments to consider how they can go beyond technical approaches of creating enterprises and increasing income, and head toward approaches that consider the kinds of labor that young people and communities value for their wellbeing.

This book will be of interest to scholars and practitioners of education and international development, youth studies, African Studies and entrepreneurship/social entrepreneurship education.

Joan G. DeJaeghere is Associate Professor of Comparative and International Development Education at the University of Minnesota, USA.

Education, Poverty and International Development series
Series Editors
Madeleine Arnot and Christopher Colclough
Centre for Education and International Development,
University of Cambridge, UK

Published titles

Education Quality and Social Justice in the Global South
Challenges for Policy, Practice and Research
Edited by Leon Tikly and Angeline Barrett

Learner-centred Education in International Perspective
Whose Pedagogy for Whose Development?
Michele Schweisfurth

Professional Education, Capabilities and the Public Good
The Role of Universities in Promoting Human Development
Melanie Walker and Monica McLean

Livelihoods and Learning
Education For All and the Marginalisation of Mobile Pastoralists
Caroline Dyer

Gender Violence in Poverty Contexts
The Educational Challenge
Edited by Jenny Parkes

The 'Poor Child'
The Cultural Politics of Education, Development and Childhood
Edited by Lucy Hopkins and Arathi Sriprakash

Educating Entrepreneurial Citizens
Neoliberalism and Youth Livelihoods in Tanzania
Joan DeJaeghere

Forthcoming titles

Gender, Education and Poverty
The Politics of Policy Implementation
Edited by Elaine Unterhalter, Jenni Karlsson and Amy North

Educating Entrepreneurial Citizens

Neoliberalism and Youth Livelihoods in Tanzania

Joan G. DeJaeghere

LONDON AND NEW YORK

First published 2017
by Routledge
2 Park Square, Milton Park, Abingdon, Oxon OX14 4RN

and by Routledge
711 Third Avenue, New York, NY 10017

Routledge is an imprint of the Taylor & Francis Group, an informa business

© 2017 Joan G. DeJaeghere

The right of Joan G. DeJaeghere to be identified as author of this work has been asserted by her in accordance with sections 77 and 78 of the Copyright, Designs and Patents Act 1988.

All rights reserved. No part of this book may be reprinted or reproduced or utilised in any form or by any electronic, mechanical, or other means, now known or hereafter invented, including photocopying and recording, or in any information storage or retrieval system, without permission in writing from the publishers.

Trademark notice: Product or corporate names may be trademarks or registered trademarks, and are used only for identification and explanation without intent to infringe.

British Library Cataloguing in Publication Data
A catalogue record for this book is available from the British Library

Library of Congress Cataloging in Publication Data
A catalog record for this book has been requested

ISBN: 978-1-138-69126-1 (hbk)
ISBN: 978-1-315-53561-6 (ebk)

Typeset in Galliard
by Cenveo Publisher Services

Contents

List of figures		vi
List of tables		vii
Acknowledgements		viii
Acronyms		xi
1	Introduction	1
2	Neo/liberal Governmentality and Citizen Subjectivities	23
3	Approaches to Entrepreneurship Education	41
4	Researching the Tanzanian experience	56
5	Governing Regimes in Tanzania	74
6	Educating for Self-sufficiency: Schools, Markets, and Social Good	92
7	Becoming Entrepreneurial Citizens: Economic Development and Social Relations	113
8	Educating Youths as Financially Responsible and Inclusive Citizens	134
9	Conclusions: Reframing Entrepreneurship Education	153
	Appendix: Selected Economic, Education, and Youth Policies 1961–2015	166
	Index	169

List of figures

2.1 Liberal and neoliberal discourses shaping citizen subjectivities   37
5.1 Youth informal employment rates by sex and area of residence   85

List of tables

4.1	Demographics of *Parka* survey participants in formal and VETA schools	67
4.2	Demographics of *Apprentice* survey participants	67
4.3	Demographics of *Parka* interview participants	68
4.4	Demographics of *Apprentice* interview participants	68
5.1	Students completing Standard 6/7 and continuing to secondary school – Mainland Tanzania, 1962-2012, by number and percentage for government and non-government schools	78
5.2	Pass rates for Form 4 exam (end of Ordinary Level), 2000–2012	84
7.1	Difference between participants' views and non-participants' views on their employability knowledge, skills and relationships, by female and male	123
7.2	Change in values that women and men hold, percentage before and after program	128
8.1	Difference between participants' views and non-participants' views on their financial knowledge and skills, by female and male	142
8.2	Use of different forms of savings, % of women and men, 2014 and 2015	146
8.3	Uses of earnings, % of women and men, 2014 and 2015	148

Acknowledgements

This book and the larger project would not have been possible without the dedicated involvement of many non-governmental organization (NGO) staff, whom I wish to thank personally but who need to remain anonymous. These NGO staff and the work they do have my deepest respect. They engaged in many interviews and discussions over five years with such dedication to their work and a commitment to learn from it and improve upon it. The young women and men who were a part of this study are the real inspiration for this work, and for many other young people in their communities, as they showed us why entrepreneurship education and training is important, and also how it served many multiple goals that they had for themselves. Conversations with local community members were also invaluable for us to understand the effects of entrepreneurship education and training in the community. I have learned so much about hope, daily struggles, self-reliance, reciprocity, and solidarity, and how the human, social and economic dimensions of development matter. *Asanteni sana*!

To my colleagues, David Chapman, who co-led this project with me and has taught me so much over the years about research and development that matter in people's lives; Nancy Pellowski Wiger, whose sure hand at managing all details of the larger evaluation project with concern and respect were exceptional; and to Frances Vavrus, whose vast knowledge of and experience in Tanzania were a guiding light for this book, and whose professional mentoring was steadfast throughout this project. I am so appreciative. My gratitude also extends to my colleagues Chris Johnstone and Heidi Eschenbacher who have worked alongside me on the larger evaluation project, bringing insights and support at all the right moments.

I am also grateful to the more than 60 graduate students who were involved in the three-country project, and particularly those who have been involved in data collection and analysis for the evaluation in Tanzania: Kristeen Chachage, Amina Jafaar, Laura Willemsen, Masanche Nelson Nkhoma, Brooke Krause, Elly Arganbright, Tamara Weiss, Kari Foley, Tatyana Venegas Swanson, Himabindu Timiri, Hanife Cakici, Emily Morris, Aryn Baxter, Anne Campbell, Ian Allen, Bior Keech, Jill Manske, Hui Bi, Chris Swanson, Humberto Guerrero, Rachel Herr-Hoyman, and Beth Lefebvre. My gratitude also extends to Amy Pekol,

Himabindu Timiri and Jenny Ernie-Steighner who provided invaluable research and analysis at different times throughout this project. And this book has particularly benefited from the valuable insights and critical eye of Emily Morris. I have learned so much from all these insights and contributions. Thank you.

The Tanzanian colleagues and researchers, some who remain anonymous here though no less appreciated, were exceptional to work with and enriched my understanding of these youths' lives. I am grateful for their expertise, commitment and care. Asanteni sana Elly J. Ligate, Laina John, Matthew Laizer, Damas Msaki, Jacqueline Ndyosi, Zawadi Kitemangu, Lilian Nsyenge, Amani Kisiza, Judith Merinyo, Mary Mwinuka, Elly Sarakikya, Wambuka Rangi, David Msola, Neema Nicodemus, Matrona Mwanja, Kalisto Lugome, Faraja Mbuduka, Andreas Mahali, Stela Kiyabo, Delta Shila, Catherine Mangare, Rosemary Maduki, and Rose Edwin.

I am most appreciative of financial support for this project, including The MasterCard Foundation that supported the data collection and our field visits with the NGOs. I greatly appreciate working with their staff; we have learned so much together. The views and opinions expressed herein are mine, and do not necessarily reflect the position or policy of The MasterCard Foundation or its partners. The University of Minnesota provided me with valuable funding and time, at just the right moments; a leave and a Fulbright fellowship in 2012–13 allowed me to begin conceptualizing this book, and subsequent funding from the College of Education and Human Development, and a sabbatical provided the time to harness the corpus of data and complete it. Thank you also to my colleague, Rebecca Ropers-Huilman who supported me personally and professionally.

Many others have provided invaluable intellectual conversations, professional mentoring and friendship over the years. To those with whom I've had many discussions about a capability approach, education and development in Africa: Leon Tikly, Melanie Walker, Elaine Unterhalter, Shirley Miske, and Erin Murphy Graham – thank you for all the generosity and insights over the years. And to other colleagues – Lesley Bartlett, Nancy Kendall and Peter Demerath – who have engaged with me about neoliberalism, governmentality, and anthropology of development, I have learned so much through our discussions. My colleagues, particularly Deborah Levinson, MJ Maynes, Frances Vavrus, Roozbeh Shirazi, Anne Meyers, and Ragui Assad, among others from the Youth as Subjects, Objects and Agents (YaSOA) research group have provided a valuable space for discussing ideas and helpful feedback on prior versions of this work. There are many others whose work in development or anthropology inspired me and whose theoretical ideas and captivating writing have informed the pages within, and whom I hope to learn from in the future: Aradhana Sharma, Daniel Mains, Anna Tsing, James Ferguson and Andrea Muehlebach.

Much appreciation goes to my longtime friends, Anne, Andrea, Lisa and Joy, whose writing and linguistic abilities have long been an inspiration and support; and a particular thanks to Becky Sun, whose keen sense of language is seen throughout this book.

Previous versions of several chapters were presented at Comparative and International Education Society (CIES) conferences and other lectures, and I have greatly benefited from the feedback of these participants. In particular I would like to thank the organizers and the participants of the CIES Citizenship and Democratic Education Special Interest Group (SIG) workshop (2016); one participant suggested Andrea Muehlebach's book at a late moment in this writing, and it was invaluable. Thank you.

Finally, I am grateful to the editors of this series, Madeleine Arnot and Christopher Colclough for considering this monograph in this series, and for all their scholarly input throughout the writing process. Thanks also to anonymous reviewers.

This book is also the product of much support, care and love from my husband, Gregor Adriany, and our two children, Noah and Dominik. They provided me with space to write, questions that clarified my thinking, and laughter along the way. I am appreciative of the support on this journey from my parents, Joe and Lorraine, and my siblings. They have often inquired about all my visits to Tanzania, and they can now see the fruit of my time there. While my children and family may not understand what governmentality is, they do appreciate how governments, communities, and friends support their hope for a better livelihood and meaningful life.

While much valuable input, resources and ideas for this project have been provided by so many, the errors are solely my own.

Acronyms

BEST	Basic Education Statistics in Tanzania
CIES	Comparative International Education Society
CRC	Convention for the Rights of the Child
DFID	Department for International Development
EFA	Education for All
EQUIP3	Educational Quality Improvement Program3
ESR	Education for Self-Reliance
ESS	Economically Self-Sufficient
FSP	Financial service provider
GDP	Gross Domestic Product
IEA	International Association for the Evaluation of Educational Achievement
ILO	International Labour Organization
IMF	International Monetary Fund
MDG	Millennium Development Goal(s)
MFI	Microfinance Institution
MoEVT	Ministry of Education and Vocational Training, Mainland
NBS	National Bureau of Statistics
NEEC	National Economic Empowerment Council
NEET	Not in Education, Employment or Training
NETF	National Entrepreneurship Training Framework
NGO	Non-governmental organization
NMB	National Microfinance Bank
NSGRP	National Strategy for Growth and Reduction of Poverty
SACCO	Savings and credit cooperatives
SAP	Structural Adjustment Program
SDG	Sustainable Development Goal(s)
SIG	Special Interest Group
SME	Small and Medium Enterprise
UN	United Nations
UNESCO	United Nations Education, Scientific, Education, and Cultural Organization

UNFPA	United Nations Population Fund
UNICEF	United Nations Children's Fund
URT	United Republic of Tanzania
USAID	United States Agency for International Development
VETA	Vocational Education and Training Authority
VSLA	Village Savings and Loan Associations
YaSOA	Youth as Subjects, Objects and Agent

Chapter 1

Introduction

> This school is very good because it saved me from a bad and vulnerable environment [and put me] into a good kind of environment. ... I'm so grateful because I had dropped out of school and lost all hope of coming back. ... But now I think I'm approaching my goals.
> – Upendo, 18 years old, 2012[1]

I first met young Tanzanian women like Upendo in 2011.[2] They were excited and nervous about returning to secondary school, as it held the promise of 'becoming an educated person' (Levinson et al., 1996). When they finished primary school, they stayed home and helped with the family *duka* (small business) or *shamba* (subsistence farm), or watched their younger siblings. Most did not imagine that they would ever have the opportunity to pursue a secondary education; they had received messages from their primary school teachers that they were not 'smart enough'. Or, their parents were not able to pay fees for a private school if their primary exam scores were too low to continue in government schools. What does it mean to be considered educated in Tanzania? Usually, having an education means completing O-levels (lower secondary) and passing enough of the exams for mathematics, biology, geography, English, physics, civics education, and Swahili to get the certificate. But if Upendo does not get her O-level certificate, what kind of educated person is she? How would she achieve her imagined future and what kind of livelihood would she have?

The secondary school that Upendo was attending was implementing a nongovernmental organization (NGO) program that was different from most secondary and vocational schools in Tanzania. The NGO program integrated entrepreneurship education into formal secondary and vocational school curriculum and extracurricular activities, including additional content and pedagogy of entrepreneurship, financial education, and business skills. The entrepreneurship curriculum and pedagogy were intricately linked with business development on the school campus. To support the school budget, the school administration and teachers developed full-scale school enterprises run by teachers and the students. There were also microenterprises that students developed to learn how to manage, sell, and calculate profit and loss. For the larger scale enterprises, administrators worked with the NGO, *Parka* (a pseudonym),[3] to develop a business plan that would help the school become self-sufficient one day. They conducted a market analysis to determine which businesses were most relevant for the area and which ones the school could operate successfully. The staff was responsible for tracking all the expenses, income, and profits of campus-based businesses. These school-wide and microenterprises served two purposes: to raise money for the school to become self-reliant and to give students practical experience in entrepreneurship.

I was skeptical of integrating entrepreneurship education into formal schooling. I wondered how families and the community would perceive secondary education that focused on business and entrepreneurial skills. Tanzania's formal school system, which evolved under British colonialism and persists today in many ways, prepares students for higher education and the formal labor market; working in agriculture and some vocational fields were not as valued and did not require a secondary school certificate. While Julius Nyerere's policy of Education for Self-Reliance (ESR) tried to change this long-held attitude, neither the labor market nor state policies prioritized vocational education, or entrepreneurship. Learning to be self-employed is not the goal of most young people or their parents for attending formal education. In addition, having young people run microenterprises is often perceived as begging, especially if they are selling on the street or in a market (Tripp, 1997). Yet the reality is that family-based microenterprises are not only common in Tanzania, but they are necessary. Without this primary or secondary source of income, many families would not be able to pay school fees, health care costs, and other expenses. I was concerned that young Tanzanians' hopes of being 'educated', which traditionally meant passing O-level exams and heading toward other educational opportunities, would be detoured by a path of entrepreneurship and business education. They would have more opportunities than if they had not had any post-primary education, but this alternate trajectory might leave them undervalued in their communities – disillusioned and struggling for their future.

In a different context in northwestern Tanzania, another international NGO, *Apprentice*, (a pseudonym) implemented a vocational and apprenticeship program that taught entrepreneurship and self-employment for young men and women who had not completed secondary school. This program includes short-term (nine months) non-formal training where the young women and men learn specific trades, and business, financial and life skills. In this case, I was concerned that while the youths would learn a specific set of skills, they would have limited opportunities to use them because of other constraints they might face, even if their skills were aligned with local market needs. In addition, I worried that if the labor and consumer markets could not support their livelihoods, these young Tanzanians would not have the literacy or numeracy skills to pursue post-secondary vocational training.

These two NGO programs are different in several ways. *Parka* takes place in formal secondary and vocational schools; thus, their curriculum, testing, and certification are aligned and regulated by the Ministry of Education and Vocational Training (MoEVT), as well as the Vocational Education and Training Authority (VETA). *Apprentice* is a non-formal training program, aligned with the national vocational/technical curriculum but not under government auspices. However, they share some common educational practices, including coursework on entrepreneurship and financial education, and a common goal: fostering entrepreneurial skills and a mindset that enables self-employment. Additionally, they are funded by the same international foundation interested in addressing youth unemployment through comprehensive livelihood and entrepreneurship education and training.[4]

I was also intrigued by a seemingly dual purpose of these NGO projects that aim, on the one hand, to offer education and training for those who are out of school, not participating in the labor market, and have few other material or social supports. In this sense, the two NGOs draw on a rights-based discourse of Education for All (EFA) in order to ensure inclusion in society and to reduce poverty and its effects. On the other hand, entrepreneurship education and training aim to integrate youths into a capitalist economy that requires them to hustle, seek profit, and fend for themselves with few supports for the educational, work, and health needs they had. It is this 'strange conjunction' of 'pro-poor' and neoliberal, which Ferguson (2010, p. 174) refers to, that prompted me to ask how entrepreneurship education and youth livelihoods training prepare young Tanzanians to be citizens,[5] and what kind of citizens they are becoming. Would this education allow marginalized youths to be included in society, to choose how they participate in the labor market, and to seek their dreams and future livelihoods that would allow them to be socially, emotionally, and materially better off than they or their families were? Or would entrepreneurship education and training put them on a path that has limited opportunities, and not necessarily transform their material or social lives as they had hoped? In this way, I see entrepreneurship education and training as a technique of governmentality, a set of ideas and ways of thinking taught through curricular and educational practices that aim to foster particular kinds of citizens (Dean, 2010).

These questions about the means and ends of education programs, such as entrepreneurship and skills for work, are at the heart of development agendas and debates. The goals of international development are multiple: to foster sustainable economic growth; to end poverty; to address inequalities; and to educate particularly the younger generation, to contribute economically and, secondarily, socially and culturally,[6] to society. The National Strategy for Growth and Reduction of Poverty (NSGRP, or MKUKUTA in Swahili) in Tanzania reflects these diverse goals, as the government must align with the international development agenda in order to receive aid. These goals are contested with regard to how to achieve them, as are the roles that international agencies and NGOs play in development and poverty reduction. For instance, does vocational and – even more recently – entrepreneurship education achieve primarily these economic goals, or does it also achieve the social and political ones? If so, which ones are achieved, for whom, and under what conditions? And what are the unintended consequences of and contradictions in achieving these goals?

The question of whether and how certain skill sets – particularly entrepreneurship – could improve the livelihood opportunities and outcomes for a burgeoning youth population is one being asked broadly in the development community. Governments in sub-Saharan Africa face increasing pressure to educate young people beyond primary school; at the same time, with the growing population of educated youths, there are insufficient job opportunities to employ them all. The development community sees entrepreneurship education as one viable solution to this 'problem'. The programs that form the basis of the analysis in this book were supported by an international foundation that aimed to address the problem of youth unemployment. The international foundation's and the NGOs' original purpose of the evaluation project that I led was to answer this question:

> Did these NGO entrepreneurship education and training programs address the problem of unemployment for youths in these communities, and if so, what were the short and long-term effects on youths?

They were particularly interested in what youths were learning, how they were earning and if and how they were saving, and in turn, investing in and sustaining their enterprises or their livelihoods (see, for example Krause et al., 2016; Krause et al., 2013).

Over time, it became clearer to me that the foundation, the NGO staff and the youths themselves had multiple goals and varying understandings of what entrepreneurship education and training meant for youth livelihoods. Additionally, these programs produced particular meanings and outcomes of entrepreneurship in local contexts (see, for example, DeJaeghere et al., 2016). I began to ask questions about how the different international and local discourses about development and purposes of education encounter each other, are changed, and in turn, effect some notion of the kind of citizens these young people are becoming (see DeJaeghere, 2013, 2014). In this book, then, I aim to examine five years of longitudinal data from these programs and youths to explore how they utilize dominant international development discourses and local Tanzanian political, economic and social practices. I explore the frictions that occur in how entrepreneurship education and training is conceptualized and implemented and how these programs produce, at times, contradictory effects on youth's lives and livelihoods (Tsing, 2005). Tsing's idea of friction considers how, in the confluence of discourses, there is not only resistance, but also transformation. When global, universalizing ideas and practices meet local ones, some energy is lost but new energy and forms emerge.

Through an analysis of NGO entrepreneurship education and training and the youths who participate in these programs, the chapters in this book show how entrepreneurship education and training is taken up and repurposed in locally specific ways in Tanzanian communities. Tanzania is a particularly interesting case to examine how global and local discourses of development and education encounter each other given its history of strong socialist governing (1962–1985) and the shifts toward neoliberal policies in the 1980s and 1990s, with vestiges of both persisting in governing, economic policies, and education practices today. I aim to illustrate throughout the book how entrepreneurship education and training, usually associated with a hegemonic neoliberal idea of the 'enterprising self' (Rose, 1998) in the wake of a retreating state (Harvey, 2005), is reshaped by the specific political and social contexts in Tanzania, its national education system, and young people's realities in specific local contexts. Similar to Mains (2012) and Ferguson (2010, 2015), this analysis is based on the assumption that neoliberalism and its effects on young people's subjectivities as citizens are not monolithic; they have many variations. On the one hand, entrepreneurship education is implemented within a neoliberal orientation, with concern for economic growth, consumerism and markets of a global capitalist economy (Gibson-Graham, 2006).[7] On the other hand, entrepreneurial mindsets, skills and enterprise development take place within social and economic relations in informal, community and moral economies in Tanzania (Tripp, 1997). These latter economic relations emphasize reciprocity, solidarity and exchange rather than individual profit, competition and regulation. These different ideas of economic and social life reveal potential convergences and contradictions in the ways that entrepreneurship education takes form among youths in poor communities.

This book has two main aims. One is to examine how global discourses frame entrepreneurship programs and how they are, in turn, implemented in local contexts in which specific political, economic, social, historical, and individual vectors meet. In analyzing how these global educational ideas and practices take form, I show how they are reshaped by some international actors and repurposed by Tanzanian governmental actors and educators to link to localized meanings and practices, particularly of *Ujamaa*[8] and self-reliance.

A second – and more specific – aim is to answer the question: How are entrepreneurship education and training initiatives, implemented by international NGOs, reshaping the purposes and means of educating young people as citizens – as social, economic, and political members – of their communities, especially in contexts of poverty and unemployment in Tanzania? I consider how these initiatives construct youths as 'educated' or 'skilled' citizens. Additionally, I ask if and how young people who participate in these programs are included in society, able to secure rights and enact responsibilities – in essence, how they construct themselves as citizens.

Educating Tanzanian youths in changing social and economic times

The education[9] of youths in a time of global economic change has prompted new reform efforts among national governments and international agencies globally.

The past two decades have seen a growing youth population worldwide, increasing the demand for education and good jobs in the labor market. At the same time, the global economy experienced a downturn since the recession of 2008, and there has been a change in economic actors, trade patterns, and labor market sectors. While most sub-Saharan African countries experienced a higher-than-average growth rate in gross domestic product (GDP) during the last decade, this has not resulted in an equivalent decline in poverty across income levels, age groups, and geographical areas. For instance, the average GDP growth rate in Tanzania has been nearly 7% each year for the past decade and the percentage of the population living below the basic needs and extreme poverty levels has decreased (NBS, 2015; World Bank, 2006–2015). Those living in rural areas and youths, however, tend to be the most vulnerable to poverty and they did not experience the same level of improvement in living standards as those in urban areas (World Bank, 2006–2015).

Despite growth in some economies, the global recession has resulted in high unemployment particularly among youths. In 2011, nearly 75 million youths were unemployed globally, and the number of unemployed youths grew considerably during the economic downturn between 2007 and 2012 (ILO, 2012). Presently, the world has the largest youth[10] demographic ever, comprising more than 30% of the working age population in many countries. Because youths are a larger percentage of the population in many countries, and even though there has been an overall increase in the creation of jobs, the percentage of employed youths has actually decreased (Elder and Koné, 2014). In addition, fewer high-skilled jobs are being created precisely at the time when there are a greater number of educated young people seeking employment. These and other statistics paint a picture of employment being the most pressing problem for youth today, and education reforms are one way to address this situation.

Economic recession and unemployment are global phenomena (Elder and Koné, 2014), but the 'youth bulge' affecting participation in education and the labor force is especially acute in sub-Saharan Africa. A secondary school certificate is often necessary for entry into the formal labor market in East Africa.[11] Youths in this region are increasingly attending secondary school; however, many do not complete a basic education – completion through year 11 or Form 4 – because they fail to pass exams, or drop out before taking them (UWEZO, 2012). Those with only a primary school education are disadvantaged when it comes to formal employment, and most end up working in the informal sector or in informal employment in the formal sector, i.e., jobs without social security benefits, paid leave or sick leave entitlements. At the same time, those who have secondary or tertiary levels of education also experience unemployment, or a longer wait for a good job in the formal sector, due to a lack of skilled jobs in the labor market or their desire for better pay (Elder and Koné, 2014). For instance, Tanzania has seen a growth in job creation, but those roles are low-skilled, resulting in a mismatch for the educated class and the kinds of available employment (Shamchiyeva et al., 2014). In 2014, 66% of youths aged 15–24 and

84% of those who were 25–34 years old were employed in the labor markets in Tanzania, with lower participation rates of women than men; and these participation rates declined slightly from 2006 to 2014 (NBS, 2015, p. 37). However, the majority of young people work in informal employment, including in non-contractual and poorly paid work in the formal sector and as unpaid family helpers in family enterprises and agriculture (but still classified as employed under ILO definitions) (NBS, 2015, p. 41).[12] High unemployment is regarded by international agencies[13] and national governments as a problem to be addressed through entrepreneurship and self-employment, even though problems also exist for the many youths who are employed in poor and unstable labor conditions in the formal sector and unstable consumer markets in the informal sector. International agencies and governments frame the solution as one of developing skills for a changing global economy instead of attending to the issues of volatile labor and consumer markets.

The World Bank and other donors advocate policies and programs that emphasize job creation and skills training. Tanzania's 2010 National Strategy for Growth and Poverty Reduction (NSGRP II/MKUKUTA II) (URT, 2010a), created to meet the Millennium Development Goals and supported through international aid from the World Bank and other donors to achieve these goals, states that skills and entrepreneurship are necessary to achieve the goal of ensuring the creation of productive and decent employment for youths (p. 57). International agencies, corporations and NGOs have all argued that such education requires a fundamental shift in the Tanzanian education system by being more employer and market-driven and integrating skills and an entrepreneurial mindset at all levels (e.g., Muhura, 2012; Volkmann et al., 2009). In addition to development strategies and economic policies in Tanzania that call for skills development and entrepreneurship, education and youth policies also echo these themes when addressing the lack of skills and employability. For example, the National Youth Development Policy (URT, 2007) documents how the problem of youth unemployment has persisted since the early 2000s, and proposes that entrepreneurship skills training is one avenue for job creation (p. 2). Relatedly, a civic education strategy asked stakeholders about development accelerators, and education was the most highly ranked as a development accelerator, with entrepreneurship education in third place (URT, 2010b, p. 154).[14] These documents show the increasing importance of entrepreneurship education and training in economic, youth and education policies and practices in Tanzania.

Entrepreneurship education and training comes in many forms and definitions and is linked with different rationalities; still, there is some consensus among development organizations as to the core purposes, skills, and mindset to be achieved through such education and training. In a recent review of literature on entrepreneurship education and training for the World Bank, Valerio et al. (2014) offer the following commonly used definition: 'entrepreneurship education and training represents academic education or formal training interventions that share the broad objective of providing individuals with the entrepreneurial mindset and skills to support participation and performance in a range of entrepreneurial activities' (p. 21). This mindset includes 'the practical application of enterprising qualities, such as initiative, innovation, creativity, and risk-taking into the work environment' (Chigunta, 2002, p. v). Entrepreneurship education and training for many international agencies and NGOs is more than simply achieving enterprise development; they give particular attention to developing the mindset as well as technical, work and life skills. As entrepreneurship education and training is increasingly offered to youths and others who are unemployed and living in conditions of poverty, there is recognition that the outcomes may be as varied as a reduction of poverty through household enterprises (informal sector), contributing an entrepreneurial mindset to formal labor markets, or starting or expanding micro-, small or medium-size enterprises.

Entrepreneurship education and training, as discussed in this book, is more than a single course or a supplemental set of activities; it is an educational technique that is reframing the link between education and participation in the economy and society. And as it is used more and more with vulnerable youths living in conditions of poverty, the goals and practices of such education and training are becoming highly diverse; and their achievement is uncertain. The agencies that fund entrepreneurship education and training programs, and the NGOs that implement them, draw on a set of hegemonic development discourses about education's ability to foster human capital and economic growth. They also draw on rationales about education as a right and its ability to alleviate poverty and promote social mobility. At the same time, entrepreneurship education and training programs, when implemented, encounter the social and economic realities affecting young people's livelihoods in specific contexts. It is important, therefore, to ask: How do these different discourses shape the kind of citizen whom youths are becoming? My contention in this book is that dominant discourses of liberalism and neoliberalism, which I discuss in the next section, influence how these education programs are implemented to achieve these diverse goals of economic growth, poverty alleviation and social justice, and they also often result in contradictory effects.

Liberal and neoliberal discourses in education and development

The global agendas and debates that influence education and development programs and practices are based in liberal and neoliberal rationalities and ideas. There are many uses, and potential misuses, of these concepts of liberalism and neoliberalism. For the purposes of this book, it is helpful to draw on Ferguson's (2010) distinctions among the many uses of neoliberalism and, relatedly, liberalism to understand the framework used to analyze these educational programs and their effects on youth's lives. One such use is as a set of philosophical ideas and political doctrine, such as John Locke's (1988) ideas on political society, rights, and consent as the foundation of liberalism, and contemporary scholarship on political liberalism, such as Nussbaum's (1997, 2014) arguments for a universal set of human rights and capabilities to be guaranteed by the state. In contrast, neoliberalism emerged from the classical economic theories of Adam Smith (1904) and the arguments of contemporary scholars, such as Friedrich Hayek (1948) and Milton Friedman (1962), for the central role of markets to ensure economic development and the wellbeing of individuals and society, with minimal interference from the state.[15]

A second example of the use of both liberal and neoliberal ideas is as a set of policies and practices, usually of a state, such as in Harvey's (2005) analysis of the emergence of neoliberal economic policies as they took shape in the USA and elsewhere. These policies and practices may differ from the philosophical ideal, but they tend to draw on the key ideas and arguments related to the state, its citizens, and the economy. Liberal policies have generally been associated with state welfare reforms, which play a critical role in ensuring social and economic equality; neoliberal policies are grounded in the belief that the capitalist market creates maximum choices and fosters economic equality, and they use tools, such as privatizing social and human services, to create choice.

A third and different way in which liberalism or neoliberalism can be understood is through the concept of governmentality. Foucault's (1988, 1991) tradition of governmentality considers the rationalities and mechanisms of governing through diverse institutions as well as through individual behaviors and ways of thinking. In this approach, it is not simply that liberal or neoliberal philosophies or policies exist, but whether and how new forms of governing through institutions and individuals are created. For example, Ferguson (2010) argues that many neoliberal policies of privatization were imposed upon African states during the 1980s, but those actions did not necessarily result in new forms of governing or subjectivities. This means that policies might have existed, but mindsets and daily practices may not have dramatically shifted. It is this third usage – of liberalism and neoliberalism as 'ways of thinking and regimes of practices' (Dean, 2010) that exert power through state and non-state institutions, policies, and everyday practices – that I take up in this analysis of entrepreneurship education and training.

In my study of entrepreneurship education and citizenship I found it valuable to consider the concept of governmentality. It allowed me to consider the ways of thinking and practices – that may be liberal, neoliberal, or even alternative forms – embodied in international agencies, NGOs, and schools as well as the daily practices of Tanzanian youths. Governmentality is practiced through 'technologies of power', or programs of government and the market in an effort to dominate and shape the conduct of the population toward desired effects (Rose, 1999; Tikly, 2003). Governmentality also includes 'technologies of the self' as techniques that individuals use to change their own mind, soul, and body to attain a certain quality of life (Foucault, 1988, p. 18; Rose, 1999).[16] In this way, an analysis of rationalities and practices of governing is less concerned with pure liberalism and neoliberalism, and more interested in identifying the practices of and effects from these technologies of power and self. Entrepreneurship education and training can be regarded as a technology of power, a program implemented through government schools and non-formal training that draws on a set of global discourses and practices related to the economy to shape how youths might be entrepreneurs. It is also a technology of the self through the various techniques it employs to shape an entrepreneurial mindset that assesses and regulates how these youths act in relation to society and economy. The different discourses and practices a program uses can be analyzed to understand the kinds of citizens they produce and the material and social consequences on citizens' lives. Before explaining how I use governmentality analytically to examine liberal and neoliberal practices used by NGO entrepreneurship education and training programs, I first explain how liberalism and neoliberalism are technologies of power and of self.

Liberalism, as a form of governmentality, emerged in nineteenth-century Europe as an effort to define and limit relationships between government,[17] citizens, and the economy, and to allow for governing of the self (Miller and Rose, 2008). Knowledge, expertise, and regulations were diffused in the non-political sphere, and, particularly, through civil society organizations and the economy. Rather than knowledge being controlled by those who rule, as it was in monarchies, it is used by many throughout society to both limit the rule of government and to govern oneself through securing one's rights. Liberalism, as a way of thinking and as a set of practices, relies on experts applying their knowledge and techniques to problems of 'the social' – issues surrounding health, labor, and urban and rural life that need to be addressed or solved in order to live well together and obtain social solidarity and prosperity. For example, governments and civil society implement interventions that deal with disease, criminality, or labor conditions to ensure not only the wellbeing of citizens, but also that of the nation. These interventions ensure citizens' rights and protect them from harm. Education, then, is a powerful technology of governing aimed at producing knowledgeable citizens who can solve social problems and ensure their own wellbeing. As Miller and Rose (2008) state, 'Liberal strategies of government thus become dependent upon devices (schooling ...) that promise to create individuals who do not need to be governed by others, but will govern themselves, master themselves, care for themselves' (p. 204). Liberal practices engage civil society, including communities and NGOs, in addressing social problems, such as the gap in youth education and employment that exists in Tanzania and elsewhere, to ensure people's rights to an education and sustainable livelihood.

Neoliberalism as a governing practice deepens the distinctions between government, citizens, and the economy by prioritizing capitalist goals, capitalist practices, and related techniques as the mechanism to ensure choice, freedom, and economic wellbeing. Neoliberalism – or *advanced liberalism*, as Rose (1999) calls it – first arose during the 1950s in European and US economic thought, and then again in policies during the 1970s as a response to the welfare state and as an attempt to deepen the role of the capitalist free market to ensure social good (Harvey, 2005). Rather than relying on civil society, social programs, and knowledge of human sciences to improve how individuals live together in society, policymakers and governing institutions use mechanisms of management and the capitalist market, such as budgeting, accounting, and auditing, to limit the state and ensure individual freedom (Miller and Rose, 2008). Governing institutions, including international agencies, governments, and local schools, all use targets, indicators, and performance measures as tools to affect the conduct of citizens, while ostensibly fostering autonomy and accountability. For example, governments aiming to improve educational quality use targets, indicators, and financial incentives as mechanisms for performance and accountability, such as testing children to see if they hit targets for learning and tying these learning results to monetary rewards for teachers. In addition to addressing societal issues through management techniques, the logic of neoliberalism is for societies and citizens to integrate into the global capitalist economy through expertise, exports, and jobs that are increasingly tied to businesses (global corporations and export processing zones) operating near the communities and in the country. Through these relationships as producers and consumers, and increasingly as financiers, citizens can secure their own economic welfare.

For many international agencies using entrepreneurship as an accelerator of development, their programs exemplify this economic logic through efforts to create new enterprises connected with global value chains, to engage in financial borrowing and investing to expand business and wealth, and to produce surplus (profits beyond what is required for one's needs and wellbeing). Entrepreneurship education and training programs also teach techniques of budgeting, accounting, and auditing as ways to regulate participants into ensuring their own financial wellbeing. Finally, an economic logic also pervades the 'social space', where problems of living together and fostering development are governed through the private sector, NGOs, communities, and individuals (Miller and Rose, 2008). For instance, the private sector and employers, rather than government, have greater influence in how young people are educated. In sum, neoliberalism, as a set of practices and ways of thinking, believes capitalism is the most effective means of governing behavior, ensuring choice and creating economic security.

As philosophies and practices, liberalism and neoliberalism exist alongside each other in development discourses, education policies, and programs aiming to foster economic growth, alleviate poverty, and address inequalities. The ideas of choice, rights, (civic) participation, and economic empowerment are invoked with different meanings and end goals. However, by examining these practices and their outcomes, we can discern the resulting 'double meanings' – some more seemingly liberal, others more neoliberal – and the ways in which they are linked with each other (Muehlebach, 2012). To examine these double meanings as they are used by and implemented in entrepreneurship education and training programs, I use the terms *neo/liberal* and *neo/liberalisms*. These words allow us to examine the multiplicity of meanings and effects among these two ways of thinking and practices of governing. Such an analysis of neo/liberalisms sheds light on how entrepreneurship in one place and time may be associated with the global capitalist markets and profits, and somewhere else and in some other time certain NGO staff may regard entrepreneurship as fulfilling rights to an education. I intentionally use neo/liberalisms in the plural, as that allows for consideration of various forms of neoliberalism and liberalism at work in societies, including how alternative forms of governing may influence meanings and practices of entrepreneurship education (Dean, 2010; Ferguson, 2010). As Ferguson (2010) eloquently argues, neoliberalism means many different things, and 'yet [there is] some utility in words that bring together more than one meaning', allowing us to be more specific about the forms it takes and the alternatives it may present (p. 172).

Frictions with local governing and a moral economy

My study of Tanzanian models of entrepreneurship education and training offers an excellent opportunity to explore the 'friction' between neo/liberalisms used in global discourses on education and development and how they get enacted in the social, political and economic practices of a community (Tsing, 2005). While most analyses of liberal and neoliberal governmentality have been related to governments in the Global North (see Dean, 2010; Peters, 2009), a few contemporary studies have examined neoliberal governmentality in the Global South (Ferguson, 2015; Mains, 2012; Ong, 2006, 2008; Tikly, 2003) and argue that the practices and effects are contingent on local histories and social, cultural, and economic practices. As Mains (2012) and Ferguson (2015) argue, neoliberalism is not homogenous; it takes on many forms in local contexts. Similarly, liberalism does not display the same characteristics in postcolonial contexts as in Europe where it originated (Aminzade, 2013; Tikly, 2003). For example, Tikly (2003) argues that many states in sub-Saharan Africa cannot be characterized by a liberal governmentality in that rights of citizens were not secured; rather, the illiberal governmentality of colonial governments continued through the apartheid regime in South Africa and persists in some forms in governmental policy and practices today. In this way, education and development initiatives that aim to foster economic growth or address poverty encounter political and social practices that are unjust and inequitable.

Analyzing neoliberalism's influence in the policies of South Africa, Ferguson (2010) asserts that even if some political projects borrow from the 'neoliberal bag of tricks', it 'doesn't mean that these political projects are in league with the ideological project of neoliberalism, … only that they appropriate certain characteristic neoliberal 'moves.' … These moves are recognizable enough to look "neoliberal," but they can, I suggest, be used for quite different purposes than that term usually implies' (p. 174). He suggests that ideas of individual choice, entrepreneurship, and market efficiency may be valorized in public discourse about the economy, but those ideas are used alongside political and social initiatives and goals that are purposefully pro-poor and equity oriented. In a sense, illiberal, liberal, and neoliberal approaches co-exist in governing policies and practices.

Ferguson's analysis highlights the multiplicity of forms of governing and economic relations occurring at different scales – international, national, and local – that affect people's lives in sub-Saharan African countries. In a similar argument, Gibson-Graham (2006) calls for a different language other than neoliberalism to describe the kinds of economic relations that exist in societies today. They prefer the term *diverse economies* to include markets, non-markets, and alternative markets. Both non-markets and alternative markets are situated in social relations and practices, such as cultural norms of reciprocity or community agreements about commensurability of transactions.

Tripp (1997) refers to economic practices in the informal economy in Tanzania as a moral economy.[18] A moral economy consists of socially embedded transactions that operate from a symbolic–cultural logic different from a capitalist economy or even the rationality of the socialist-planned economy of the Tanzanian state at the time of her study (see Tripp, 1997, p. 17; Mains, 2012). A moral economy follows a logic that one's survival is inseparable from that of others, be that of one's village or the nation; 'survival strategies are collective efforts rather than individual ones' (Tripp, 1997, p. 14). Social relations in a moral economy entail reciprocity, reliance on one another, and an egalitarian ethos that everyone is entitled to at least a subsistence standard of living. Transactions in the informal economy tend to be characterized by high levels of trust and accountability to each other (to pay what you owe, to watch someone's goods). Earning in this economy also requires cooperation and networking, such as when groups of shopkeepers or craft workers share goods, tools, and even customers. On the one hand, cooperation may seem to reduce competition and even profits for any one individual. But on the other hand, it serves as a mechanism to create alternatives, such as getting access to sufficient goods, credit, and even demand when the government or other private entities inhibit these services. Thus, entrepreneurship education and training programs that seek to develop enterprises and economic transactions in a capitalist economy also encounter a moral economy's existing financial and social relations. It is these encounters, and their resulting frictions and alternatives that I examine in this book.

The Tanzanian experience: entrepreneurship education in situ

This book explores these political and social dilemmas of how to address the continuing poverty experienced in countries in the Global South through entrepreneurship education programs. It uses a study of two different NGO entrepreneurship education and training programs implemented in semi-urban and rural communities in Tanzanian supported by an international foundation. By examining and comparing these two entrepreneurship education and training programs, I explore their varied rationalities, goals and practices that 'make' youths particular kinds of citizens (Ong, 2006). I also consider throughout the various chapters how NGO staff and youths give diverse meanings to entrepreneurship in these communities.

In Chapter 2, I begin by elaborating how global education and development discourses are influenced by both liberal and neoliberal discourses – what I call *neo/liberal* – or double, and at times contradictory, ways of thinking and practices of liberalism and neoliberalism. I then use neo/liberalisms as an analytical concept to examine the double meanings of rights, responsibilities, participation, and empowerment that are present in development and education discourses and practices. I analyze how these ideas take on particular meanings in sub-Saharan African contexts by drawing on literature from African scholars of citizenship and governance, such as Mamdani, Mensah, and Ndegwa, and on studies of citizenship education in the region. These perspectives offer a critique of liberalism and neoliberalism; they also put forth local conditions, perspectives, and practices affecting citizenship in postcolonial contexts.

In the third chapter, I identify the different approaches to entrepreneurship education and training taken by the international donor community, foundations, and NGOs. I review two distinct and dominant approaches used by the World Bank, International Labour Organization (ILO), and the United States Agency for International Development (USAID). One approach focuses on job creation and economic development, and the other is aimed at poverty reduction and addressing social ills. The former is aligned with neoliberal rationalities in which economic practices ensure wellbeing, while the latter draws on more liberal discourses of equity and pro-poor policies, while still promoting economic practices to address social ills. In contrast to these two approaches, a capability approach calls for the consideration of valued livelihoods, social outcomes, and overall wellbeing. This approach to policy emphasizes the governmental and social supports needed to be an entrepreneur, including social policies that support self-employment and enterprise development. Additionally, a capability approach recognizes that many entrepreneurship programs for youths may not necessarily result in business development or stable employment, so it also considers social outcomes, such as the wellbeing of family and community, as important. The analysis of these three approaches to entrepreneurship education and training provides a valuable context within which to examine how these different approaches are articulated in the policies and practices in Tanzania (discussed briefly in Chapter 5), and used by the NGO programs (analyzed in Chapters 6, 7 and 8).

While an analysis of these global institutions and their approaches allows us to know the politics that surrounds entrepreneurship education, such programs take very different shape within local contexts. With that in mind, I describe in the rest of the book, the findings of a major research program of two NGO entrepreneurship education and training programs supported by an international foundation. In Chapter 4, I explain the methodological approach and sites of two case studies used to examine how political discourses and approaches to entrepreneurship education encounter local Tanzanian practices of entrepreneurship and the economy. I describe the different sites, including the institutional context of the international foundation, the NGOs, and the communities. I briefly present the curriculum and practices of the two different NGO entrepreneurship education and training programs, illustrating certain common features across sites and types of education programs, and describing distinctions in the specific technical and business skills cultivated to fit local market needs. Finally, I discuss the methods used, the participants involved in the study, and the analyses of five years of longitudinal data conducted for this book using the framework of frictions between neo/liberal and local discourses set out in Chapters 2 and 5, respectively.

The challenge of addressing poverty alleviation while creating national unity, prosperity and global integration through different governing regimes and practices in Tanzania is the focus of Chapter 5. I describe how governing regimes in Tanzania emerged over time from Nyerere's 1960s decolonization efforts to the present day. I highlight the philosophical influences and policies and practices of Nyerere's (1967, 1968) alternative approach to development, that of *Ujamaa* – African socialism – and education for self-reliance (ESR). In particular, I examine how ESR policies and practices achieved outcomes in primary and secondary education, and also the challenges ESR encountered. I then turn to global influences and national macro-economic policy shifts in the mid-1980s and new education policies as the nation's ideology of governance changed from socialism to capitalism. These shifting policies are also examined in relation to the changing formal and informal labor market in Tanzania, characterized by both capitalist and moral economic relations. Finally, I detail the emergence of entrepreneurship education and training in contemporary policy and practice. This chapter sets the stage for analyzing frictions between neo/liberal discourses in entrepreneurship education and training initiatives and the governing practices of the Tanzanian government and local communities. Considering these local practices allows for an analysis of how entrepreneurship education and training programs may have, at times, contradictory effects.

Entrepreneurship education and training programs take different shapes in semi-urban and rural communities, and in formal, vocational and non-formal education programs. The programs are also mediated by the varied and contradictory ways that NGO staff, educators and youths enact them in their contexts. In Chapter 6, I analyze how NGO secondary schools implement *Parka*'s economically self-sufficient (ESS) model that uses on-campus businesses to teach entrepreneurship and to generate profits. I examine the discourses that staff utilize to explain the goals, practices, and outcomes of the ESS model and entrepreneurship education. The ESS model uses the concept of self-reliance, and this analysis aims to illustrate how the NGO staff and school teachers appropriate this concept in relation to the consumer market and profit for the school, as well as to students' future wellbeing. I show the tensions that the schools and staff face between providing tuition-free education and being dependent on either private funding or the consumer market for its business goods. In this analysis, I illustrate how staff increasingly employed neoliberal techniques of financial management as well as cultivated a mindset of innovativeness and resiliency even while profit remained elusive.

In Chapter 7, I analyze *Apprentice*'s entrepreneurship training for out-of-school youths to understand the livelihood outcomes of the program. I describe how *Apprentice*'s program in Kagera, a region along Lake Victoria that has little formal employment, aims to promote self-employment or work in others' small enterprises. I use longitudinal survey and interview data from youths who participated in the program to illustrate their multiple work and enterprise-related outcomes. In this analysis, I identify the neo/liberal influences on youths' livelihood development and how these also encounter local practices of reciprocity and solidarity. I show how these young people were excluded as citizens or members of society because they were regarded as uneducated and unemployed. In effect, they did not have 'work membership' through being employed in recognized wage labor (Ferguson, 2013). I then explore the friction between the program's emphasis on creating individual enterprises and the youths' uses of their enterprises for family and community development. Another friction I examine is the program's desired outcome of enterprises that create profit and economic development, and the youths' goals of social inclusion and becoming valued members of the community. In these frictions, I argue that an 'entrepreneurial citizen' emerges, one who aims to claim both economic and social rights in their community.

Chapter 8 offers a different angle on *Apprentice*'s non-formal training project to examine the effects of financial education on youths' lives. One aim of entrepreneurship education and training programs is to teach youths to be financially responsible, assuming this will have long-term effects on their economic wellbeing – both in starting and sustaining enterprises and in increasing their household income. I situate this analysis in the contested concept of financial inclusion, an outcome of financial education – one that has a double meaning of integrating youths into financial markets and teaching them to become productive citizens that contribute economically as consumers and socially to their community. In this chapter, I present longitudinal data to show the double meanings of financial inclusion for these youths, which, on the one hand, responsibilizes them through knowledge and practices of saving and lending that make them good customers for financial institutions. On the other hand, they use their financial knowledge to create alternative financial mechanisms and practices in their community. I also examine the friction produced between goals of borrowing for, and investing in, their enterprises, and using their financial resources to support peers, family members, and the community.

I conclude the book with a discussion of the multiplicity of, and at times unexpected, effects when global discourses of entrepreneurship education and training encountered national governing rationalities, and local discourses and practices of self-reliance, solidarity, and reciprocity – all elements of a moral economy in Tanzania. The analysis of this study suggests a need for international agencies, governments, and NGOs to shift the gaze beyond an economic framing of youth livelihood programs, those oriented toward economic growth discussed in Chapter 3, to see the alternatives that arise and are produced when implemented in local contexts. Entrepreneurship, called *ujasiriamali* in recent Tanzanian policy, is more than earning an income or starting an enterprise; it is also related to existing moral beliefs and practices of *kujitegemea*, or Nyerere's idea of self-reliance, which emphasizes being an included member of the community and, in turn, supporting the community. By bringing these ideas together, I suggest that these programs have the effect of making Tanzanian youths into a new form of citizen, a *social–economic citizen* who is neither the enterprising self nor a socialist citizen harkening to Nyerere's project. The social–economic citizen is the result of a transformative potential in entrepreneurship education and training, but this transformation is contingent on a continual reframing and reshaping of these programs to consider the long-term wellbeing effects on youth livelihoods and lives.

Finally, I consider the implications of this analysis for the global agenda focused on skills and employment, and for actors and organizations that advocate for and implement entrepreneurship education and training. I call for the reframing of entrepreneurship skills and knowledge as social capabilities, ones that consider and address the social, historical, and cultural inequalities that affect these youths and their communities, rather than purely as economic outcomes focused on development and growth. Such a framing goes some way toward reshaping the social relations that constrain economic participation and wellbeing, and it offers some progressive possibilities of reclaiming – in new and different ways than in the past – social and economic welfare in low-resourced communities and societies.

***

Upendo did not do well on her O-level exams and, therefore, she was not able to continue her education. But she had acquired social, technical, and entrepreneurial knowledge and skills that allowed her to work with various businesses at the school and to care for her family. From her labor, Upendo was able to pay her child's school fees and to support and care for her mother. In these ways, she was being made, and was making herself, as an entrepreneurial citizen, contributing to the social and economic wellbeing of her family and community.

Notes

1 Upendo is a pseudonym, as all are names throughout the book, for a young woman who participated in one of the entrepreneurship education programs. A fuller story of

her experiences over the years is discussed in DeJaeghere, Pellowski Wiger, and Willemsen (2016).
2 Starting in 2011, I led a five-year longitudinal study of NGO programs aimed at incorporating skills, particularly work and entrepreneurship skills, in education and training of secondary-age youths in Tanzania. The project included an international team of US-based graduate students and researchers, and Tanzanian researchers. They are listed in the acknowledgments.
3 *Parka* is a pseudonym for this international NGO that implements what I have called the economically self-sufficient schools (ESS) program. I use pseudonyms for all NGOs, staff and youths discussed in this study.
4 Throughout this chapter and the book, I use both *education* and *training*. Education generally refers to the teaching and learning of entrepreneurship in formal education systems (basic and higher education), while training refers to non-formal settings.
5 By *citizen*, I mean the social construction of an identity in relation to a community, including how one is included and excluded from political, social, and economic means of power. Chapter 2 discusses my theoretical orientation to being made and self-making as citizens.
6 These broad goals have been articulated and championed through the Millennium Development Goals (MDGs) and now the Sustainable Development Goals (SDGs).
7 I use the term *global capitalist economy* rather than market to more specifically show how economic relations are framed in terms of global capital, not simply any market, including community economic markets, a distinction made in Gibson-Graham (2006). Gibson-Graham are two feminist economists who have hyphenated their last names as authors. I refer to them in the plural throughout the book to recognize their combined identities and ideas.
8 *Ujamaa* stems from the term *ujamii*, or social relations/social life. It is used both as a value underlying social life in Tanzania, and as Nyerere's strategy for economic and social development.
9 Education often connotes schooling, but it is a broader term that also refers to non-formal and informal ways of learning. Because this research includes both non-formal education and training as well as formal schools, I generally use the broader term of *education*. I also use education and training to denote the two types of entrepreneurship programs, those that take place in formal schools and those in non-formal settings
10 The United Nations (UN) defines youths as those between the ages of 15–24, for purposes of consistency in statistics. However, the African Youth Charter defines youths as those between the ages of 15–35. In this research, youth refers to program participants, who were generally between the ages of 12 (those beginning formal lower secondary) and 24 at the beginning of our research.
11 While some without an O-level certificate may be informally employed in the formal sector, most formal sector work with contracts and benefits requires a certificate. Other scholars have noted that '[h]aving 12 years of schooling [equivalent to Form 4 education] lowers the probability of entering low pay and of low-pay persistence by more than 90 percent' (Falco, 2014, p. 46).
12 I use definitions of employment, formal employment and informal employment recommended by the International Conference of Labour Statistics (2003) and used in International Labour Organization reports for Tanzania (see Shamchiyeva et al., 2014). Those considered *employed* includes all persons who did some work in the reference period, either for pay in cash or in kind, or who were in self-employment for profit or family gain. *Informal employment* includes persons working as paid employees in 'informal jobs', i.e. jobs without a social security entitlement, paid annual leave or paid sick leave; (b) paid employees in an unregistered enterprise with size classification below five employees; (c) own-account workers in an unregistered enterprise with size classification below five employees; (d) employers in an

unregistered enterprise with size classification below five employees; and (e) contributing family workers. Categories (b–d) refer to the informal sector, while (a) refers to informal job/work in the formal sector.

13 I use the term *international agencies* here to refer to the assemblage of international institutions, including financial institutions, such as the World Bank; bilateral donors, such as the Department for International Development (DfID); and international organizations that are not directly donors, affiliated with the United Nations, such as UNESCO. This term also refers to foundations and large international NGOs that also fund large and small development programs. While having different missions and scope, they share a common commitment to the SDGs and the EFA agenda.

14 Entrepreneurship is not an explicit concept used in the civic education syllabus, nor is it taught as a separate subject in primary or secondary education in Tanzania, as it is in some other countries in sub-Saharan Africa, such as Mozambique. Still, as will be discussed in Chapter 5, there is an increasing number of policy initiatives in Tanzania that aim to include entrepreneurship education and training, including the National Entrepreneurship Training Framework (NEEC, 2013), at all levels.

15 Other scholars provide a rich discussion of the different philosophical ideas that are shared by and that also distinguish liberalism and neoliberalism. See, for example, Gordon (1991) for a discussion of Foucault's analysis of liberalism, drawing on John Locke's ideas of civil society and Adam's Smith's ideas related to the 'economic man' (sic) and the 'invisible hand'. Harvey (2005) provides a discussion of the distinctions among contemporary theorists, such as Hayek's (1948) neoliberalism with an opposition to state intervention in contrast to Polanyi's (1944) ideas of the economy embedded within culture and society. Muehlenbach (2012) provides a nuanced treatment of Adam Smith's works, including reading his *Theory of Moral Sentiments* in relation to *The Wealth of Nations*, suggesting that he gave due consideration to moral action as it relates to economic, political and social life. Muehlenbach argues that Smith makes affect toward others, and not only rationality, the basis of self-regulation in the capitalist market.

16 Foucault's work included both an analysis of governments as technologies of power, such as how institutions like schools or prisons disciplined people, as well as technologies of the self, or the creation of subjects that governed themselves through freedoms and choices. An analytics of governmentality, then, not only describes how government works, but considers the effects of these technologies for the kind of life that is led. See also Foucault (1997).

17 I use the term *government* or *governing* rather than *state* in line with the analytical perspective of Dean's governmentality. This analytical usage allows for governing not to be limited to the state, as it occurs at all levels, and it also focuses on the processes of governing. Some scholars that I discuss will refer to the state, particularly in relation to nation-building in Africa. In these cases, I use the term state.

18 I use *moral economy* here to signify the types of social relations that are embedded within economic relations and transactions, not as a term that signifies some 'traditional' or pre-modern economy, as it is sometimes used (e.g., Scott's reference to the moral economy of peasants). Similar to Tripp (1997) and drawing on Booth (1994), I regard the moral economy as existing in relation to and, at times, influencing how the capitalist economy operates in Tanzanian communities.

References

Aminzade, R. (2013). *Race, nation, and citizenship in postcolonial Africa: The case of Tanzania*. Cambridge, UK: Cambridge University Press.

Booth, W. J. (1994). On the idea of the moral economy. *American Political Science Review*, 88(3), 653–667.

Chigunta, F. (2002). The socio-economic situation of youth in Africa: Problems, prospects and options. *World*, *32*(27.3).

Dean, M. (2010). *Governmentality: Power and rule in modern society* (second edition). Thousand Oaks, CA: SAGE Publications.

DeJaeghere, J. (2013). Education, skills and citizenship: An emerging model of entrepreneurship in Tanzania. *Comparative Education*, *49*(4), 503–519.

DeJaeghere, J. (2014) Encountering friction between liberal and neoliberal discourses of citizenship: A non-governmental organization's entrepreneurship education in Tanzania. *Education, Citizenship and Social Justice*, *9*(3), 226–238.

DeJaeghere, J., Pellowski Wiger, N., and Willemsen, L. (2016). Broadening educational outcomes: Social relations, skills development and employability for youth. *Comparative Education Review*, *60*(3), 457–479.

Elder, S., and Koné, K. S. (2014). *Labour market transitions of young women and men in sub-Saharan Africa*. (Work4Youth Publication Series No. 9). Geneva, Switzerland: ILO. Retrieved from http://www.ilo.org/employment/areas/youth-employment/work-for-youth/publications/regional-reports/WCMS_235754/lang–en/index.htm

Falco, P., Kerr, A., Pierella, P., Paci, P., and Rijkers, B. (2014). *Working toward better pay: Earnings dynamics in Ghana and Tanzania*. Washington, DC: World Bank Publications.

Ferguson, J. (2010). The uses of neoliberalism. *Antipode*, *41*(s1), 166–184.

Ferguson, J. (2013). Declarations of dependence: Labour, personhood, and welfare in southern Africa. *Journal of the Royal Anthropological Institute*, *19*(2), 223–242.

Ferguson, J. (2015). *Give a man a fish: Reflections on the new politics of distribution*. Durham, NC: Duke University Press.

Foucault, M. (1988). Technologies of the self. In M. Foucault, L. H. Martin, H. Gutman, and P. H. Hutton (Eds.) *Technologies of the self: A seminar with Michel Foucault* (pp. 16–49). Amherst, MA: University of Massachusetts Press.

Foucault, M. (1991). Governmentality. In M. Foucault, G. Burchell, C. Gordon, and P. Miller. *The Foucault effect: Studies in governmentality* (pp. 87–104). Chicago, IL: University of Chicago Press.

Foucault, M. (1997). *Ethics: Subjectivity and truth (Essential works of Michel Foucault, 1954–1984, Vol. 1)*. New York, NY: The New Press.

Friedman, M. (1962). *Capitalism and freedom*. Chicago, IL: University of Chicago Press.

Gibson-Graham, J. K. (2006). *A postcapitalist politics*. Minneapolis, MN: University of Minnesota Press.

Gordon, C. (1991). Governmental rationality: An introduction. In G. Burchell, C. Gordon, and P. Miller (Eds.), *The Foucault effect: Studies in governmentality*, (pp. 1–52). Chicago, IL: University of Chicago Press.

Harvey, D. (2005). *A brief history of neoliberalism*. Oxford, UK: Oxford University Press.

Hayek, F. A. (1948). *Individualism and economic order*. Chicago, IL: University of Chicago Press.

International Labour Organization. (ILO) (2012). *The youth employment crisis: Time for action*. Report prepared by youth for the Youth Employment Forum (Geneva, 23–25 May 2012). Geneva, Switzerland: ILO.

Krause, B., Chapman, D., and DeJaeghere, J. (2013). High aspirations, limited capabilities, challenging context: An empirical look at a youth entrepreneurship training program in a low income setting. *World Studies in Education*, 14(2), 63–78.

Krause, B. L., McCarthy, A. S., and Chapman, D. (2016). Fuelling financial literacy: Estimating the impact of youth entrepreneurship training in Tanzania. *Journal of Development Effectiveness*, 8(2), 234–256.

Levinson, B. A., Foley, D. E., and Holland, D. C. (1996). *The cultural production of the educated person: Critical ethnographies of schooling and local practice*. Albany, NY: State University of New York Press.

Locke, J. (1988). *Two treatises of government*, P. Laslett (Ed.), Cambridge, UK: Cambridge University Press. (Original work published 1689)

Mains, D. (2012). *Hope is cut: Youth, unemployment, and the future in urban Ethiopia*. Philadelphia, PA: Temple University Press.

Miller, P., and Rose, N. (2008). *Governing the present: Administering economic, social and personal life*. Cambridge, UK: Polity.

Muehlenbach, A. (2012). *The moral neoliberal: Welfare and citizenship in Italy*. Chicago, IL: University of Chicago Press.

Muhura, C. (2012). *Elimu ya Ujasiriamali: Kuelekea kwenye Maendeleo Endelevu Tanzania*. [Entrepreneurship education: Towards sustainable development Tanzania, Report 12.2.k]. Dar es Salaam, Tanzania: Haki Elimu.

The National Economic Empowerment Council (NEEC) [Tanzania]. (2013). *National Entrepreneurship Training Framework (NETF)*. Dar es Salaam, Tanzania: The Prime Minister's Office.

Nussbaum, M. C. (1997). Capabilities and human rights. *Fordham Law Review*, 66, 273.

Nussbaum, M. C. (2014). Perfectionist liberalism and political liberalism. In F. Comin and M. Nussbaum (Eds.) *Capabilities, gender, equality: Towards fundamental entitlements* (pp. 19–56). Cambridge, UK: Cambridge University Press.

Nyerere, J. K. (1967). Education for self-reliance. *The Ecumenical Review*, 19(4), 382–403.

Nyerere, J. K. (1968). *Freedom and socialism/Uhuru na Ujamaa: A selection from writings and speeches, 1965–1967*. Oxford, UK: Oxford University Press.

Ong, A. (2006). *Neoliberalism as exception: Mutations in citizenship and sovereignty*. Duke, NC: Duke University Press.

Peters, M. (2009). Education, enterprise culture and the entrepreneurial self: A Foucauldian perspective. *The Journal of Educational Enquiry*, 2(2), 58–71.

Polanyi, K. (1944). *The great transformation: The political and economic origins of our time*. Boston, MA: Beacon Press.

Rose, N. (1998). *Inventing ourselves: Psychology, power and personhood*. Cambridge, UK: Cambridge University Press.

Rose, N. (1999). *Powers of freedom: Reframing political thought*. Cambridge, UK: Cambridge University Press.

Shamchiyeva, L., Kizu, T., and Kahyarara, G. (2014). *Labour market transitions of young women and men in the United Republic of Tanzania*. (Work4Youth Publication Series No. 26). Geneva, Switzerland: ILO. Retrieved from http://www.ilo.org/employment/areas/youth-employment/work-for-youth/publications/regional-reports/WCMS_235754/lang–en/index.htm

Smith, A. (1904). *An inquiry into the nature and causes of the wealth of nations*. E. Cannan (Ed.). London, UK: Methuen. (Original work published 1776)

The National Bureau of Statistics (NBS) [Tanzania]. (2015). *Analytical Report for Integrated Labour Force Survey 2014*. Dar es Salaam, Tanzania: NBS.

Tikly, L. (2003). Governmentality and the study of education policy in South Africa. *Journal of Education Policy*, 18(2), 161–174.

Tripp, A. M. (1997). *Changing the rules: The politics of liberalization and the urban informal economy in Tanzania*. Berkeley, CA: University of California Press.
Tsing, A. L. (2005). *Friction: An ethnography of global connection*. Princeton, NJ: Princeton University Press.
United Republic of Tanzania (URT). (2007). *National Youth Development Policy*. Dar es Salaam, Tanzania: Ministry of Labour, Employment and Youth Development.
United Republic of Tanzania (URT). (2010a). *National Strategy for Growth and Reduction of Poverty II, Mkukuta II*. Dar es Salaam: Ministry of Finance and Economic Affairs.
United Republic of Tanzania (URT). (2010b). *National Strategy for Civic Education*. (draft). Dar es Salaam: URT.
UWEZO (2012). *Are our children learning?* (Annual Learning Assessment Report 2012), Dar es Salaam, Tanzania: UWEZO Tanzania.
Valerio, A., Parton, B., and Robb, A. (2014). *Entrepreneurship education and training programs around the world: Dimensions for success*. Washington, DC: World Bank Group.
Vavrus, F. and Bartlett, L. (2016). *Rethinking case study research: A comparative approach*. London, UK: Routledge.
Volkmann, C., Wilson, K. E., Mariotti, S., Rabuzzi, D., Vyakarnam, S., and Sepulveda, A. (2009). *Educating the next wave of entrepreneurs: Unlocking entrepreneurial capabilities to meet the global challenges of the 21st century*. (A report for the World Economic Forum, Global Education Initiative). Geneva, Switzerland: World Economic Forum.
World Bank. (2006–2015). *World development indicators*. Washington, DC: World Bank Group.

Chapter 2

Neo/liberal Governmentality and Citizen Subjectivities

Education policies and initiatives related to skills development and entrepreneurship education and training are (re)emerging[1] in many sub-Saharan African countries, employing a multitude of rationalities and discourses that are present at different scales – in international development agendas, national education and development goals, and local education and economic practices. This chapter sets out a framework with which to analyze the ways various international, national, and local actors who fund and implement entrepreneurship education and training programs and how they relate to dominant liberal and neoliberal ways of thinking and practices of governing. I explore how international agencies and global discourses use rationalities of rights to education and work, and how they also call on a discourse of responsibilization, which is the moralization of individual responsibility for economic insecurities and social risks. I consider how entrepreneurship education programs use double meanings of participation in, and empowerment through, education and the economy. By framing liberalism and neoliberalism as neo/liberalisms, it allows for the exploration of the plurality of rationalities, ideas, and meanings – and the tensions among them – as they are used in entrepreneurship education and training programs. Finally, I critique the ideas of rights, responsibilities, and participation, as associated with both liberal and neoliberal governing, from the perspective of scholars writing on governing and citizenship in sub-Saharan African countries.

Neo/liberal discourses and practices influence the construction of citizenship in diverse and contradictory ways. Entrepreneurship education and training is a technology of governing and a technology of self, used by international agencies, governments, and communities to shape and produce citizens toward specific ends. Ong (2003, 2006) refers to these as processes of being made and self-making in relation to governing regimes. As a technology of power, entrepreneurship education and training is embedded in laws, institutional practices, and programs that allow for the creation of microenterprises and savings and lending groups that endeavor to support youths' businesses. These technologies offer economic and social incentives and protections that aim to ensure economic rights and participation. Technologies of the self are educational techniques (such as life skills or financial education) that programs use to foster self-discipline, goal setting, and resiliency by creating entrepreneurial youths. These technologies support participation, responsibilization, and empowerment in economic and social life. Thus, young people are not only 'made', but they are remaking and reshaping the meaning of these practices for their own identities as entrepreneurs and as citizens in society (Ong, 2003). By exploring the different meanings of *rights, responsibilities, participation*, and *empowerment* as used in neo/liberal discourses, I have been able to establish a framework for the analysis of empirical data, not least an understanding of the multiple meanings that are present in the NGO entrepreneurship education and training programs in Tanzania in this study. Before I discuss how these concepts are used in and shaped by neo/liberal discourses, I briefly describe how global institutions and the global agenda on education utilize these discourses to frame the goals of economic growth and poverty alleviation, and how skills development, and entrepreneurship education programs in particular, are called on to address these problems in Tanzania.

Global governing: Neo/liberal discourses of development and education

Global institutions, goals, and strategies produce and reproduce neo/liberal discourses – meaning they draw on both liberal and neoliberal ways of thinking and practices – related to development and education through various mechanisms and techniques. The most dominant actors in education and development are the United Nations' (UN) organizations and international financial institutions, which, although distinct in their approaches, have together led the creation of and funded Education for All (EFA), Millennium Development Goals (MDGs), and Sustainable Development Goals (SDGs). The UN has played a critical role in defining the relationship and rights between states and its citizens – for those states that become signatories – through its declarations and conventions, such as the Universal Declaration of Human Rights (UDHR) and the Convention on the Rights of the Child (CRC). These declarations and conventions also informed the goals and targets established in the global education and development agendas – EFA, the MDGs, and SDGs – deepening governing commitments and practices of ensuring the right to a quality education (Mundy, 2006; McCowan, 2013; Tikly, 2017). For example, the UN's perspective on education as a right and necessary for fostering equality and poverty alleviation can be seen in the preamble to a new vision for EFA in the Incheon Declaration (UNESCO, 2015):

> Our vision is to transform lives through education, recognizing the important role of education as a main driver of development and in achieving the other proposed SDGs. ... This new vision is fully captured by the proposed SDG 4 'Ensure inclusive and equitable quality education and promote

life-long learning opportunities for all' and its corresponding targets. ... It is inspired by a humanistic vision of education and development based on human rights and dignity; social justice; inclusion; protection; cultural, linguistic and ethnic diversity; and shared responsibility and accountability. We reaffirm that education is a public good, a fundamental human right and a basis for guaranteeing the realization of other rights. It is essential for peace, tolerance, human fulfilment and sustainable development. We recognize education as key to achieving full employment and poverty eradication. (p. 1)

Here, UNESCO's declaration on EFA, which influences policies and practices of member states, draws on the declaration of human rights. It also states that education is a public good, an effort to shape the relationship between states' roles in providing for the right to education. In addition, it signals education's role in employment, drawing, in part, on human capital rationales for education.

Some scholars have argued that while EFA has been framed by UN organizations and a rights discourse, international agencies and financial institutions such as the World Bank, and organizations like the Organization for Economic Development Cooperation (OECD) have had a powerful influence on the discourse and strategies for achieving EFA (Mundy, 2006) and the education goal in the SDGs (Tikly, 2017). Mundy (2006) argues that there has long been a diffuse and contradictory set of actors and discourses that comprise the global education-for-development regime, and Tikly (2017) shows that there has been both a shift in the discourse and in the norms used to govern and implement EFA over time, and in its relationship with the SDGs.[2] In particular, the World Bank influences the implementation of EFA through its strategies and discourses aligned with a human capital approach and a neoliberal orientation to the role of government and the economy, rather than a human rights approach. The following goals and strategy set out in the World Bank *Learning for All* (2011), which supports the achievement of the global education goals, represent a contrast with the UNESCO statement above.

The state of education and the expectation of leaders, citizens, and students of national education systems – that education can be an engine of economic progress and a chance for people to transform and improve their lives. ... The new strategy focuses on learning for a simple reason: growth, development, and poverty reduction depend on the knowledge and skills that people acquire. ... [A]t the societal level, recent research shows that the level of skills in a workforce – as measured by performance on international student assessments such as PISA and TIMSS – predicts economic growth rates. (p. 25)

After discussing its approach to life-long learning, quality, and equity, it concludes this section with this statement: 'While most governments consider basic education part of their mandate, learning opportunities – from preschool to universities and training programs – are not provided only by governments. The role of the nonstate, or private, sector is discussed in the next section' (p. 26).

The World Bank strategy does not deny that education is a right, but it quickly adds that it is a strategic development investment (p. 1). It also argues that it 'promotes the equity goals that underlie the education MDG' (p. 4), but this statement seems to suggest that the World Bank does not give the same priority to equity as do UNESCO EFA documents. Mundy (2006) describes the current approach taken by international agencies as 'a third way', or new global consensus, in which financial institutions endorse equity, and UN institutions are 'less skeptical of the role of the market and private sector in development' (p. 19). But, she argues that despite the common use of these discourses across institutions, many differences exist in these various institutions' education programs, their specific practices, and their effects.

These plural rationalities, enshrined in global governance and discourses, have had a dominating influence on governing in Tanzania. For instance, neoliberal policies of privatization, deregulation, and free trade were instituted in many developing countries, including Tanzania, during the 1980s and 1990s, prompted by IMF conditionalities and the World Bank programs that implemented them. These conditionalities, which included privatization of public and the parastatal sectors, gave rise to increased fees for schooling and an expanded private education sector (Samoff, 1987; Vavrus, 2003). In the 2000s, with EFA and the MDGs, there was a turn toward rights to and equity in education and ensuring free primary education for all (Vavrus and Moshi, 2009). At that time, there was greater coordination among UN organizations and the IMF and World Bank to achieve the MDGs, and countries were required to develop Poverty Reduction Strategy Papers (PRSPs), a document that countries prepared – with World Bank support – to set out their social and economic goals. Mundy (2006) describes the use of the PRSP as a 'pivotal turn' in committing the IMF and World Bank to equity *and* economic growth goals, but she also says it had contradictory effects because it allowed international donors and, to a lesser extent, citizens to hold governments accountable for their targets and plans, rather than governments owning the process of development (p. 26). This use of specific economic and financial targets to manage development and social issues also aligns with a neoliberal governmentality, as described in Chapter 1.

In Tanzania, the National Strategy for Growth and Reduction of Poverty II (MKUKUTA II) (URT, 2010) reflects these multiple approaches and goals, stating that it aims to strengthen government and national ownership and implementation. But a major shift in the current strategy from the previous one is the scaling up of the role and participation of the private sector in priority areas – education being one of them (p. 27). It acknowledges the importance of education for social wellbeing, with a particular emphasis on ensuring equitable access to quality education, in line with EFA goals. It also specifically describes education as 'skills demanded by the labour market' (p. 27) and notes that entrepreneurship programs are particularly important for youth employment (p. 58).

These global institutions and the state, through governing mechanisms such as the PRSP, established technologies of the capitalist market through greater private involvement in education, including through families' contributions through fees and industry's input into policies and curriculum. They also include technologies of the state aimed at ensuring equity and social welfare through universal primary education. In effect, rationalities of governing in Tanzania have increasingly drawn on global neo/liberal discourses and practices to achieve the multiple development goals. But these goals and their related discourses and practices are also embedded in local values and discourses. The MKUKUTA II includes a particular Tanzanian emphasis, stating that it aims to 'foster changes in mind-set toward hard work, patriotism, and self-reliance' (p. ix), which suggest that national unity and development continue to be important. At the same time, it acknowledges a challenge in implementing reforms in Tanzania (URT, 2010), stating that a wider definition of culture needs to be adopted, which includes 'self reliance, confidence and patriotism, environmental conservation, the reading culture, adherence to ethical conduct, work ethics, entrepreneurship, savings …' (p. 21). This statement brings together a combination of local norms of self-reliance and patriotism with global ones relating to the environment, entrepreneurship, and saving.

These neo/liberal ways of thinking and practices that govern education, while hegemonic and distributed through international agencies and agendas, are resisted and adapted as they take form in sub-Saharan African countries. African studies scholars provide critiques of how liberalism and neoliberalism have influenced the role of the state, economy, and citizens, and they argue that social, economic, and political life does not necessarily conform to the dominant practices of liberalism and neoliberalism. For instance, Mamdani (1996) argues that the relationship between the 'state' and 'individuals'[3] must be understood through a postcolonial perspective of how colonial regimes[4] created political subjectivities based on race and ethnicity. Mamdani contends that colonial governments granted rights based on racial groups in which, he says, 'non-natives' were citizens, while 'natives' were subjects governed under customary law or local (and ethnic) groups, thus dividing the population as political and social members. Through the process of decolonization, most states, in political efforts toward nation-building, moved closer to inclusiveness and became deracialized; however, 'historically accumulated privilege, usually racial, was embedded and defended in civil society' or among local chiefs and customary law (Mamdani, 1996, p. 20). This process of creating new relations between the state, citizens, and the economy during decolonization resulted in citizens being inscribed as political subjects, though elites had economic, social, and political power tied to both local and international forms of governing, including the global economy. In addition, citizen subjectivities continued to be differentiated, at times, among ethnic and racial groups, and liberal notions of individual rights (and responsibilities) were not centrally important.

African scholars also critique the idea that citizenship is based on individually held rights prior to belonging to a community. Halisi et al. (1998) contend that this liberal notion did not recognize 'indigenous' conceptions and practices of citizenship present in African societies that are based on the community or group. They further argue that inclusiveness – or being part of a community – is a value separate from democratization and economic development in African countries: 'The tendency to overemphasize liberal citizenship with its emphasis on legal-rational factors while ignoring populist and communitarian conceptions of citizenship may be conditioned by a bias with which Africanists are familiar – the arbitrary distinction drawn between tradition and modernity' (pp. 341–342). Liberalism, they suggest, assumes that populist and communal perspectives of involvement in society are pre-modern and, thus, the purview of tribal or community governance, not the state. This differentiation between states and communities governing citizens, and its related inequalities, persisted through decolonization.

Citizenship education also reflects these tensions between citizens as individual political members of the state and as collective groups participating in social and economic life of communities. In addition, national values of equality, social change, and unity are often contrasted with participation in an unequal global capitalist economy. Scholars have argued that in recent decades, there has been a distinct shift in the curriculum toward individualism and participation in the global economy. For instance, Wainaina et al. (2011) analyze how citizenship education evolved in Kenya from post-independence to present day. Kenya's decolonization project propagated Democratic African Socialism as a guiding philosophy for the development of the nation. This philosophy recognized all members of society equally, with social responsibility toward others, and all groups equally, without one group having undue influence in society. From this perspective, education in Kenya was given the task of inculcating inclusive citizenship by both fostering a sense of national identity and unity, and eradicating divisions of race, tribe, and religion. Wainaina et al. suggest that in the early years of the nation, the aim was focused on political and social inclusion in efforts to erase the citizen–subject and native–non-native divides. To achieve this aim, the Kenyan government introduced social education and ethics as a subject in 1976 in order to develop national identity as well as the ethics deemed critical for addressing social divisions. In the 1980s, a clear shift occurred away from ethics and social equality to the development of the individual, skills, and knowledge (Wainaina et al., 2011, p. 185). By the 1990s, ethics education declined in its visibility, and the state gave increasing attention to policies that supported Education for All. These shifts resulted in a structural and political approach to equality over a discursive and social approach, meaning policies espoused political inclusion but local practices shifted away from norms of equity and unity and diminished social and economic rights over time and for some ethnic groups.

In South Africa, Hammett and Staeheli (2013) also find competing logics of educating for citizenship, those of 'the pursuance of state-guided, communal racial and social equality, and market-led socioeconomic individualism and responsibilization' (p. 310). They argue that despite policy efforts to foster equality, particularly in educational participation among racial groups, the economic conditions of schools and families overwhelmingly negated this equality and inclusion discourse. Differential funding and material conditions affected how young people related to schooling and the citizenship values they learned. The authors conclude that neoliberal policies aimed to develop skills for use in the economy and affected students' values and identities in a 'quest for quick money, respect, and social success through alternative means', in contrast to values related to the social, civic, and public good (p. 318). In sum, ways of governing citizen subjectivities, particularly through education in sub-Saharan Africa, attempt to construct a social and community-oriented[5] citizen based on principles of equality, but competing discourses also emphasize political and economic subjectivities oriented toward the state and the global economy.

Rights and responsibilization

Rights and responsibilization are invoked by various actors who advocate, fund, and implement entrepreneurship education and training programs, and these international agencies and NGOs often use these ideas with double meanings. Rights are used by governing regimes for the dual purposes of establishing citizen inclusion and participation in society, and also limiting the role of government in individuals' lives. One of the tensions that exists in the meaning of rights is whether they are conceived as moral rights (the rights of every human being to be protected by one's own or other governments and other private individuals), or as liberties granted and protected only by one's own state (Pogge, 2002).[6] In the first instance, rights are *universal* and the duty of everyone to protect. In the second, rights are *official*, established in laws and protected by governments. However, even within a state, there may be different abilities to secure the claims of rights.

Therein lies the contradiction between universal human rights, or those codified in international human rights conventions, and those granted by the state. Rights granted and protected by the state seek to be inclusive of citizens, but they also exclude, or do not protect all rights for all citizens. For example, the right to basic education may be considered applicable to all citizens – in this case a moral right (as set out in the Universal Declaration of Human Rights) granted and protected by the state. Currently, Tanzanian policy provides for the right to fee-free primary and now secondary education, but many students cannot afford to attend, as there are other costs – uniforms, books, test fees, and so on – to consider, even when schooling is considered 'free' and a right. Even when other governments or international agencies aim to protect this right within Tanzania through granting aid or providing educational programs, these rights are not fully ensured. The result is two groups: educated citizens who, consequently, have access to the formal labor market, and uneducated (or undereducated) citizens, many of whom are relegated to the informal labor sector with fewer social protections.

Global institutions and states also conjointly utilize ideas of positive and negative rights, often with contradictory meanings of freedom and choice. Positive rights refer to granting and protecting economic, social, and political rights through the state as the main governing institution, generally a liberal rationality (e.g., Marshall, 1964). This discourse regards the state – but increasingly other governing institutions, too – as benevolent and aiming to foster equality among individuals. Negative rights are used to ensure the autonomy of individuals and to limit government, such as prohibiting state-sponsored religion. This perspective tends to assume that private individuals and the economy can ensure social and economic development, and social equality becomes achievable through economic equality and means.[7]

Neoliberal discourses gave new meaning to negative rights, associating them with ideas of individual freedom, choice, and responsibilities. Miller and Rose (2008) argue that the idea of a state ensuring citizen rights came under critique for fostering passivity and dependency, particularly in the contexts of social welfare states in the USA and Europe. In response, a new discourse emerged in these contexts that associated rights with individual responsibilities and articulated citizens as active and exercising personal choice, in contrast to the meaning of responsibility as the duty of the state and all citizens to ensure wellbeing. Choice became associated with individuals being self-reliant and enterprising (Peters, 2009). This discourse also portrays those 'at risk' and not active in pursuing their choices, such as not going to secondary school, as in need of responsibilization. Responsibilitization in this sense means the moral obligation to be active and enterprising to ensure one's individual wellbeing, and not to rely on the state or community to protect rights. These ideas of 'youth-at-risk' and responsibilization are in tension with the ideas of community care and support, such as through education, health care, and other social welfare policies (Kelly, 2001). Miller and Rose (2008) capture this shift toward responsibilization as: 'active entrepreneurship is to replace the dependency of responsible solidarity as individuals are encouraged to strive to optimize their own quality of life and that of their families' (p. 79). Responsibilization has gained currency and spread globally in part because youths, particularly those who are ascribed as NEET (not in employment, education, or training), are regarded as a cost to society.

Skills development and entrepreneurship education and training are techniques used to foster responsibilization of youths for their own economic and social wellbeing. An underlying assumption of these initiatives is that education as presently offered (by the state) does not adequately prepare young people for jobs in a changing global economy; if they had skills aligned with the capitalist market, they would be employable or self-employed. The neologism 'skills for the twenty-first century', which broadly includes technological, communication, and life skills, among others, suggest that these abilities are necessary for integration into and further development of the global economy (King and McGrath, 2002; King and Palmer, 2006; UNESCO, 2012). Additionally, socio-emotional skills, such as resiliency and risk-taking, included in many entrepreneurship education and training programs, are increasingly advocated as necessary for getting youths out of poverty and ensuring they are productively engaged. The suggestion is that 'at risk' youths – those who live in poor material conditions but also are socially marginalized – need these skills to achieve the global goals of poverty reduction and, relatedly, economic growth.

African scholars offer strong critiques of hegemonic discourses of individual rights and, by extension, individual responsibilization (Halisi et al., 1998; Nyamnjoh, 2004). Nyamnjoh (2004), drawing on work in Botswana, challenges this 'rhetoric of rights', or rights as set out philosophically as if they are a *fait accompli*, but not practiced. He states: 'Being a rights-bearing independent individual is indeed neither as natural nor as affordable as is often presented' (p. 39). Here he makes the distinction between a philosophical ideal of universal moral rights, and rights being granted and protected by governments. Halisi et al. (1998) argue that colonial rule bisected the relationship between rights and obligations, meaning that rights were regarded as inherent to the individual and could be ensured by government without necessarily any obligations of citizens, in effect separating individuals and their political status from the community and social responsibilities. Relatedly, Ndegwa (1998) explains that for many African postcolonial societies, citizens hold rights and obligations to two entities: the state and their community. These two citizenship spaces, affiliation to the nation-state and obligations to kin-groups, also correspond to different values of participation in these spaces. For instance, political and economic power are necessary for participation in the state, whereas relationships and harmony are critical in kin and community relationships (Wainaina et al., 2011). While the Tanzanian state has long attempted to integrate political, social, and economic rights and responsibilities (Aminzade, 2013), social relations and status in different communities and the state still leave some, for instance uneducated young people, excluded from claiming many of these rights from their government. Likewise they may not have sufficient social relations or power to participate within their communities.

The universalization of human rights, as Englund (2006) shows in his ethnographic study in Malawi, also gets translated and interpreted as individual freedoms and responsibilities, and not necessarily that of the duty of the state or others in the community. He argues that the process of implementing human rights initiatives through NGO and government programs has left them 'prisoners of individual freedoms, their prime definition of human rights' (loc. 2656) and 'gives priority to political and civil rights at the expense of social and economic rights' (loc. 2667). Different from other scholars who have argued that international and national elites are to blame for such a narrow enactment of rights, Englund suggests that human rights activists, who are on the ground and part of these communities, have regulated themselves as certain kinds of subjects. Englund shows that civic educators used language and relationships with 'the poor' in their communities that ultimately made them responsible for their poverty. He concludes that interrogating how discourses of rights take on meanings in local contexts allows for actors to reflect and consider the tensions that emerge in their work. In sum, rights as universal (in content) and individually held are disputed by these scholars as necessarily explaining how governing happens in sub-Saharan African societies; relatedly, individual responsibility to ensure one's wellbeing also contrasts with local practices in which obligations are embedded in social relations in most sub-Saharan African communities.

Citizenship education is also a site where both individual rights and communitarian values are reflected and refracted. Preece and Mosweunyane's (2006) analysis of citizenship among youths in Botswana shows how ideas of communitarianism, civic republicanism, and individualism and self-interest are present in youths' citizenship practices. They define communitarianism as a community that is unified and the self is identified with the community. They argue this idea fits with Tswana 'culture' within the depoliticized space of family, where there is an emphasis on consensus and commitment to each other. Civic republicanism, on the other hand, places more emphasis on participation in civil society, and in the case of Botswana, they suggest is constituted by ethnic groups and patron–client networks. In their analysis, they find that youths learn values aligned with communitarianism through *botho*, or giving respect, particularly to elders; they imply this practice constructs citizen subjectivities related to harmony and unity within this community. Youths also learn values of individualism through schooling practices that emphasize critical analysis and diversity of thought over unity. They conclude that Batswana youths were situated in a tension in which citizen identities were neither solely communitarian as a part of family relations, nor were they necessarily individualistic and self-interested.

Arnot et al. (2009), in their review of citizenship education in Kenya and Ghana, also find tensions between individualism and communitarianism in the curriculum and in how youths practice their citizenship. They cite Kubow's (2007) study to show how both teachers and students find it difficult at times to navigate cultural norms that emphasize consensus, communality, and respect, as well as liberal values that advocate individual freedom and responsibility. Still, both communitarian values (through teaching about local cultures, religions, and ethics) and individual human rights are integrated in the curriculum. For instance, in Ghana, they note that the National Civic Education Programme integrates concepts that attend to both unity and diversity.

While both individualism and communitarianism as values are present in citizenship education in sub-Saharan African countries, these ideas hold a multiplicity of meanings that are dynamically changing. At times, individualism seems to be associated with moral rights of every human, and at other times with the enterprising-self who participates in an uncertain economy. Similarly, communitarian values at times refer to ethnic or kin-group norms and values, and at other times to the construction of a national identity, solidarity, and unity among a diversity of social groups. These scholars argue that even though social relations in families and communities are changing and the global economy and culture are more pervasive, communitarian and individual values are being practiced in new sets of relations and spaces, suggesting a need to understand how citizen subjectivities are formed in relation to diverse values and changing governing regimes (Preece and Mosweunyane, 2006; Honwana, 2012).

Participation and empowerment

As ideas, participation and empowerment are perhaps the most 'semantically versatile', to adapt Muehlebach (2012), used in education and development discourses and programs, and these ideas are often reinterpreted in contradictory ways over time and contexts. From a narrow political (liberalism) perspective, participation is a necessary component of enacting citizenship through engaging in political institutions and civil society. Such participation serves as a check on the authority of the state and as an enactment of individual freedom. This form of participation is most commonly fostered through civic education in schools. Political participation in postcolonial societies, however, was affected by a confluence of efforts to build the nation and those that limited international influences on society and the economy. Aminzade (2013) argues that Nyerere's initiatives to foster national identity and solidify the nation-tate through the national civil service limited political parties as the primary technique for citizen participation. In this way, political participation may also be regulated by the state.

In contrast to this more limited notion of participation, education and development initiatives give considerable attention to citizen participation to address social issues and to contribute to the economy. Participation, particularly of marginalized people, has been a development buzzword used by international agencies since the 1990s and particularly following the establishment of the MDGs. These efforts combined the goal of ensuring rights to education along with individuals' own role in their development. In the strange conjunction of neo/liberalisms, 'active' has become conjoined with participation, and its meaning has shifted toward individuals being responsible for addressing social problems, such as school dropout, and ensuring economic development. From this perspective, youths who are economically and socially marginalized are to actively participate in programs, such as entrepreneurship education and training, to ensure their own economic and social wellbeing and to contribute to national development. These different uses of participation reveal distinct purposes, means, and ends of being a citizen.

Many development practitioners and educators believe empowerment to be an outcome of citizen participation, assuming that by participating in political, social, and economic life, citizens have the power to address social and economic problems. Like the concept of 'rights', international agencies, NGOs, and citizens ascribe very different meanings to 'empowerment'. One reason for these different uses is the semantic versatility of choice as central to empowerment.

Kabeer (1999) provides a definition of empowerment used in many education and poverty programs: 'those who have been denied the ability to make choices acquire such an ability' (p. 2). She ties empowerment, or the ability to make choices, inextricably to disempowerment within a social and economic context, though it does not mean one is necessarily powerless. She further clarifies that choice has to be qualified. On the one hand, choice can mean simply having the freedom to choose; in this way, it is necessarily individual in that it espouses that if a young woman has the requisite self-esteem or knowledge, she can make choices. On the other hand – and Kabeer's definition tends toward this perspective – choice implies a young woman has access to alternatives and thus is able to choose from different options within her social and economic context. Therefore, it is not simply choice but alternatives that impact future livelihoods and wellbeing differently. This perspective, grounded in critical and feminist scholarship, assumes that empowerment requires the removal of obstacles that either inhibit choice as a psychological and cognitive function, or inhibit the options and the provision of both material (e.g., access to a school) and social (e.g., relationships that encourage attending school) alternatives.

In her book, *Logics of Empowerment,* Sharma (2008) argues that empowerment is a contested discourse and technology (through education or other training programs), used by NGOs, governments, and communities to express a process of including those who are excluded and disempowered economically, politically, or socially. This hegemonic discourse of empowerment calls for 'including' those who are 'in poverty' or 'at risk', as they are regarded as not being able to participate in political, civil, or social life (Kelly, 2001). Many empowerment programs designed particularly for youths and women emphasize individual psychological and cognitive characteristics of increasing self-esteem and knowledge so that 'poor people' are able to participate and choose. Unequal political or economic structures as causes of disempowerment or lack of alternatives are often overlooked or not substantively addressed in education models for empowerment. From this perspective, disempowerment, usually equated with 'the poor', is regarded as a symptom of individual attributes and failure. Sharma (2008) offers an important distinction between the meaning of empowerment used by sub-altern groups and feminists, such as Kabeer, and that of hegemonic development agencies. Critical perspectives of empowerment

> [e]mphasize the active processes of subordination carried out by people in positions of dominance and by social, political, and economic structures ... Empowerment, under current neoliberal orthodoxy, becomes a benign and programmatic way to train improper and deficient subjects in the ways of the market and civil society and to include them in these institutions. (pp. 26–27)

Empowerment is pervasive in development discourses and projects in Tanzania, from health to education to micro-finance. Vavrus (2003) argues that empowerment is most often used to emphasize a woman's agency and responsibility to improve the economic wellbeing of the nation. In this regard, empowerment is explicitly understood as economic. In education initiatives, empowerment is also linked to social changes, including how an educated and empowered woman improves health and wellbeing outcomes for herself and her family. Whether oriented toward economic or social outcomes, a nearly ubiquitous use of empowerment draws on a belief that youths and women are 'deficient individuals' and that with skills and attitudes imparted by these programs, their lives can be changed so they have better control over their wellbeing. Education in general, and programs targeting youths, such as entrepreneurship training for out-of-school youths, are tools used for empowering young people – sometimes with this rationale of fostering individuals' skills and choices to improve their own lives and other times with the logic discussed above of removing obstacles and creating alternatives. Despite this pervasive individualistic meaning of empowerment, some scholars have begun to show that education can both draw on and produce collective efforts toward social change, even if in small ways (Murphy-Graham, 2007, 2012).

Although citizenship and citizenship education scholarship in sub-Saharan Africa tends to emphasize practices of participation rather than empowerment, there is a clear critique of how power relates to citizen subjectivities and participation. Governing regimes in postcolonial sub-Saharan Africa emphasize political rights and participation over social, civil, and economic participation in society (Ndegwa, 1998; Englund, 2006; Aminzade, 2013). However, Ndegwa (1998) argues that political participation may be more symbolic than actual because participation in governance and society carries colonial vestiges of primarily engaging only powerful and privileged groups. He contends that during decolonization, a small group of elites worked for the development of the state, and, without societal struggle for rights, postcolonial governments maintained more power than the population to claim these rights. His argument draws on Mamdani's (1996) distinction that only select 'citizens' of the regime negotiated independence, the forms of governance, and the rights granted, and that many 'subjects' – generally the uneducated rural populace – were left out of the struggle. This bifurcation of political participation from economic or social power persists, creating greater emphasis in education, particularly civic education, on fostering political subjectivities in relation to the state with less attention to social and economic rights and participation.

Studies on youths and citizenship in sub-Saharan Africa also examine youths' participation, and how education may empower youths. Preece and Mosweunyane's (2006) study on how youths constructed citizenship and participated in civic ways responded to a concern raised in public discourse that youth participation in and responsibility to communities and the nation were waning. They found that young people's participation tended to be with local youth or self-sponsored groups and less with national or civic-related organizations, though Preece and Mosweunyane did not characterize youths' participation as declining or apathetic. Furthermore, youths regarded their participation as informed by communitarian rather than individualistic values in that they aimed to help and benefit others in their groups. Participation in local groups and their community, however, did not always signify decision-making power. The authors state that 'many expressed tensions about how they were excluded from participation in decision-making [particularly in traditional community structures]' (p. 12). Their findings show that young people care about and aim to affect political and social concerns, but usually through participation in peer groups or youth organizations where they presumably have more power and decision-making authority than in community and political institutions.

The changing meanings of youth participation and citizen subjectivities are further addressed in Honwana's (2012) analysis of young people across four countries in sub-Saharan Africa. Similar to Preece and Mosweunyane, she concludes that participation in the 'traditional' political structures of society has been disenchanting for youths, in part because these institutions lack the dynamism of the broader cultural, social, and economic environment in which youths live. She argues, however, that young people are critically engaged in societal issues and seek to foster social change toward greater democracy and equality, but not through ossified political structures. She makes the distinction between 'state citizenship', or the legal status for membership in a community, and 'participatory citizenship', or the extent and quality of one's citizenship as a function of participation in that community (Kymlicka and Norman, 1994, p. 111). Political participation and inclusion are important for youths in sub-Saharan African societies, but such participation is not necessarily empowering in the sense of creating social change that improves their lives. At the same time, youths also seek power through participation in the economic and social life of society, which is dramatically changing for many young people in sub-Saharan African countries. Hammett and Staeheli (2013) conclude that the task of educating citizens amidst these diverse purposes needs to attend to the value that young people place on education for their future: '[E]ducation may be tasked with creating new citizens, but ... citizens' engagement with the content and aims of education depends, to a great extent, upon their aspirations for the future and the value attached to formal schooling to those ends' (p. 327). This quote captures the importance of trying to understand young people's aspirations and what they value from their education and training that will enable them to participate socially, economically and politically as citizens.

Conclusion

In sum, neo/liberal governing technologies and techniques that produce citizen subjectivities utilize multiple and different meanings of the relationship between state, citizen and the economy; the rights granted and protected; the responsibilities needed to ensure wellbeing; and political and economic participation and empowerment. While these ideas may be more discretely associated philosophically or in policies with liberalism or neoliberalism, I suggest that there is great semantic versatility employed by diverse actors to achieve different means and ends. In sub-Saharan African societies, rights that are aligned with liberalism, as in the state granting and protecting the right to education, have at times hinged on a neoliberal use of the private sector as integral to governing and ensuring this right. In a similar way, NGO programs that utilize a neoliberal meaning of empowerment, one that is primarily about achieving economic outcomes, may produce effects of greater political participation (see Sharma, 2008).

Educational programs and the subjectivities they produce often conjoin liberal and neoliberal ideas, producing contradictory meanings and effects. Figure 2.1 represents some distinct and yet at times overlapping concepts in liberalism and neoliberalism as they are enacted through governing practices and ways of thinking. These concepts presented here are not meant to be comprehensive; rather they are used analytically in the subsequent chapters analyzing these programs. While there are many concetpual differences between liberalism and neoliberalism, including notions of freedom, liberty and property ownership, I have focused here on the concepts discussed above of rights, participation, responsibilization and empowerment because international agencies, NGOs and governments use them as rationalities for education programs, and particularly entrepreneurship education and training. These various actors use these ideas with semantic ambiguity and versatility, and the outcomes of their programs and practices are equally not clear. They bring together these ideas which, represented at the center of the figure, are where neo/liberal citizen subjectivities are produced.

To recognize the double and, at times, contradictory meanings of these neo/liberal ideas, in the rest of the book I examine how international agencies, NGOs and local communities implement education initiatives and use similar terms of participation or empowerment, but diverge in the kind of citizen they aim to create in Tanzania. I also explore how the young people who participate in these education and training projects are repurposing the skills and knowledge they have

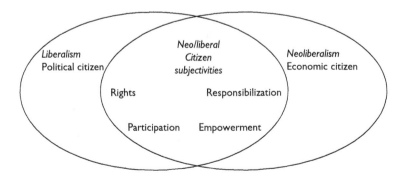

Figure 2.1 Liberal and neoliberal discourses shaping citizen subjectivities

learned to be responsible and empowered young people toward a livelihood that has economic value and social meaning to them, their families, and community. But the meanings of and outcomes from being responsible, empowered and included into social and economic life are complex and multiple. Turning next to consider entrepreneurship education and training programs, we can see these neo/ liberal discourses are present in international agencies' programs and practices.

Notes

1 I suggest they are re-emerging in some cases because skills development was advocated by donors in the 1970s and 1980s for many developing countries as a way to promote economic development, especially after independence. However, skills development, and in particular entrepreneurship, is different today as it is more strongly related to integration into a global economy rather than the development of the national labor force.
2 See Tikly (2017) for a more detailed analysis of the norms and practices that have shaped the SDGs and the different actors' influences.
3 I use quotes here because Mamdani (1996) is problematizing what is meant by the *state*, given the vestiges of colonialism; he is also reframing the idea that citizenship status as individuals is only one way of thinking about citizens; citizenship also includes the rights and protection of groups.
4 Mamdani does not differentiate between colonial regimes, though there were differences in practice. Rather, he gives examples of this citizen–subject and race–ethnicity divides across several countries and colonial governments.
5 *Community*, as used in these studies and citizenship education curricula usually refers to fostering solidarity among diverse community members in nation-building efforts. It can also refer to communities represented by ethnic or kin groups.
6 In this instance, I use the *state* as the governing entity that is most often associated with granting rights, particularly in relation to the nation-building project, and in contrast to governing institutions at the international or community level, which may draw on either human rights discourses or collective/communitarian values of inclusion.
7 Dean (2010) and Harvey (2005) provide rich discussions on Hayek's (1948) related ideas of negative freedoms, in which he argued that government should play no role in the regulation of individuals; in contrast, he argued, freedoms can be best achieved through individual moral discipline and the social order of the economy.

References

Arnot, M., Casely-Hayford, L., Wainaina, P. K., Chege, F., and Dovie, D. A. (2009). *Youth citizenship, national unity and poverty alleviation: East and West African approaches to the education of a new generation (No. 26)*. RECOUP Working Paper.
Aminzade, R. (2013). *Race, nation, and citizenship in postcolonial Africa: The case of Tanzania*. Cambridge, UK: Cambridge University Press.
Dean, M. (2010). *Governmentality: Power and rule in modern society* (second edition). Thousand Oaks, CA: SAGE Publications.
Englund, H. (2006). *Prisoners of freedom: Human rights and the African poor*. Berkeley, CA: University of California Press.
Halisi, C. R. D., Kaiser, P. J., and Ndegwa, S. N. (1998) (Eds.) Introduction: The multiple meanings of citizenship: Rights, identity, and social Justice in Africa. *Africa Today*, 45(3/4), 337–349.

Hammett, D., and Staeheli, L. (2013). Transition and the education of the new South African citizen. *Comparative Education Review, 57*(2), 309–331.

Harvey, D. (2005). *A brief history of neoliberalism.* Oxford, UK: Oxford University Press.

Hayek, F. A. (1948). *Individualism and economic order.* Chicago, IL: University of Chicago Press.

Honwana, A. M. (2012). *The time of youth: Work, social change, and politics in Africa.* Sterling, VA: Kumarian Press Publishers.

Kabeer, N. (1999). Resources, agency, achievements: Reflections on the measurement of women's empowerment. *Development and change, 30*(3), 435–464.

Kelly, P. (2001). Youth at risk: Processes of individualisation and responsibilisation in the risk society. *Discourse, 22*(1), 23–33.

King, K., and McGrath, S. (2002). *Globalisation, enterprise and knowledge: Education, training and development in Africa.* Oxford, UK: Symposium Books Ltd.

King, K., and Palmer, R. (2006). *Skills development and poverty reduction: The state of the art.* Post-Basic Education and Training Working Paper Series, No. 9. University of Edinburgh, Centre for African Studies.

Kubow, P. K. (2007). Teachers' constructions of democracy: Intersections of Western and indigenous knowledge in South Africa and Kenya. *Comparative education review, 51*(3), 307–328.

Kymlicka, W. and Norman, W. (1994). Return of the citizen: A survey of recent work on citizenship theory. *Ethics, 104*(2), 352–381.

Marshall, T. H. (1964). *Class, citizenship and social development.* New York, NY: Praeger.

Mamdani, M. (1996). *Citizen and subject: Contemporary Africa and the legacy of late colonialism.* Princeton, NJ: Princeton University Press.

McCowan, T. (2013). *Education as a human right: Principles for a universal entitlement to learning.* London, UK: Bloomsbury.

Miller, P. and Rose, N. (2008). *Governing the present: Administering economic, social and personal life.* Cambridge, UK: Polity.

Muehlebach, A. (2012). *The moral neoliberal: Welfare and citizenship in Italy.* Chicago, IL: University of Chicago Press.

Mundy, K. (2006). Education for all and the new development compact. *International Review of Education, 52,* 23–48.

Murphy-Graham, E. (2007). Promoting participation in public life through secondary education: Evidence from Honduras. *Prospects, 37*(1), 95–111.

Murphy-Graham, E. (2012). *Opening minds, improving lives: Education and women's empowerment in Honduras.* Nashville, TN: Vanderbilt University Press.

Ndegwa, S. N. (1998). Citizenship amid economic and political change in Kenya. *Africa Today, 45*(3/4), 351–367.

Nyamnjoh, F. B. (2004). Reconciling the rhetoric of rights with competing notions of personhood and agency in Botswana. In H. Englund, and F. B. Nyamnjoh (Eds.) *Rights and the politics of recognition in Africa.* London, UK: Zed Books.

Ong, A. (2003). *Buddha is hiding: Refugees, citizenship, the new America.* Berkeley, CA: Univeristy of California Press.

Ong, A (2006). *Neoliberalism as exception: Mutations in citizenship and sovereignty.* Raleigh, NC: Duke University Press.

Peters, M. (2009). Education, enterprise culture and the entrepreneurial self: A Foucauldian perspective. *The Journal of Educational Enquiry, 2*(2), 58–71.

Pogge, T. (2002). Human rights and human responsibilities. *Global justice and transnational politics*, 151, 3–35.

Preece, J., and Mosweunyane, D. (2006). What citizenship responsibility means to Botswana's young adults: Implications for adult education. *Compare*, 36(1), 5–21.

Samoff, J. (1987). School expansion in Tanzania: Private initiatives and public policy. *Comparative Education Review*, 31(3), 333–360.

Sharma, A. (2008). *Logics of empowerment: Development, gender, and governance in neoliberal India*. Minneapolis, MN: University of Minnesota Press.

Tikly, L. (forthcoming, 2017). The future of Education for All as a global regime of educational governance. *Comparative Education Review*.

UNESCO (2015). *Incheon Declaration*. Unesdoc. Unesco.org. http://unesdoc.unesco.org/images/0023/002331/233137E.pdf.

UNESCO (2012). *Youth and skills: Putting education to work*. EFA Global Monitoring Report. Paris, France: UNESCO.

United Republic of Tanzania (URT). (2010). *National Strategy for Growth and Reduction of Poverty II, Mkukuta II*. Dar es Salaam: Ministry of Finance and Economic Affairs.

Vavrus, F. (2003). *Desire and decline: Schooling amid crisis in Tanzania* (Vol. 13). New York: Peter Lang Publishers.

Vavrus, F., and Moshi, G. (2009). The cost of a 'free' primary education in Tanzania. *International Critical Childhood Policy Studies Journal*, 2(1), 31–42.

Wainaina, P. K., Arnot, M., and Chege, F. (2011). Developing ethical and democratic citizens in a post-colonial context: Citizenship education in Kenya. *Educational Research*, 53(2), 179–192.

World Bank. (2011). *Sector Strategy 2020: Learning for all: Investing in people's knowledge and skills to promote development*. Washington, DC: World Bank Group.

Chapter 3

Approaches to Entrepreneurship Education

[An entrepreneur is] the inspirational figure of our age ... creating wealth and prosperity for him/herself and others.
(ILO and UNESCO, 2006, p. 5)

Economists first defined entrepreneurship to refer to people who found alternative ways of using resources productively for higher yield or value (Say, 1855). The term, as Schumpeter (1934) used it, evolved to include innovativeness in business practices in order to grow the economy and create profit, a foundation of capitalism. While entrepreneurship is associated with financial gain, people in many diverse societies have long conceived new ideas and products and engaged in economic activity to earn money for themselves and to create wealth and opportunities for others. However, the purposes and forms of entrepreneurship that are practiced differ depending on the economic and social structures. For example, Tripp (1997) shows that entrepreneurship has been used as a strategy for economic survival in Tanzania, particularly when political and economic structures constrict labor options and provide little support and stability in securing livelihoods. While entrepreneurship emerged in Tanzania to address the family's basic needs and livelihoods, foundations and NGOs have adopted entrepreneurship as one of their core mechanisms for national economic development.

From the new millennium, in the face of growing youth population and the 2008 global economic recession, international agencies, nongovernmental organizations, and governments became increasingly interested in entrepreneurship education and training as a way to address the 'employment crisis' among youth (Volkmann et al., 2009; World Bank, 2009; Bohoney, 2011; USAID, 2012). The recent focus on youth unemployment is a shift in approach from many entrepreneurship education and training programs, which were initially oriented toward helping current or potential business owners develop small and medium-size businesses primed for expansion and technological innovation. Youths became a target group in part because more young people are attending secondary school, but they are not necessarily getting their certificates or learning skills applicable to the changing labor market. At the same time, the downturn in the global economy has resulted in fewer jobs in the formal sector. Thus, entrepreneurship education and training is regarded as one way to increase job creation and lower unemployment for the youth population. Until recently, we knew little about entrepreneurship education and training programs for youths, nor whether – and how – they foster job creation or future employment (Chigunta et al., 2005). Programs have proliferated in the past decade (see, for example, a review of programs by Valerio et al., 2014), suggesting that entrepreneurship education and training has emerged as a bona fide development idea and practice.

The growing interest in entrepreneurship education and training parallels the reemergence of skills development and technical and vocational education in global development agendas (King and Palmer, 2006, 2008; King, 2011; McGrath, 2012). Entrepreneurship education and training is a specific skills initiative that combines technical and business skills with attitudes and values, such as resiliency and risk-taking – often referred to as non-cognitive or life skills in these programs. The skills agenda, particularly supported by the World Bank, has evolved since the 1960s from one of specific vocational and technical skill sets for modern labor sectors toward market-driven and flexible skills that can be used across different types of jobs in today's changing global economy (King and Palmer, 2006). Formal technical and vocational skills training was largely deemed a failure, particularly in Tanzania, due to the high costs of training for certain specializations (Psacharopoulos and Loxley, 1984). More recently, non-cognitive skills, regarded as necessary and flexible in their use across many types of employment, have emerged as a major area of skill development. These skills, such as conscientiousness, communication, and self-esteem, can be individually cultivated and, therefore, are not as costly to teach as technical skills are (See Kautz et al., 2014). Donors, such as the World Bank, are also now giving particular attention to skills training for growing the informal economy and for poverty reduction, in contrast to earlier initiatives aimed at the formal economy (King and Palmer, 2006). Similarly, entrepreneurship education and training cultivates these non-cognitive and flexible skills, and prepares young people for creating jobs in the informal economy.

Entrepreneurship education and training is distinct from earlier vocational and skills development approaches, as it shifts the purpose of education to one in which entrepreneurial knowledge and skills are to be used *for creating jobs*, not simply applying one's knowledge and skills *to a job* (Valerio et al., 2014). As the joint ILO and UNESCO (2006) report on entrepreneurship education in secondary schools states:

> [T]he outcomes of entrepreneurship or enterprise education programmes at secondary level should not only be to stimulate employment opportunities, but to prepare young people for the complexities of life in today's urban and rural communities. Through the acquisition of practical learning, work and

life skills, programmes should improve the ability of students to anticipate and respond to societal changes more easily. (p. 3)

From this perspective, international agencies and governments use entrepreneurship education and training to create particular kinds of citizens.

International agencies, governments, and local actors utilize different underlying logics of entrepreneurship education and training in Tanzania, with varying goals, content, and outcomes. These approaches to entrepreneurship education and training parallel different approaches to development: those of creating human capital for economic growth, addressing equity and alleviating poverty, and fostering human development. In this chapter, I first provide a context for the Tanzanian study by discussing the dominant approach to entrepreneurship education and training, which is aimed at stimulating job creation and economic growth, contrasting it in the second section with a different approach that has the objective of reducing poverty and addressing other social ills that particularly affect youths. I examine these two distinct approaches drawing on the World Bank, ILO, and USAID documents and initiatives, because these actors dominate development discourses and practices through the documents they publish, the programs they finance, and the partnerships they create with Tanzanian governments and international NGOs working there. While I draw out distinctions among these approaches, in reality, the actors – international agencies, governments and NGOs – often bring together these different approaches in their programs.

Dominant framings of entrepreneurship are powerful, but alternative frameworks exist that position entrepreneurship education and training programs within a social justice perspective. In the third section, I consider a different model: the capability approach to entrepreneurship education and training, in contrast to the dominant neoliberal human capital perspective, is discussed. It prioritizes what individuals' value for their wellbeing such that livelihood outcomes are not a priori determined as economic wealth. It also attends to economic and social inequalities that exist and the supports that youths need to be educated and employed. The description of these three different approaches to entrepreneurship education and training, which draw on elements of liberal and neoliberal discourses, is helpful in identifying the heterogeneous goals and practices at play in the NGO entrepreneurship education and training programs that operate in Tanzania, which I analyze in the subsequent chapters.

Entrepreneurship education and training as job creation and economic growth

The most influential approach to entrepreneurship education and training has been that of the international agencies, such as the World Bank, the ILO, USAID, and the Kauffmann Foundation, which advocate it as a development effort to grow the global economy. In 2010, the US government, through the

Department of State and USAID, launched a Global Entrepreneurship Program. Program documents stated that entrepreneurship was the most effective way to address high unemployment and sluggish labor market growth: 'Entrepreneurship is now recognized as one of the strongest drivers of global job creation, with an important impact on economic growth and political stability' (Bohoney, 2011). But while some entrepreneurship programs have previously focused primarily on seed money and mentorship to existing entrepreneurs, this initiative and others began to put more emphasis on educating people to give them the necessary skills and mindset.

The argument that entrepreneurial attitudes and skills can be learned prompted initiatives to move from the realm of business and economic development into youth and education programs (Kuratko, 2005). International agencies have strongly advocated for entrepreneurship education and training for youths to be included in formal, vocational, and non-formal programs (ILO and UNESCO, 2006). The ILO has been an early leader of this agenda,[1] but this approach is supported throughout the international agencies. For instance, in the World Bank's (2011) Education Strategy 2020, entrepreneurship training emerges as a goal to address unemployment, particularly among youths who do not complete basic education.[2] In addition, entrepreneurship education in formal schooling is advocated based on the assumption that it can address the problem of creating more jobs if only more young people learned these skills and had an entrepreneurial mindset. For instance, a report for the World Economic Forum, *Educating the Next Wave of Entrepreneurs* (Volkmann et al., 2009), claims that anyone can be an entrepreneur and that everyone needs to be more entrepreneurial, particularly in a changing global economy: 'Entrepreneurial potential is in all of us. ... [T]he only difference is in the age of the entrepreneur. What differs between youth and adult entrepreneurship – given the inherently different levels of intellectual and behavioral maturity – is how entrepreneurship is taught and how it is learned' (p. 25). This report, in both the model it proposes and the case studies it reviews, puts much emphasis on learning entrepreneurship while giving little attention to the material and social conditions in societies that may not support entrepreneurship.

The proliferation of entrepreneurship education and training has prompted recent analyses to determine 'what works' for effective outcomes (e.g., Valerio et al., 2014; World Bank, 2013). A World Bank report, *Entrepreneurship Education and Training Programs around the World: Dimensions for Success* (Valerio et al., 2014), documents the increasing diversity of entrepreneurship education and training programs, their goals, target groups, and outcomes. They show that most programs are oriented toward promoting job creation and economic growth, particularly among 'high growth or opportunity driven entrepreneurs' (p. 7). The logic of this approach is to expand profits, create additional jobs, expand business products and customer base, achieve greater productivity, and reinvest in businesses. Programs achieve these desired outcomes by usually targeting 'opportunity entrepreneurs', or those who own an enterprise and show the propensity to expand and engage in a global value chain. These programs also address government regulations that inhibit growth, or alternatively promote private sector initiatives to expand entrepreneurship opportunities. While these programs have predominantly targeted older or opportunity entrepreneurs, the same logic and ideas are often incorporated into curricula that are being increasingly used with youths.

These programs rest on a belief that young people can be created as entrepreneurs through learning certain skills and cultivating a certain mindset – one of innovativeness, risk-taking, and creativity. While there is considerable debate about whether this mindset[3] can be taught, the ILO and UNESCO (2006) report advocates for both business and non-cognitive skills to be taught in secondary education.[4] These programs also teach young people to improve their locus of control and discipline, two aspects of inculcating a mindset among young people that prepares them to be enterprising individuals. These non-cognitive skills have gained prominence in the new global agenda[5] and are being taught in numerous youth livelihood programs.[6]

Resources and networks are also critical to achieving the desired outcomes of job creation and economic growth. A key premise of achieving economic growth is that enterprises are incorporated into a global value chain, or a set of activities that affect both supply and demand of products for any given business, in order to be competitive and make a profit. Being part of a global value chain requires assessing the markets, determining alternative markets as well as suppliers and competitors, and understanding how to add value. Most entrepreneurship education and training programs, even those targeting girls and boys through formal schooling, include how to assess consumer markets and determine one's competitiveness (see, for example, ILO and UNESCO (2006) for key skills to be included in entrepreneurship education in secondary schooling). But capital investment is needed to effectively engage in the value chain, and these programs often offer 'angel money' or 'seed money' at a level that will move the business beyond a small producing enterprise, such as food production stalls, to one that creates and adds value (Bohoney, 2011). Entrepreneurship education and training programs for youths, however, tend to provide little direct access to seed funding and microloans; rather, these programs tend to emphasize financial literacy and indirect access to loans, possibly because youths are regarded as 'too risky' for financial institutions.

Finally, entrepreneurship education and training programs oriented toward job creation and growth bolster government regulations and policies that support business development and growth. For example, *The Entrepreneurship Toolkit* (Bohoney, 2011) supports program implementers to consider how governments can spur enterprise development by removing constraints for private sector investment, such as reducing taxation on profits or providing contract regulation and enforcement. In addition, these initiatives are undergirded by a belief and some evidence from World Bank projects that involving the private sector in the delivery of education and training produces better effects on participants (Cho and Honorati, 2014). These World Bank and USAID programs give priority to private sector initiatives over government policies that provide greater social security to entrepreneurs.

This approach to entrepreneurship education reflects a neoliberal agenda, like the broader mission and strategies of the World Bank (see Sharma, 2008) in targeting individuals to become successful entrepreneurs by integrating them into a global capitalist economy. Governments' role in fostering such entrepreneurship is relegated to ensuring the freedoms of individuals and delimiting obstacles to private enterprise and growth. In addition, entrepreneurship education and training programs are used not only to achieve economic growth, they also seek to permeate social life and address social problems by advocating individual responsibility, encouraging entrepreneurs to be risk-takers, and teaching them how to be resilient in the face of economic instability and uncertainty. Relatively little attention is given to policies and programs that can foster social supports for greater income security or address income inequalities. For youths, and particularly marginalized young men and women, this approach is problematic. There is a disconnect between the assumption that entrepreneurship education and training can address the problem of unemployment by providing job creation and expanding businesses and the reality that most youths will not start new enterprises that are able to grow, at least in the short term. These programs do not often account for high business failure rates; rather, they assume that perseverance will result in eventual success. Still, the assumption persists that by educating youths, they will become entrepreneurs.

Entrepreneurship education and training as poverty alleviation

It is important to note the assumption that entrepreneurship programs can improve job creation and income, particularly for vulnerable groups, has been challenged by recent studies, even from within the World Bank (Valerio et al., 2014). The World Bank acknowledged recent research showing that the majority of jobs created is through microenterprises, which have high failure rates,[7] and they further stated that the driver of growth remains in the formal employment sectors (World Bank, 2013; Valerio et al., 2014). These debates have resulted in a differentiation between 'opportunity' and 'necessity' entrepreneurs. Opportunity entrepreneurs are those who are engaged in enterprises and could expand them; necessity entrepreneurs are those who have to start a microenterprise in order to generate income to survive. Thus, entrepreneurship education and training programs target these two different groups to achieve different outcomes.[8] Valerio et al.'s (2014) review of entrepreneurship education and training programs shows that programs targeting necessity entrepreneurs often do not result in improving income, employability, and growth, particularly long-term sustainable growth. The evidence from various studies led the authors to conclude that programs for 'vulnerable groups' are a means to poverty alleviation rather than as a means to '[foster] entrepreneurs and entrepreneurship' (p. 83).

Education programs for necessity entrepreneurs tend to be short term and nonformal, with most training focused on starting household enterprises or engaging in the informal economy.[9] These initiatives are oriented toward pro-poor development and poverty alleviation, which the World Bank and other international agencies also promote in addition to those oriented toward economic growth. This pro-poor or poverty alleviation discourse is linked with assumptions of reducing inequalities and ensuring the rights of the poor to have a decent livelihood. There is less evidence, however, of the long-term effects of such programs on getting the 'poor' out of poverty and having sustainable livelihoods.

The difference between entrepreneurship programs for economic growth and those for poverty alleviation is the groups they target and the outcomes they aim to achieve. The former promotes participation in the formal labor market and contribution to economic growth; the latter targets out-of-school youths or other disadvantaged groups and creates enterprises in the informal economy to generate income to meet basic needs. Programs aiming to alleviate poverty are often labeled youth livelihood[10] programs, though they teach similar skills and mindsets as entrepreneurship programs. And, increasingly, these programs incorporate an explicit entrepreneurship component and outcome of starting a microenterprise (e.g., Butler et al., 2012). For example, the USAID consortium EQUIP3 is designed to address youth livelihoods through workforce development, education, and engagement in the economy to improve the school-to-work transition. Their program documents state that it 'evolved to incorporate new components … [including] entrepreneurship' (p. 135). Preparing youths to work in the informal economy has emerged as the desired outcome of these programs, and evidence is increasingly showing this to be more probable than getting employment in the formal sector (Valerio et al., 2014). When these programs target 'at risk' or 'poor' groups for training, they perpetuate status differences and relegate these youths to the sector of the economy that is most unprotected by government social programs. Thus, while they use the language of addressing inequalities or ensuring youths' right to work, the programs do not promote equitable and favorable work conditions or work that supports youths' wellbeing.

Entrepreneurship education and training for poverty alleviation also aims to promote development by reducing social costs, as the groups targeted are deemed as idle, risky, and a 'profoundly destabilizing force' (James-Wilson, 2008, p. 2). Kelly (2001) argues that these programs perpetuate a binary between at-risk youths and entrepreneurial youths. He states, the 'population of Youth at-risk, in its negativity, illuminates the positivity that is the entrepreneurial Self' (p. 18). These programs claim that targeting 'at-risk' youths – those who are out of school or unemployed – not only reduces poverty, but also prevents social ills by responsibilizing youths to engage in productive work in the informal economy.

This logic of addressing 'social ills', such as ethnic conflict and political instability, attributes these problems to youths and their behaviors rather than to larger political and economic challenges of the government. The skills these programs teach (literacy, numeracy, financial, and vocational) and an array of life skills, such as discipline, communication, and resilience, are deemed necessary to ensure that youths contribute to society in constructive and productive ways. For instance, the USAID Youth Livelihoods Guide states that an aim of these programs is to foster positive youth outcomes in terms of democratic participation, public safety, education, and health (James-Wilson, 2008, p. v). Relatedly, EQUIP3 made a change in its youth leadership component of these programs to emphasize projects related to community needs. The consortium state that this change represented a shift away from 'power and payment', as in giving youths money and power to initiate projects they wanted to achieve, to one that 'instill[ed] in youths an understanding of their responsibilities to communities and families' (p. 142). This rationale suggests a concern about youths' dependency and a need to responsibilize, but not necessarily empower, them to make social change. EQUIP3 also note that civic engagement has become a common and important component of the program in order to 'strengthen youth's participation in project management and implementation and also because greater youth participation in governance and civil society is viewed as a potential strategy to stem political instability' (p. 144). Here, youth participation is a necessary component in solving community problems – in this case, political instability – rather than addressing the problem of youth exclusion in economic and political life.[11]

The logic of entrepreneurship education and training for poverty alleviation and addressing social ills, while seemingly influenced more by liberal discourses of pro-poor equity, also articulates neoliberal discourses, particularly the ideas of individual responsibility through learning life skills. The ultimate goal for most of these programs is for youths to participate in the informal economy by increasing private, albeit micro-scale, enterprise. In this model, less attention is given to the regulations that affect youths in conditions of poverty in distinct ways, such as national and city taxes and local neighborhood informal taxes, or to the barriers to enterprise development and financial resources for youths who have little access to financial institutions. While there is some recognition by the ILO[12] and the World Bank of the complicated environment in which youths secure jobs, and while they stress that other factors beyond the individual need to be accounted for, a considerable emphasis remains on youths and their household resources as efforts to reduce poverty (Elder and Koné, 2014). In effect, these programs emphasize youths and their skills rather than labor market reforms and employment programs as the way out of poverty (Robilino et al., 2013).[13]

Entrepreneurship education for human development and wellbeing

The above two approaches to entrepreneurship education and training assume that young people can, and need to, be entrepreneurs, and in turn, they can improve their lives. However, not everyone is able or wants to be an entrepreneur. While an entrepreneurship mindset is regarded as something that can be learned, there are other factors that 'make' or constrain entrepreneurs. Banerjee and Duflo (2012), two renowned economists whose research has focused on initiatives to end poverty and particularly micro-finance programs, make a strong statement against microenterprise development as the way to alleviate poverty: 'There are more than a billion people who run their own farm or business, but most of them do this because they have no other options. ... [W]e are kidding ourselves if we think that they [small enterprises] can pave the way for a mass exit from poverty' (p. 233–234). A related argument for a different approach to development comes from Gries and Naudé (2011), who state that a singular focus in the development agenda on economic growth overlooks the importance of human development, or how education and employment can expand freedoms and improve overall wellbeing of individuals, families, and communities. This third approach, a capability approach to human development, has a different logic than the other two, that of reducing inequality *and* improving welfare. It draws attention to whether and how individuals and societies value entrepreneurship education and training, and whether its outcomes enhance wellbeing, in addition to creating jobs or income.

Reducing inequalities is not central to many international agencies' strategies that promote entrepreneurship education and/or training, even if they are oriented toward 'pro-poor' programs. In fact, a pro-poor and poverty alleviation approach may actually exacerbate income inequality by differentiating and limiting the outcomes to work in the informal economy. Programs for economic growth target and support an already economically successful group, while programs for poverty alleviation limit opportunities to move into growth areas or into the formal economy. The first two approaches both assume that inequality and failure are necessary for entrepreneurship to thrive. The USAID Entrepreneurship Toolkit (Bohoney, 2011) specifically states, '[a] culture that is less critical of inequality, business failure, and personal independence may be more conducive to entrepreneurship' (p. 9). These above approaches do not take into account the lack of social supports and structures in some societies when businesses fail and when an individual assumes all the risks. In contrast, framing entrepreneurship education and training from a capability approach raises the concern for equality and focuses on achieving valued wellbeing, in addition to economic outcomes (Sen, 1992, 1999). A capability approach draws attention to youth livelihoods as more than a means of sustaining life on the verge of poverty, but rather as a pathway to stable, more equitable, and sustainable earning opportunities. This means policies are needed to reduce necessity entrepreneurship so that innovation and employability in the formal labor market can be achieved (Naudé, 2012). The logic of a capability approach to entrepreneurship education and training is that sustainable development is not achieved when entrepreneurial activities are limited to, or rely primarily on, the informal economy, which, when unregulated and unsupported by government policy, can exacerbate economic and social inequalities.

In using this approach to inform policy, it follows then that government social policies need to attend to historical inequalities and ensure that disadvantaged individuals and their households do not have to incur all the economic risks. These policies include job creation and labor market expansion, wage and labor market protections, and social security – regulations that are not typically associated with entrepreneurship in its neoliberal form (Naudé, 2012). Entrepreneurship education and training programs in middle- and high-income countries give more attention to improving the labor market and regulatory environment while those implemented in East Africa often include access to micro-finance and sociocultural constraints, usually related to participation in the informal economy (DeJaeghere and Baxter, 2014). Scholars argue that the informal economy is informal precisely because public policies do not offer certain social benefits, such as health insurance and social security, to micro-business owners or their households as they do in the formal sector (Balwanz, 2012). Without these social protections, informal employment is not an attractive option for future livelihood and wellbeing. Those who frame entrepreneurship education and related skills development from a capability approach argue that state policies and programmatic support for safety nets and employability are central to fostering entrepreneurship, rather than a singular focus on the individual characteristics, initiative, and resources. Social protection policies can foster greater confidence and motivation among new entrepreneurs; they also reduce costs for starting an enterprise and increase the range of business opportunities (Gries and Naudé, 2011). Such social policies include those that promote greater gender equality, given constraining gender norms for entrepreneurship (e.g., access to land, credit) and, at the same time, the over-representation of women in the informal economy. In addition, policies directed at youths include paid apprenticeships and employability programs, and policies directed at the macro-environment include equitable access to formal and informal sectors and financial services (Gries and Naudé, 2011; Balwanz, 2012). From a capability approach, these policies are a necessary component of entrepreneurship education and training programs; as DeJaeghere and Baxter (2014) conclude:

> Without governments committed to leveling the playing field, necessity entrepreneurs will not succeed as they transition out of programs and into competitive and struggling marketplaces. The chance of failure and its associated risks are far greater for youth from households and communities with limited and fragile safety nets. (p. 75)

A capability approach also positions entrepreneurship as something that should be valued and chosen, rather than being undertaken out of necessity to survive (Naudé, 2012; DeJaeghere and Baxter, 2014). In an unstable economy, youths learn that they have few choices and they have to create opportunities for themselves. Powell (2012), in her use of a capability approach for analyzing vocational and technical education policies in South Africa, argues that such education needs to foster the ability to aspire – to imagine and create a future that has meaning and is sustainable. A capability approach, then, shifts the lens away from the ends of income and economic development to the means of choosing and creating meaningful livelihoods. Powell, seeking to understand what youths valued and why they chose vocational/technical education, notes, 'For these students, colleges are not simply an opportunity to access the labour market; colleges are an opportunity to gain satisfying work in workplaces where they will be respected and where they can make a contribution' (p. 21).

A capability approach to framing entrepreneurship education and training can be best summed up in McGrath's (2012) terms: It replaces a 'productionist' framework aimed at developing human capital for employability by putting the wellbeing of people first and removing any 'unfreedoms' to achieving their wellbeing. Wellbeing is also not simply individualistic; rather, a capability approach considers the wellbeing of self and others, in the present and the future (Deneulin and McGregor, 2010; DeJaeghere, 2016). Thus, a capability approach points to how individuals are socially embedded and that their value to society is based on their social contribution, not only their work productivity (DeJaeghere and Baxter, 2014; DeJaeghere, 2016). A capability approach, while sharing some commonalities with the first two approaches, in that it does not discount the importance of job creation, economic growth and reducing poverty, is also an alternative to these approaches. It primarily focuses on what form of wellbeing is valued by participants of development policies and programs, and it considers the social and economic context that hinders or supports such wellbeing. In doing so, it allows for understanding historical inequalities and locally determined values of wellbeing.

Conclusion

As the analysis of these different approaches show, entrepreneurship is, foremost, an economic idea with a purpose of creating alternative means for economic growth; it also permeates social life through the values and attitudes it cultivates. It is used to promote economic development of society and it shapes individual development and identity to be an entrepreneur. Entrepreneurship education is used as an exogenous tool for development, promoted by international agencies, and it is practiced endogenously in communities. But within these different agencies and communities, entrepreneurship education and training is manifested in many different ways. The polyvalent framings of entrepreneurship education and training emerge from various ideas of the state and society, and how development occurs in specific times and places. For example, the USAID and the Kauffmann Foundation replicate strategies which are effective in the economic structure and environment and with entrepreneurs in high-income countries. These entrepreneurs are the 'ideal' of risk-takers and innovators, creating alternative business options where markets for other large businesses may fail.

In transferring these programs to low-income and poorly resourced contexts, as well as with groups that are vulnerable to global capital market failures, the ideal of starting and sustaining an enterprise may not be realized.

To see how these approaches are reshaped, we need to understand alternative and local regimes of governing, including the political ideals and practices, changing social life and relations, and moral economy and community practices in a country such as Tanzania. Sharma (2008) captures the distinctions between dominant economic and alternative approaches in a comparison of neoliberalism and Gandhi's perspectives on empowerment and self-rule in India. She argues that Gandhi's governance was firmly grounded in local moral and relational worldviews, whereas neoliberalism is an abstract and rational logic of the capitalist market and the state. She states:

> [N]eoliberal approaches focus more on individual entrepreneurialism and de-emphasize the dialectical relationship between self and society and between the individual and the collective, which is precisely what counterhegemonic frames highlight. ... [T]hey diverge in the terms of the social subjects they want to create and the kind of 'end' society they seek to establish. (p. 22)

To examine these alternative and local discourses and practices of governing, in the next chapter I discuss the historical context of Nyerere's approach to political economy, development and education, and the subsequent and changing influences on education, the labor market, and development in Tanzania.

Notes

1 The ILO adopted a resolution on youth unemployment in 1998. Starting in the early 2000s, strategies and programs for entrepreneurship education began to take shape, and the ILO has subsequently worked in many developing countries to implement its programs. See http://www.ilo.org/empent/areas/youth-entrepreneurship/lang–en/inde.htm
2 Entrepreneurship education is also included as one of five critical steps in the World Bank's framework of skills development (World Bank, 2010).
3 Non-cognitive skills, also referred to as socio-emotional skills, include attitudes and personality characteristics, such as resiliency, risk-taking, and perseverance, which are regarded as critical for entrepreneurs.
4 In 2004, the ILO started Know your Business (KAB), a program that has been used to educate young people about entrepreneurship around the world. KAB has been active in Tanzania, working with NGOs in programs such as the Y2Y Fund, which specifically aims to foster enterprise development for the creation of jobs, preferably ones that are longer term and pay well. See http://www.y2ytoolkit.org/what-is-the-y2y-fund.html
5 The SDG 4 on education includes a number of targets related to skills, including target 4.3, which is related to ensuring youths have access to vocational and technical skills for employment, decent jobs, and entrepreneurship. Target 4.7 also includes knowledge and skills to promote a sustainable development, including gender equality and global citizenship. Within these targets, various non-cognitive skills have been proposed as necessary for achieving sustainable development.

6 See, for example, the International Youth Foundation's Passport to Success, a skills training program that includes a broad set of non-cognitive skills, not only entrepreneurial skills or an entrepreneurial mindset. The aim of Passport to Success is to fill the gap between cognitive skills learned in formal education and those skills needed for employment. Indeed, there is a strong overlap between many of the non-cognitive skills taught in school-to-work and employability initiatives, and those taught in entrepreneurship education and training.
7 This World Bank report on entrepreneurship is citing other research they conduct on jobs globally. See World Bank (2012). World Development Report 2013: Jobs. Washington, DC: World Bank Group.
8 Scholars debate the distinction between necessity and opportunity entrepreneurs, and their ability to create jobs and generate growth. Some argue there is the potential for movement along this continuum, and that even household enterprises create jobs and income that is necessary. Still, many programs make the distinction in terms of whom they target and what they emphasize as program outcomes.
9 I use the term *informal economy* to reference those working in the informal sector *and* those who are in informal employment, which includes laboring as nonwage workers, working employers, unpaid family workers, apprentices, and self-employed workers. I also use the term to signify, as Gibson-Graham (2006) does, that there are different kinds of economies regulated by different laws, but also norms and forms of exchange that occur in the informal economy versus the formal economy.
10 The term *livelihood* is broader than employment and is used specifically by international agencies to refer to basic education/preparation for youths to secure any kind of work, usually in the informal economy, that will provide for necessities and possibly 'abundance for individuals and the family' (see USAID-sponsored EQUIP3, *Youth Livelihood Toolkit*, 2005).
11 For example, the USAID-funded Garissa youth livelihood project in the Somali region in Kenya had a notable component on citizen engagement of youths. Some funding in support of this initiative was given by the Department of Defense. Clearly the goal of political stability in the region was emphasized, and such citizen engagement tends to place the responsibility on youths for these "social ills."
12 It is important to note that the ILO approach to entrepreneurship education is distinct from the World Bank and USAID in their primary focus of creating employment outcomes, including starting enterprises. The ILO is also concerned about the conditions of employment for youths, including government regulations for wages and social policies for those working in the informal economy (see, for example, ILO, 2013).
13 The World Bank, along with other donors, has developed a Youth Employment Inventory that catalogs more than 500 programs globally. Robilino et al. (2013) show that 86% of these programs focus on training, while only a few address labor market reform.

References

Balwanz, D. (2012). Youth skills development, informal employment and the enabling environment in Kenya: Trends and tensions. *Journal of International Cooperation in Education*, 15(2), 69–91.

Banerjee, A. and Duflo, E. (2012). *Poor economics: A radical rethinking of the way to fight global poverty*. New York, NY: Public Affairs.

Bohoney, J. (2011). *The entrepreneurship toolkit: Successful approaches to fostering entrepreneurship*. Washington, DC: USAID, Economic Growth and Trade.

Butler, E. P., Taggart, N. and Chervin, N. (2012). *Education, earning, and engagement for out-of-school youth in 26 developing countries: What has been learned from nine years of EQUIP3?* Washington, DC: EQUIP3 Education Development Center.

Chigunta, F., Schnurr, J., James-Wilson, D., Torres, V. and Creation, J. (2005). Being 'real' about youth entrepreneurship in eastern and southern Africa. *SEED working paper, 72* Geneva, Switzerland: International Labour Office..

Cho, Y. and Honorati, M. (2014). Entrepreneurship programs in developing countries: A meta regression analysis. *Labour Economics, 28*(c), 110–130.

DeJaeghere, J. (2016). Girls' educational aspirations and agency: The critical role of imagining alternative futures through schooling in low-resourced Tanzanian communities. *Critical Studies in Education*, 1–19. DOI: 10.1080/17508487.2016.1188835

DeJaeghere, J. and Baxter, A. (2014). Entrepreneurship education for youth in sub-Saharan Africa: A capabilities approach as an alternative framework to neoliberalism's individualizing risks. *Progress in Development Studies, 14*(1), 61–76.

Deneulin, S. and McGregor, J. A. (2010). The capability approach and the politics of a social conception of wellbeing. *European Journal of Social Theory. 13*(4): 501–519.

Elder, S., and Koné, K. S. (2014). *Labour market transitions of young women and men in sub-Saharan Africa*. (Work4Youth Publication Series No. 9). Geneva, Switzerland: ILO. Retrieved from http://www.ilo.org/employment/areas/youth-employment/work-for-youth/publications/regional-reports/WCMS_235754/lang–en/index.htm

Gibson-Graham, J. K. (2006). *A postcapitalist politics.* Minneapolis: University of Minnesota Press.

Gries, T. and Naudé, W. (2011). Entrepreneurship and human development: A capabilities approach. *Journal of Public Economics. 95*, 216–224.

James-Wilson, D. (2008). *Youth livelihood program development guide.* Washington, DC: EQUIP3 Education Development Center, Inc. (EDC).

International Labour Organization (ILO). (2013). *Global employment trends for youth 2013: A generation at risk.* Geneva, Switzerland: ILO.

International Labour Organization (ILO) and United Nations Educational, Scientific and Cultural Organization (UNESCO). (2006). *Towards an entrepreneurial culture for the twenty-first century: Stimulating entrepreneurial spirit through entrepreneurship education in secondary schools.* Secondary Education in the 21st Century Series. Retrieved from http://unesdoc.unesco.org/images/0014/001470/147057e.pdf

Kautz, T., Heckman, J. J., Diris, R., Ter Weel, B. and Borghans, L. (2014). *Fostering and measuring skills: Improving cognitive and non-cognitive skills to promote lifetime success* (Report No. w20749). National Bureau of Economic Research.

Kelly, P. (2001). Youth at risk: Processes of individualisation and responsibilisation in the risk society. *Discourse, 22*(1), 23–33.

King, K. (2011). Skills and education for all from Jomtien (1990) to the GMR of 2012: A policy history. *International Journal of Training Research, 9*(1-2), 16–34.

King, K., and Palmer, R. (2006). *Education, training and their enabling environments: A review of research and policy.* Edinburgh, UK: Centre of African Studies, University of Edinburgh.

King, K. and Palmer, R. (2008). *Skills for work, growth and poverty reduction; Challenges and opportunities in the global analysis and monitoring of skills.* (Report TD/TNC 105.350). London, UK: British Council and UK National Commission for UNESCO.

Kuratko, D. F. (2005). The emergence of entrepreneurship education: Development, trends, and challenges. *Entrepreneurship Theory and Practice, 29*(5), 577–598.

McGrath, S. (2012). Vocational Education and Training for Development: A policy in need of a theory? *International Journal of Educational Development, 32*(5), 623–631.

Naudé, W. (2012). *Entrepreneurship and economic development: Theory, evidence and policy.* (Discussion Paper No. 7507). Bonn, Germany: University of Maastricht.

Powell, L. (2012). Reimagining the purpose of VET – Expanding the capability to aspire in South African Further Education and Training students. *International Journal of Educational Development, 32*(5), 643–653.

Psacharopoulos, G. and Loxley, W. (1984). *Diversified secondary education and development: A report on the diversified secondary curriculum study.* Washington, DC: World Bank Group.

Robilino, D., Margolis, D., Rother, F., Newhouse, D. and Lundberg, M. (2013). *Youth employment: A human development agenda for the next decade.* (Social Protection and Labor Discussion Paper No. 1308). Washington, DC: World Bank Group.

Say, J. B. (1855). *A treatise on political economy* (sixth edition). (C.R. Prinsep, Trans.). Philadelphia, PA: Lippincott, Grambo and Co.

Schumpeter, J. A. (1912/1934). *The theory of economic development: An inquiry into profits, capital, credit, interest, and the business cycle.* Volume 55. New Brunswick, NJ: Transaction Publishers.

Sen, A. (1992). *Inequality reexamined.* Oxford, UK: Clarendon Press.

Sen, A. (1999). *Development as freedom.* Oxford, UK: Oxford University Press.

Sharma, A. (2008). *Logics of empowerment: Development, gender, and governance in neoliberal India.* Minneapolis, MN: University of Minnesota Press.

Tripp, A. M. (1997). *Changing the rules: The politics of liberalization and the urban informal economy in Tanzania.* Berkeley, CA: University of California Press.

United States Agency for International Development (USAID). (2012, October). *Youth in development: Realizing the demographic opportunity.* (USAID Youth Policy). Washington, DC: USAID.

Valerio, A., Parton, B. and Robb, A. (2014). *Entrepreneurship education and training programs around the world: Dimensions for success.* Washington, DC: World Bank Group. doi: 10.1596/978-1-4648-0202-7.

Volkmann, C., Wilson, K.E., Mariotti, S., Rabuzzi, D. Vyakarnam, D.S. and Sepulveda, A. (2009). *Educating the next wave of entrepreneurs unlocking entrepreneurial capabilities to meet the global challenges of the 21st century.* (A report of the Global Education Initiative). Cologny, Switzerland: World Economic Forum.

World Bank (2009). *Youth and employment in Africa: The potential, the problem, the promise.* Washington, DC: World Bank Group.

World Bank (2010). *Stepping up skills: For more jobs and higher productivity.* Washington, DC: World Bank Group.

World Bank (2011a). *Learning for all: Investing in people's knowledge and skills to promote development.* (Education Strategy 2020). Washington, DC: World Bank Group.

World Bank. (2012). *World Development Report 2013: Jobs.* Washington, DC: World Bank Group.

World Bank (2013). *Framing the global landscape of entrepreneurship education and training programs.* (Report No. 78983). Washington, DC: World Bank Group.

Chapter 4

Researching the Tanzanian experience

To understand the effects that entrepreneurship education and training programs have in local contexts, we need to see how these programs move through various organizations, sites and actors. Researchers have analyzed the globalization of education reforms and practices – or the movement and engagement of global ideas and practices over time and space – through different theoretical and methodological perspectives. Some of those analyses perpetuate a universalizing narrative, while others critique how local actors take up, translate, or resist dominant ideas and practices. For example, neo-institutional scholars and approaches attempt to understand the convergence of educational practices globally by analyzing similarities in policies or curriculum at the national level (see, for example, Boli et al., 1985; Baker and LeTendre, 2005). These studies tend to ask what has been globalized, with less emphasis on the processes of how global educational discourses and practices move, converge, and diverge. From another perspective, some scholars utilize in-depth ethnographic studies of specific localities, in which educational practices take shape (see for example, Stambach, 2000; Anderson-Levitt, 2003). These local studies have been critiqued for their singular focus on the micro-level without consideration of meso- and macro-levels (Bray, 2007; Vavrus and Bartlett, 2009). These two different approaches tend to reinforce a binary between global and local influences and practices.

The approach I use in this book can best be described as a comparative case study of entrepreneurship education projects (Bartlett and Vavrus 2017),[1] which brings these different scales together through 'its concomitant commitment to micro-level understanding and to macro-level analysis. It strives to situate local action and interpretation within a broader cultural, historical, and political investigation' (Vavrus and Bartlett, 2006 p. 96). They further argue that local understandings and social interactions are not demographically or geographically bounded; they are part of larger structures and forces that occur nationally and globally. In this way, local practices and knowledge are regarded on a more equal footing with ideas and knowledge that is generated and disseminated by national governments and international agencies.

I use a comparative case study to analyze entrepreneurship discourses and practices across different scales, locations, and time, or as Vavrus and Bartlett

(2009) term it: to compare vertically, horizontally, and transversally. This approach attends to at least four important epistemological and methodological assumptions of the analysis in this book. First, my assumption is that while there are hegemonic discourses influencing entrepreneurship education and training programs, actors at all levels also have agency in shaping and rearticulating these discourses in specific social, political, and economic contexts. In this sense, the analysis assumes that structures and agency are 'mutually constituted across social practice' (Bartlett and Vavrus, 2017, p. 2). The comparative case study approach does not assume a singular or one-way influence of the globalization of education ideas. Rather, it allows for a deep and rich analysis of 'how global processes are shaped by and, in turn, influence social action in various locales' (Bartlett and Vavrus, 2009, p. 9).

Second, in this conceptualization of the relationship between the global and local, the comparative case study approach allows for a dialectical analysis, one that focuses on processes and relations that are heterogeneous and, at times, contradictory. Tsing's (2005) metaphor of friction is useful as a way to view these processes. Bartlett and Vavrus (2009) also draw on Tsing and conceptualize this approach as 'global encounters', stating that when studied in this way, we can examine how 'new and unanticipated cultural and political forms that exclude as well as enable' emerge (p. 10).

Third, this approach draws attention to the vertical scales of education discourse and practices. Vavrus and Bartlett (2006) state that such a methodological approach also has epistemological implication for 'situat[ing] the nationstate within a world marked by global agencies and agendas. ...Yet the national–global relationship is only one part of a vertical case because the local–national and the local–global connections are of equal importance' (p. 97). Analyzing vertically, I aim to understand how youths in local contexts make sense of the global ideas represented in the programs in which they participate, and simultaneously, how the international staff of the NGOs come to understand and adapt their programs to reflect the local contexts.

Fourth, this approach responds to the concern that a case study is not comparative and does not offer knowledge that is transferrable elsewhere. Bartlett and Vavrus (2014) suggest that a comparative case study that employs in-depth qualitative or ethnographic data, both compares vertically by examining how education policies and practices take shape across different scales or levels, and also compares horizontally across sites and time. They state that 'the horizontal axis compares how similar policies unfold in distinct locations that are socially produced (Massey 2005) and simultaneously and complexly connected (Tsing, 2005, p. 6)' (2014, p. 131). Thus multiple sites, as in this study, can be compared for similarities and differences in the processes and relations that allow for educational practices to take shape. Additionally, they term the comparison across time as the 'transversal', which 'reminds us to study across and through levels to explore how globalizing processes intersect and interconnect people and policies that come into focus at different scales' (Bartlett and Vavrus, 2014, p. 131).

Through these different analyses, comparisons of meanings and practices of entrepreneurship for development are made across time, space and scales.

By giving attention to these different scales and sites, I am able to examine the processes by which these entrepreneurship education and training programs become implemented, take on multiple meanings, and have, at times, unexpected and contradictory effects. While the emphasis is in part on understanding convergence and divergence across the vertical scales in which entrepreneurship education and training is funded and implemented, equally important are horizontal comparisons – between different communities and types of education – that allow me to comparatively examine differences and similarities, and the transversal dimension of how these programs create new meanings and practices related to citizenship, education, and livelihoods over time.

The international, national and local sites

The sites examined in this study, over the period of 2011 to 2016, include the international discourse used by those who fund entrepreneurship education and training programs more broadly, two international NGOs (*Parka* and *Apprentice*), and three different communities and education sites – a formal NGO all-girls secondary school (Sasema) in a semi-urban community, an NGO co-ed vocational/technical secondary school (Usawa) in a rural community, and a non-formal training project in mostly rural communities.[2] As I indicate below, I also draw on data from youths as well as interviews from teachers, facilitators, and local community members in each of the three communities and education settings.

The analysis of the *Parka* and *Apprentice* models of entrepreneurship education and training programs, the convergent and divergent goals and practices of these programs, and the various effects they have needs to be examined from a vertical perspective – of how international agencies influence the design and implementation of programs implemented at the national and local levels (Chapter 3). These programs also take place within a changing national political, social, and economic context, which is discussed in more length in Chapter 5. The local communities, staff and participants also all influence how these projects take shape. Below, I briefly describe the international agency that funded these entrepreneurship education and training programs, as well as some description of the NGOs, their programs and the local community and schools setting in which they are implemented.

International agencies

Many international agencies, including the World Bank, the ILO as well as bilateral donors and international NGOs, fund initiatives in Tanzania[3] to address the double-edged problem of inadequate knowledge and skills among youths for a changing labor market, and insufficient jobs in the formal sector for educated youths. This study involves one international foundation[4] that has a mission to provide learning opportunities, financial education, and services to improve the quality of life for those living in poor and under-resourced countries. The foundation supports a broad portfolio of projects in education/secondary schools and youth livelihoods in sub-Saharan Africa. Some of these projects include short-term training, technical skills, employability skills, entrepreneurship, and financial literacy aimed at facilitating the transition from education to self-employment or employment and better livelihoods. The projects funded in this study are not exclusively entrepreneurship education; rather, they employ holistic models of education, training, financial literacy, and skills development. A common feature, however, is a focus on the entrepreneurial mindset – the attributes of someone who is seeking and creating alternative livelihoods – and on skills to employ oneself through starting an enterprise. The projects do not necessarily have as a goal that all youth participants will start an enterprise or income-generating activity, though acquiring the knowledge and skills to do so is a goal. Through these programs, the donor is hoping to affect the kinds of knowledge and skills learned through education and training in sub-Saharan African countries, and to change attitudes and mechanisms by which livelihoods are secured in these communities.

The international foundation is well networked with other donors, as well as with a large array of international and local NGOs implementing projects in the areas of skills development, financial education, and employment for youths in sub-Saharan Africa. The foundation is influenced by and influences the larger development discourses related to youth, education, financial literacy, and livelihoods. The power this foundation wields in the international education and development agenda and in the discourses of these programs is evident: it commits millions of dollars to organizations small and large, local and international, and the knowledge created and learned from their projects is shared by a network of global actors. In addition, the knowledge generated from past projects is utilized to inform promising practices and models that they will fund in future initiatives. I draw on the institutional context of the donor and its related networks to illustrate how ideas and practices among international agencies influence other actors, but these donor strategies and programs are also reshaped by the ways of thinking and actions of others who implement and participate in the projects. These discourses, and the goals and practices of these diverse entrepreneurship and livelihood programs for youths were discussed in depth in Chapter 3. The final chapter of the book considers how our learning from these projects can inform donor approaches and the larger global agenda related to skills development and youth employment.

Entrepreneurship education and training projects: Parka and Apprentice

Parka and *Apprentice* are international NGOs whose entrepreneurship education and training models have been implemented in many different countries and social and economic contexts. *Parka*, originating in the Global South, has long implemented similar schools in other low-income contexts and countries. *Apprentice*, based in Europe, started implementing vocational education programs in sub-Saharan Africa in the 1960s. Their models have also been adapted and integrated into the interests and needs of specific communities within Tanzania, meaning they have identified community partners and settings that seek similar goals and processes for addressing skills development and youth unemployment. These organizations and their project models might be what Steiner-Khamsi (2006) calls 'travelling reforms', as they come from another context and are being implemented in a new one. *Parka* and *Apprentice*'s ideas of entrepreneurship education, financial education, and skills development are also considered as 'floating signifiers', meaning that they take on new meanings in local communities. Thus, I discuss the NGOs, their models, and the communities as sites in which the global and local discourses and practices meet, result in friction and are reshaped by different actors implementing the ideas of entrepreneurship education and training.

As international NGOs, *Parka* and *Apprentice* represent global discourses of education and development in at least three ways. First, they were deemed by donors to have a 'proven model' that could be adapted and scaled in other countries. The scaling of the organization's program is, in part, propelled by international donors whose funds support these models and ideas to travel to specific localities (Steiner-Khamsi, 2006; Silova and Steiner-Khamsi, 2008). Second, *Parka* and *Apprentice* are each broadly connected to international networks of development agencies, donors, and social entrepreneurs, and they have been recognized in international forums for their innovativeness in regard to youth and entrepreneurship. For example, *Parka* has been recognized by Ashoka, a global organization that supports social entrepreneurs and innovation to foster change and address social problems. This recognition gives *Parka* symbolic capital, such as meeting other similar organizations through their networks and credibility with donors that they have a recognized model. Third, their models draw on 'best practices' – program components that have been tried and sometimes researched, and then argued to be an effective 'universal practice' in promoting youth education and employment. For example, other organizations have already successfully implemented financial literacy training, internships and mentoring, and market scans to determine needed skills and training for the private sector, and *Parka* and *Apprentice* include these three practices in their projects. Finally, *Parka* and *Apprentice*'s mission and related projects align with global agendas concerned with poverty alleviation, education, and employment in that they seek funding or partnership with other global organizations, and they relate their programs and goals to these agendas by targeting 'marginalized' youths – youths who are/have been out of school and/or are unemployed. In sum, these entrepreneurship education and training projects, implemented by NGOs with different origins, philosophies, and histories, share goals and common practices related to skills, entrepreneurship, and livelihoods.

While *Parka* and *Apprentice* are international NGOs, their projects are situated in local communities and schools, in peri-urban and rural areas, serving girls and boys who have not (yet) completed secondary school. *Parka*'s economically self-sufficient schools (ESS) model operates within the formal education system, collaborating with other internationally funded NGO-supported and managed schools. These NGO schools require external funding to operate, often drawing on donations from international agencies or NGOs. These forms of funding make the school's sustainability precarious; thus, they have an incentive to develop an economically sustainable model, and collaborating with *Parka* aims to achieve this goal. *Parka* has also implemented its entrepreneurship and financial education through a business club model in government secondary schools in urban and peri-urban areas.

One of the NGO schools with whom *Parka* collaborates, Sasema, is a formal lower secondary (O-level) school located several miles outside a thriving city with a history of international influence and aid presence.[5] Currently, the area sees considerable donor aid aimed at increasing agricultural production for local and international export. Local industries, including masonry, carpentry, and rubber and textile factories, employ some graduates of local secondary and vocational/technical schools. Two well-regarded universities, one agricultural and one business oriented, serve the region; in addition, a college of education and several technical and vocational centers provide additional training and certification. In the neighborhoods and towns around the school, there is one other government secondary school available for all the youths who wish to attend – and are able to afford – secondary school. Other private (usually church-affiliated or NGO-sponsored) secondary schools provide much needed access to secondary education in the district. Sasema also serves a particular niche as an all-girls boarding school, enrolling girls aged 12–19 years who previously had little opportunity to participate in secondary school due to low primary test scores, poverty, pregnancy, or the need to work or care for family members. A female academic director and a psychosocial counselor serve as role models to these girls. The school integrates entrepreneurship education in the business and commerce classes of the formal secondary curriculum, as well as in an after-school business club required for all students in Form 3. As a part of the ESS model, Sasema operates businesses, such as raising chickens for egg production and tending a vegetable garden, and students are involved in producing and selling these goods. One of the business education teachers oversees the business clubs and the enterprises' financial management; Sasema also hires other staff with expertise in the different production areas, such as a poultry manager.

The second school, Usawa, is located in a recently formed region in Tanzania. The region receives considerable government and private support for developing its production and export of natural resources, including timber and tea. In addition to export products, agricultural production serves local markets. For instance, a milk production plant is owned by an international private company and, in part, by a local farmer cooperative. The region has a number of international and local NGOs working in the areas of sustainable agriculture and forestry production. Usawa is a vocational and technical school serving male and female youths aged 13–19 years who had not been able to continue their formal secondary schooling. Usawa started as a collaborative effort between an international NGO and the local church diocese that sought to establish educational institutions in the growing area. It offers certificates in technical trades, including masonry, carpentry, and agriculture; the course curricula are based on the VETA's national curriculum. The technical training areas were identified through a market survey of local company/community needs, as well as availability of teachers and curricula. For example, community leaders, local businesses, and the school are interested in developing a forestry program, but there is no VETA curriculum for forestry. At Usawa the ESS model integrates business and entrepreneurship content within the VETA courses, expanding upon the requirements and content of VETA curricula with more emphasis on practice-based skills working in school-operated businesses. As examples, the carpentry technical area aims not only to train students in carpentry techniques and skills, but also to develop products under contract with local businesses. The agricultural production unit teaches students how to care for cows and chickens, while also selling milk to the local milk factory and chickens to the local market. The school employs an academic director to oversee the academic training of students and a financial director to ensure the financial viability of the school. In addition, the *Parka* staff assist with marketing, production planning, and financial management to achieve an economically sustainable school. Sasema and Usawa's curricula and entrepreneurship education practices are further described in Chapter 6.

Apprentice implements a community-based entrepreneurial training program for non-completers of secondary education, usually those between the ages of 14 and 22 years. The program is non-formal and the different modules are taught over a nine-month period. *Apprentice*'s model creates collaborative learning groups in villages, utilizing local community trainers with expertise in specific trades to facilitate classroom and apprenticeship learning. Its model includes the following training modules:

- Vocational training
- Financial education, including a group saving and lending program
- Entrepreneurship skills
- Life skills
- Trade apprenticeships with community experts

The technical trades, again identified through a market survey of local needs and businesses, include auto and motorbike repair, carpentry, masonry, cooking, tailoring and sewing, among a few others that are added each session. As there exist few opportunities for formal employment in the communities where this project is implemented, the desired outcome for youths is to start microenterprises, individually or in groups.

The *Apprentice* project is implemented in several locations around Lake Victoria in Tanzania. The chapters in this book focus on the non-formal learning groups in two different locations: a small urban area that is also the region's capital, and a rural village. Being close to Lake Victoria, fishing is a major form of labor and food production for many households. Another is agriculture, both food and cash-crops with coffee being the primary export crop. In addition, some residents migrate temporarily to neighboring Uganda for employment or cross the border to trade with Ugandans; this is an option particularly for men working in auto mechanics and other trades. In the urban area, there is access to alternative education and training opportunities, such as vocational education colleges that provide training in agriculture, horticulture, and other trades. However, these programs may require the completion of secondary school or obtaining a certain score on primary school exams. They also charge tuition, making enrollment beyond many youths' means. In contrast, *Apprentice* targets secondary school non-completers and presently does not charge fees due to the international foundation's financial support. There are some financial institutions and community services in the urban community, so youths can access loans and savings mechanisms when starting and operating their businesses. In the rural village, few other training opportunities exist, except for formal schools and a few NGO training programs. In addition, there are no financial institutions, so financial services tend to be community-based mechanisms. *Apprentice*'s project in these two communities is the focus of Chapters 7 and 8.

While *Parka* and *Apprentice*'s models differ, they shared some similar goals and curricular features. Both include entrepreneurship education and training, and courses on life skills and finances, including practices to save and lend together in groups. Both projects aim to improve the employment or self-employment of youth, though *Parka* includes continued education and formal employment as possible outcomes of their program because they work with secondary school students. In addition, *Parka* and *Apprentice* staff have met with each other over the past five years to share ideas, curricula, practices, and challenges. This engagement, supported by the donor and facilitated by my evaluation team, has resulted in a convergence of discourses and practices. At the same time, differences have also become more apparent.

Research methods, participants and analyses

The study in this book is based on longitudinal quantitative and qualitative data collected over five years, from 2011 to 2016. While it is not an ethnography, the international research team employed ethnographic tools that allowed us to see and understand the perspectives of various actors from within their own socially situated contexts. For example, US-based and Tanzanian based researchers worked together, many of them over the five years, to draw on their language and cultural knowledge, as well as to co-construct meanings from the interviews. Some of the Tanzanian researchers were from the local communities; others worked in education or community and NGO projects. They often drew on their knowledge of the communities and education to both gather data during the interviews and to interpret it with us. Furthermore, the US-based team of researchers included several colleagues who had lived, taught, or worked in Tanzania for extended period of time (2–20 years). In this way, our combined knowledge and experiences, both within the country and outside it, were used to interrogate ideas and meanings.

My involvement in the evaluation project included leading and working with a US-based and Tanzanian research team to carry out the different types and waves of data collection. Over the five-year period, I engaged with the international foundation in regular (monthly) conversations, sharing what we were learning about the implementation and outcomes of these NGO programs. I also participated in large meetings and workshops the foundation held in Africa that brought together government officials, NGOs, the private sector, youths and other global and local partners with whom they work. I worked closely with *Parka* staff, planning data collection, interviewing them, and discussing the data analysis and interpretations to use in implementation of their ESS program. This included meeting with the NGO staff and youths, usually twice a year, for a total of nine visits to their organization and school sites. I met with the *Apprentice* staff on an annual basis to analyze and interpret data from their program. I relied on the international research team to conduct the annual data collection in the *Apprentice* sites, and I visited the training sites and communities once to interview staff and some youths during the five years.

Overall, our iterative approach to this evaluation – in which we engaged with the donor and NGO staff to design the survey and interviews, to collect the data, and to interpret the data for their use – revealed the unfolding of different discourses and practices related to their entrepreneurship education and training projects. The collaborative nature of the evaluation also allowed for co-constructing these discourses and trying new practices over time as the NGOs continued to reshape their projects. In the design of the surveys and interviews and the analysis of the data, I brought the perspective of a capability approach, one which sought to understand what youths valued for their future lives and livelihoods. This approach allowed us to examine their wellbeing broadly rather than assume a priori that their livelihoods would be defined and measured by their employment and earnings, as so many evaluations of these projects do (see DeJaeghere and Baxter, 2014). A capability approach also draws attention to the local values and meanings that shaped staff and participants' thinking and practices, as well as the constraints they face in their contexts. From this perspective, the data allowed for discussion and debate about the outcomes achieved, and it prompted the NGO staff to consider different conceptualizations of youth livelihoods as well as different practices in achieving them. For example, *Apprentice* was initially most interested in achieving self-employment for the youths in the trade they were trained, and they collected monitoring data on the number of youth employed or earning. Over time, these youths also sought other forms of education and training so they could expand the types of employment and earnings they could access. This prompted discussions among NGO staff about additional training as well as various outcomes that might be achieved, including fostering further education.

Methods

To understand changes over time and the effects of the youths' participation in the program, we utilized quantitative surveys at the beginning and end of the non-formal *Apprentice* program with three cohorts of youths. As participants in the *Parka* program participated in a formal school setting for four years, we administered the survey each year that they attended the school (with two to four different time points). Survey data provided information on programmatic components, such as financial, business, and entrepreneurship skills, knowledge, and values. Questions were also asked about youths' values for their future livelihoods; their goals, confidence level, and resilience toward their future; the supports they had to achieve their goals; and the attitudes they held about women's and men's abilities to secure their livelihoods, particularly through self-employment. These data allowed us to discern short-term outcomes of the program, as well as the youths' values and aspirations. In addition to the survey questions, each year we collected demographic data on the employment, educational, and financial statuses from a subset of the youths who participated in the qualitative interviews. These data provided a more detailed picture of the changes in their livelihoods. Over the years, we gathered more data about how they used their earnings to support themselves and their family, thus providing a richer understanding of how employment does or does not support their wellbeing.

The field research with the youths, NGO staff, and community actors took place over a one-month visit each year. We used qualitative semi-structured interviews with considerable probing of specific areas regarding youths' experiences in the programs and their current livelihoods. The main interview questions asked about their goals and aspirations; their current education or work status; supports from family, peers, and program staff; their current financial status, including what they spend and save; and the challenges they face. Each year, the interview questions changed slightly to capture emerging themes related to their livelihoods and the constraints they faced. We sought to understand the youths' family and community context, and how that shaped their livelihoods. In addition to interviewing program participants, we visited some of the microenterprises they had started in the community and met with the peers with whom they were trained or worked.

Semi-structured interviews with school staff, teachers, facilitators, and community members were also conducted each year. These interviews gave us further insight into how the programs were implemented; their perceptions of the youths and their current livelihoods (as many of the staff and community members had ongoing contact with the youths); and the supports and challenges in the community for these youths and their livelihoods. The semi-structured nature of the interview allowed us to ask community members, such as employers or financial providers, specific questions related to these youths' employment or to loans they may have taken to support their livelihoods. In addition to these interviews, the research team conducted interviews with the NGO staff three times each year in an effort to understand how the program was being implemented and any changes that were made. Again, using semi-structured interviews, we inquired about specific responsibilities of each staff. In the analysis, I supplemented the NGO staff interviews with available public documents, including curricula, regarding *Parka* and *Apprentice* programs in Tanzania and other countries where they work.

While the interviews provided the basis for understanding the goals and practices of these NGO entrepreneurship education and training programs and their effects on youths, to undertake the vertical and transversal analyses of the encounter of global, national, and local discourses, I enriched this analysis with a review of select documents. These included international agencies' strategies and programs – such as those of the World Bank, USAID, ILO, and other foundations – related to entrepreneurship and youth livelihoods, as well as from Tanzanian government policies, strategies, and programs. The analysis of the international agencies' documents and their discourses is discussed in Chapter 3. The changing discourses in Tanzanian government policies and programs over time are described in Chapter 5. These texts included government development strategies, including Tanzania's poverty reduction and strategy plans, education policies, recent youth development policies, vocational and technical training policies, and documents related to workforce development and entrepreneurship. (A more complete list of these documents is listed in Appendix A.)

Participants

In *Parka*'s economically sustainable schools program, we collected yearly survey and demographic data from cohorts of youths who attended the formal and vocational schools, Sasema and Usawa. In total, we had data from 244 (192 females and 52 males) secondary school-age youths[6] who completed the survey at least at two different, and some four, time points. In *Apprentice*'s non-formal program, we surveyed 712 (320 female and 392 males) youth participants at the start and end of the nine-month non-formal training program. This dataset includes three different cohorts of youths who completed the program in different training fields. Tables 4.1 and 4.2 provide general demographic data on the youths at the time they began their participation in these schools and programs.

Qualitative interviews were conducted with a subset of youths who participated in the program and for whom we had survey and demographic data. In the first year of evaluating the projects, we identified 60 youths participating in *Parka*'s ESS model, 30 from the formal secondary school, and 30 from the vocational/technical school; two years later we added another 10 youths from the vocational

Table 4.1 Demographics of *Parka* survey participants in formal and VETA schools

Age	12–22
Married	<1%
Children	5%
Median household size	6
Caring for one or more dependents	35%
Mother not living	16%
Father not living	32%
Previously started enterprise	12%
Currently working for pay	3%
Only one household member earns income	38%

N = 244
Source: DeJaeghere, Chapman and Pellowski Wiger and Learn, Earn, Save Project Team at University of Minnesota survey

Table 4.2 Demographics of *Apprentice* survey participants

Age	14–28
Married	14%
Children	19%
Median household size	6
Caring for one or more dependents	40%
Mother not living	15%
Father not living	32%
Previously started enterprise	22%
Currently working for pay	14%
Only one household member earns income	46%

N = 712
Source: DeJaeghere, Chapman and Pellowski Wiger and Learn, Earn, Save Project Team at University of Minnesota survey

school, for a total of 70 youths in the *Parka* program. We selected 30 youths participating in *Apprentice*'s non-formal training program; we included another 10 youths who began the program two years later, for a total of 40 youths in the *Apprentice* program in Tanzania. We conducted in-depth interviews with these youths for five years.[7] In total, 110 youths were interviewed from these two programs. I draw on four years of data, or a total of 222 interviews with youths from ESS schools, and 126 interviews from the non-formal training project. Tables 4.3 and 4.4 provide additional demographic data on these interviewed youths at the beginning of their program and four years later. As expected based on their maturation, more youths were married and with children in the fourth year, particularly those who had been out-of-school. Many were also responsible for at least one, and sometimes up to five, dependents. The brief narratives of Sudi and Marini below illustrate the lives of the youths in our study.

Sudi and Marini are typical youths from each of these programs and communities, and I met them at different points in their life trajectory. When I encountered Sudi, he was working as a mechanic in a local shop along with a

Table 4.3 Demographics of *Parka* interview participants

	No. of participants, first year of interview (N = 70)	No. of participants, final year of interview (N = 52)	
Married	1	1	
Children	5	5	
Caring for one or more dependents	31*	12	
Trade trained in (VETA school); Subject area studied (formal secondary)**		Carpentry:	5
		Masonry:	6
		Livestock/Ag.:	11
		Science:	14
		Arts:	2
		Commerce/Business:	9
		Dropped out:	4

Source: DeJaeghere, Chapman and Pellowski Wiger and Learn, Earn, Save Project Team at University of Minnesota interview

*These data were collected from only 60 of the interviews. In addition, it is not clear if the youths understood this question well regarding being responsible for dependents. Most of these youths were in school, so they could not be financially responsible for others. They might have, however, been taking care of others before returning to school. The demographic data over the years shows a lower number of the youths stating they were responsible for others, but we know from the qualitative interviews that once youths started working, either after completing school or during their breaks, they had more responsibilities to care for others in their family.

**These data are provided only for their final year as some youths had not selected an area/trade to study in the first interview.

Table 4.4 Demographics of *Apprentice* interview participants

	No. of participants, first year of interview (N = 39)		No. of participants, final year of interview (N = 31)
Married	2		7
Children	2		8
Educational level completed	Primary Grade 7:	24	No additional formal education completed
	Secondary Year 1:	1	
	Secondary Year 2:	1	
	Secondary Year 3:	2	
	Secondary Year 4:	11	
Caring for one or more dependents	19		28
Trade, trained, and working in	Auto-mechanics:	2	All work in areas where trained
	Carpentry:	4	
	Cooking:	2	
	Phone repair:	1	
	Embroidery:	2	
	Fish hatchery:	1	
	Furniture making:	1	
	Knitting:	5	
	Masonry:	2	
	Motorbike mechanics:	4	
	Tailoring:	4	
	Welding:	3	

Source: DeJaeghere, Chapman and Pellowski Wiger and Learn, Earn, Save Project Team at University of Minnesota interview

group of other young men. Sudi joined the *Apprentice* program at 20 years old, having been out of school for several years after completing primary school and not continuing to secondary school, like many of his peers in the program. He came from a village, as did the majority of youths in these programs. He was orphaned and living with his uncle, who did not provide emotional or financial support, similar to many youths in both the *Parka* and *Apprentice* programs. Sudi was, therefore, the main income earner, as were between one-third to nearly one-half of program participants. Sudi was also typical of many youths in these programs in that one of his major challenges was unexpected illness, either his own or others, and he had to pay for health care and medicine.

Marini, aged 17 years, was studying in Form 2 at Sasema when *Parka*'s entrepreneurship education program was first implemented. She came from a typical-size family of six in a village in the far north of Tanzania. (Some other girls who attended Sasema also came from faraway regions.) Unlike Sudi, Marini's parents were still alive, and they supported her financially and emotionally to pursue her education. She was married, which was not typical for many attending the secondary and vocational schools, but 15% of the youths in the *Apprentice* program were married, perhaps because, like Marini, they were older than the typical secondary student. She also had a child; between 5 and 15% of the youths, usually women, told us they had a child when starting the program, though others may have had a child but did not want to reveal this. In addition, more than a third of the youths were financially responsible for at least one dependent, often a sibling that they supported by paying school fees. Over the five years of this study, Sudi and Marini – along with other youths – became responsible for more dependents or became the main earners of their household.

Three times a year, we interviewed NGO staff who implemented the programs in Tanzania. The staff was mostly Tanzanian, though a few were from South America (*Parka*) or Europe (*Apprentice*). Over the five years, we interviewed 12 different staff from *Parka*, including their partner NGO school staff, and 7 staff from *Apprentice*. The staff had various roles – country director, program or site directors, and program facilitators. In the case of *Parka* (and discussed more at length in Chapter 6), it had a partnership with NGO schools and these school staff, such as directors and some teachers who implemented the entrepreneurship curriculum, and they were included in our interviews. Our engagement with the staff went beyond interviewing them; we worked with them to collect data in the schools or training sites, often spending days and weeks together in this process. In total, I drew on 120 interviews with NGO staff for this book.

In addition, we interviewed community members who were trainers or teachers, board members, business owners, financial service providers, and government educational officers. Thirty-six interviews were conducted with various community actors in the sites where *Parka* works, and 33 interviews were conducted with community actors from the Kagera region where the *Apprentice* project is being implemented. We interviewed some of the same community actors each year, as well as new ones later on. For example, in the first year, we did not interview anyone from local financial institutions, as the youths were not yet interacting with them. But in the subsequent years, we added interviews with these actors, as well as with community businesses and employers. For the analysis, I drew on 69 interviews with community members.

Analyses

In this comparative case study of different actors at the global, national, and local scales, I utilize primarily discourse analysis of the longitudinal interview alongside an analysis of policies and educational texts. I considered convergent and divergent ideas and meanings of citizenship as evident in discourses on entrepreneurship education and training, viewed across global, national, and local scales, but also across time from the socialist, nation-building period to present day. While meanings of citizenship as represented through governing technologies and techniques are analyzed through the arc of time, I give particular attention to the meanings that the NGO projects, their staff, and youth participants give to self and community, rights and responsibilities, and participation and empowerment as they construct their subjectivities as citizens.

For this book, the interviews and documents were analyzed inductively and discursively[8] to identify neo/liberal purposes and practices of education, the processes by which these practices take shape within local contexts, and the contradictions that occur across space and time. As the project evolved, I gave particular attention to the emergent possibilities within these discourses – in a sense, what new and local meanings and practices staff were giving to entrepreneurship education and training. I followed Fairclough's (2003) approach to discourse analysis: discourse as texts, discourse as discursive practice, and discourse as social practice. To analyze the discourses as text, I examined the vocabularies, semantic relations, and co-occurrence between keywords, such as *rights* and *choice*, that reveal contradictory meanings of citizenship. I first analyzed these words as found in the interviews. Fairclough (2003) states:

> The vocabularies associated with different discourses in a particular domain of social life may be partly different but are likely to substantially overlap. Different discourses may use the same words ..., but they may use them differently, and again it is only through focusing upon the semantic relations that one can identify these differences. (p. 130–131)

I then interpreted the interview discourses in relation to other discourses present in international agendas, including donor and NGO strategies and documents. For example, an NGO staff member referred to how the ESS model was related to another international organization's work, so I looked at documents from that organization to see the discourses they used, the descriptors of their program, and which international organizations they were related to (such as being supported by the World Bank). This analysis helps to understand how discourses become discursive practices across interrelated texts. Finally, I considered how the NGO, school staff, and youth participants acted upon these discourses and related them to historical and present-day practices in their local contexts. This analysis shows how the discourses become social practices with contingent, contested, and potentially transformative meanings in specific contexts (Rogers et al., 2005).

In addition to the analysis of interviews and texts, I draw on quantitative analyses of the surveys and demographic data. A propensity score matching (PSM) analysis was conducted to discern the effects of the program on youths (see Krause et al., 2016). This analytical method is particularly useful as the original study was not designed with a non-treatment group, but the PSM allowed us to analyze differences between those who had completed the program and those who were just beginning. I report data from this analysis in Chapters 7 and 8 in order to show the short-term effects of the program. I then compare and contrast these quantitative results with the analysis of the long-term interview data to understand how knowledge and skills play out in the youths' lives. This analysis helps to show that while knowledge and skills were important to their livelihoods, other social factors both during and after the program had considerable influence on their livelihoods and wellbeing. In addition to the PSM, I used descriptive statistics from the survey of all program participants, and also from the demographic data of the selected interviewees. These analyses included cross-tabs, for example, to see differences between how young women and men utilized their earnings. We conducted non-parametric tests to discern the significance of these differences between groups and over time, and we calculated effects sizes; however, the interview sample from *Apprentice* is too small to draw meaningful conclusions from statistical analyses. Thus, I present these data as descriptive statistics (in Chapters 7 and 8) and then draw on the qualitative interviews to provide an in-depth analysis and understanding of youths' entrepreneurial activities and what they meant for their lives.

Conclusion: Analyzing comparatively

In sum, a comparative case study – analyzing vertically, horizontally, and transversally – allows us to examine how policies and programs are shaped and repurposed globally, nationally, and locally, influenced by different rationalities of governing and social and economic life. In this way, as Bartlett and Vavrus (2017) argue, this approach positions culture and context as relational and spatial, socially produced through changing activities and meanings of education, livelihoods, and entrepreneurship, as discussed in this study.

Chapter 5 provides a rich analysis of education and livelihoods policy and practice over time in Tanzania – or the transversal axis of this comparative case. Key analytical concepts emerging from local discourses are presented in that chapter, including the changing meanings and practices of *Ujamaa* and self-reliance that will be drawn on in the subsequent chapters. Chapter 6 in contrast uses vertical and transversal analyses to explore how one NGO entrepreneurship education and training program, *Parka's* ESS model, was implemented over the five years in local contexts and in relation to past and present meanings of self-reliance. Chapters 7 and 8 examine *Apprentice's* model and the varied and complex effects on youths. These chapters consider the frictions between global and local approaches and discourses of entrepreneurship training. Together, these chapters allow for a comparison between these formal and non-formal NGO programs in different sites, or the horizontal comparison of programs within Tanzania. The analyses also serve as a heuristic for consideration by programs in other countries and sites.

Notes

1 Vavrus and Barlett have previously referred to this as a vertical case study approach (Vavrus and Bartlett, 2006, 2009; Bartlett and Vavrus, 2014) that aims to examine how international development policies are formulated and implemented across time and space – international, national and local levels. In their current book (Bartlett and Vavrus, 2017) they refer to this as a comparative case study, suggesting that comparisons are made at sites vertically and horizontally, as well as over time.
2 I use pseudonyms for the NGOs, the schools, and all staff and youths. This is to protect the anonymity of those who implemented and participated in these programs.
3 Sekei et al. (2015) provide a list of government as well as international agencies and NGOs working in the areas of youth employment, entrepreneurship and financial literacy in Tanzania. International agencies include DfID, Femina HIP, ILO, Plan, UNESCO, UN Women and VSO, among others.
4 The donor works specifically in the area of youth livelihoods in Africa but it shares broader goals and program designs with other international and national agencies working with youth unemployment, education and livelihoods.
5 I do not reveal the regions where *Parka* works as it would be quite easy to identify the schools, and the school staff. In contrast, *Apprentice* works in many sites in Kagera region with a larger staff.
6 We collected surveys from youths who attended the NGO schools implementing Parka's ESS model. Each year, the new Form 1/Year 1 students were added to the sample, thus we have fewer time points for those added in the second and third year of data collection; in addition, some youths dropped out of school and were no longer in the sample. In the analysis, we included only those youths for whom we have multiple time points; this resulted in a total of 244 young women and men (192 females and 52 males). The sample included more young women because one of the secondary schools was an all-girls school; the other was co-ed.
7 I used interview data from the first four years of the program, as the fifth year of interviewing had not been completed when undertaking this book.
8 While the larger study had a codebook and process for encoding the data according to the questions of our larger study, analysis for this book entailed re-reading the interviews, determining new codes, and, in particular, analyzing the data associated with codes, such as ways of saving or earning through the analytical lens of neo/liberalisms.

References

Anderson-Levitt, K. (2003). *Local meanings, global schooling: Anthropology and world culture theory*. New York, NY: Palgrave Macmillan.

Baker, D., and LeTendre, G. K. (2005). *National differences, global similarities: World culture and the future of schooling*. Palo Alto, CA: Stanford University Press.

Bartlett, L., and Vavrus, F. (2009). Introduction knowing, comparatively. In F. Vavrus and L. Bartlett (Eds.), *Critical approaches to comparative education* (pp. 1–18). New York, NY: Palgrave Macmillan.

Bartlett, L., and Vavrus, F. (2014). Transversing the vertical case study: A methodological approach to studies of educational policy as practice. *Anthropology & Education Quarterly*, 45(2), 131–147.

Bartlett, L. and Vavrus, F. (2017). *Rethinking case study research: A comparative approach*. London, UK: Routledge.

Boli, J., Ramirez, F. O. and Meyer, J. W. (1985). Explaining the origins and expansion of mass education. *Comparative education review*, 29(2), 145–170.

Bray, M. (2007). Scholarly enquiry and the field of comparative education. In M. Bray, B., Adamson, and M. Mason (Eds.). *Comparative education research: Approaches and methods* (pp. 341–361). Hong Kong: Springer.

Fairclough, N. (2003). *Analysing discourse: Textual analysis for social research*. London, UK: Routledge.

Krause, B. L., McCarthy, A. S. and Chapman, D. (2016). Fuelling financial literacy: estimating the impact of youth entrepreneurship training in Tanzania. *Journal of Development Effectiveness*, 8(2), 234–256.

Massey, D. (2005). *For Space*. London, UK: Sage Publications.

Rogers, R., Malancharuvil-Berkes, E., Mosley, M., Hui, D. and Joseph, G. O. G. (2005). Critical discourse analysis in education: A review of the literature. *Review of Educational Research*, 75(3), 365–416.

Sekei, L. Altvater, A. Kisinda A. and Chuachua, R. (2015). *Mapping study on the vocational education, skills training and entrepreneurship in Tanzania*. Baar, Switzerland: Development Pioneers Consultants.

Silova, I., and Steiner-Khamsi, G. (2008). *How NGOs react: Globalization and education reform in the Caucasus, Central Asia and Mongolia*. Bloomfield, CT: Kumarian Press.

Stambach, A. (2000). *Lessons from Mount Kilimanjaro. Schooling, community, and gender in East Africa*. New York, NY: Routledge.

Steiner-Khamsi, G. (2006). The economics of policy borrowing and lending: A study of late adopters. *Oxford Review of Education*, 32(5), 665–678.

Tsing, A.L. (2005). *Friction: An ethnography of global connection*. Princeton, NJ: Princeton University Press.

Vavrus, F. and Bartlett, L. (2006). Comparatively knowing: Making a case for the vertical case study. *Current Issues in Comparative Education*, 8(2), 95–103.

Vavrus, F. and Bartlett, L. (2009) (Eds). *Critical approaches to comparative education: Vertical case studies from Africa, Europe, the Middle East, and the Americas*. New York, NY: Palgrave Macmillan.

Chapter 5

Governing Regimes in Tanzania

Entrepreneurship education and training programs implemented by international agencies encounter governing practices that are situated in a local political economy and social life, both of which have changed over time and place in Tanzania. These local practices are rooted in the idea(l)s of Nyerere's *Ujamaa* that brought together philosophy and policies of African socialism and self-reliance. These ways of governing were an alternative to the illiberal colonial rule, as well as to liberalism's individualism and the encroaching neoliberalism of the global economy. The ideals and practices of *Ujamaa* and self-reliance arose during Nyerere's governing, and they continue to be important today; additionally, they have taken on new meanings. In this chapter, I first describe the historical emergence of *Ujamaa* and its meanings for development in Tanzania. In addition, the idea and policies of education for self-reliance were critical to development during Nyerere's governing, and I briefly illustrate Education for Self-Reliance's (ESR's) achievements, failures and the challenges that persist today. Following Nyerere's governing, the goals, policies, and practices for development shifted, and in the last section I summarize some of the main changes in policy, as well as the current status of education and employment in Tanzania. I then discuss the emergence of entrepreneurship education and training in policies and how they articulate with both global discourses and local practices of self-reliance and a moral economy. My aim is to provide a transversal analysis of sub-Saharan African and local discourses related to education, development, and the economy. By detailing these local discourses and their shifting meanings, it allows me to examine in subsequent chapters how the NGO entrepreneurship education and training programs encounter these rationalities and ideas, and the new meanings that emerge in the various communities and schools.

Ujamaa, equality, and development

During the decolonization period, Nyerere and leaders in Kenya, Nigeria, Ghana, and other new African states established a Pan-African philosophy and movement that created a new political discourse for independence, to be followed by nation building, citizenship, and governing. Campbell (2010) argues that the philosophy of Pan-Africanism, which arose from these leaders' struggles and commitment to freedom and independence, sought to do away with artificial colonial borders and asserted the self-definition and unity of people and purpose for many of these new states. Nyerere declared *Ujamaa*, informed by Pan-African Socialism, as the official state policy in his Arusha Declaration (1967). *Ujamaa* was an attempt to bring together African values and practices of social–family relations and community life, drawing particularly on the concept of *utu*, or common humanity, with political and social development (Campbell, 2010). In the Arusha Declaration, Nyerere put forth two main strategies for governing: socialism and education for self-reliance. He used both as means for promoting economic, political, and educational development and a way forward for the specific problems that Tanzania faced (Chachage, 2010). Socialism aimed to foster communal development that was neither dependent on a capitalist system nor colonial or foreign aid. It emphasized government ownership of and citizens' participation in economic development activities. Education for self-reliance was not only to prepare people to live in and serve society, but to live and work together for the common good.

Nyerere's ways of governing might best be captured in his 1986 speech, *Reflections on Africa and Its Future*:

> Our people's demand for independence, however, derived its major strength from their demand for human dignity and freedom. They wanted to govern themselves, in their own interests. And while they were demanding improvements in their conditions of life and in the provision of social services, they also wanted freedom and peace in their villages and towns and in their own lives. (in Mbilinyi, 2010, p. 79)

Nyerere's reference to freedom and governing themselves must be understood in the context of colonial rule and economic systems. His regime aimed to redress illiberal and, to a degree, liberal colonial governing regimes and, in its place, establish African values and policies in efforts to unify the nation politically and develop it economically without international and colonial influences. Pan-African Socialism resisted a capitalist market economy that was increasingly evident in political discourses and in economic practices. Nyerere saw the British colonial system as having emphasized and encouraged the individualistic instincts of humans instead of cooperative instincts or, in effect, liberal notions of individual rights over the collective and group. Mushi (2009) observes that '*Ujamaa* was to incorporate certain basic traditional principles (i.e., respect, common ownership of the means of production, and obligation to work) and marrying these to modern knowledge and technology' (p. 109). In this regard, Nyerere saw democracy (though not liberalism) as compatible with socialism, and socialism was able to incorporate some basic principles of African societies. Some scholars have critiqued Nyerere's ideas of *Ujamaa* as overly homogenizing values among diverse African societies, suggesting that governing practices and participation in society were much more diverse than could be practiced through *Ujamaa* villages and national socialist planning (see, for example, Burgess, 2005). However, in the case of Tanzania, African socialism also served as a symbolic purpose for national unity and inclusion in the new nation-state, even if political and economic participation may not have changed for many (Burgess, 2005).

Attending to social and economic rights, which had been unequally provided under colonialism, was central to Africanization efforts of the early postcolonial governments. Nyerere (1968b) articulated this approach to political and economic inclusion in his writings on *Freedom and Socialism*:

> The economic growth must be of such a kind, and so organised, that it benefits the nations and the peoples who are now suffering from poverty. This means that social and political development must go alongside economic development – or even precede it. For unless society is so organised that the people control their own economies and their own economic activity, then economic growth will result in increased injustice because it will lead to inequality both nationally and internationally ... Political independence is meaningless if a nation does not control the means by which its citizens can earn a living. (p. 88)

Linking social, political, and economic development was evident in *Ujamaa* (e.g., *Ujamaa* villages), his collective approaches to rural development through villagization, and in his strategy of Education for Self-Reliance (ESR), in which he called for education to serve as the means by which Tanzanians can reclaim control over their own development. Villagization aimed to foster economic and social development through collective agricultural means: 'they would live together in a village; they would farm together, market together, and undertake the provision of local services and small local requirements as a community' (Nyerere, 1968a, p. 351).[1] This approach was to encourage 'economic and social communities where people live together and work together for the good of all' (p. 348). Through ESR, Nyerere also placed importance on the role of schooling in facilitating the economic and social development of these villages.

Education, self-reliance, and citizenship

Education became an important tool for postcolonial leaders to reshape the colonial regimes that had limited who was a citizen and what the rights they had. Under colonial rule in Tanzania, attaining a secondary school certificate was a privilege reserved for only a few. Nyerere noted that in 1961, right before independence, just 11,832 Tanzanians were in secondary schools while there were more than 490,000 students attending primary schools (Nyerere, 1968a, pp. 270–271).[2] Additionally, more than a quarter of secondary students attended private schools, many of which were colonial schools established in the north (Nyerere, 1968a; Samoff, 1987).

Nyerere's Education for Self-Reliance (ESR) policy was prominently about promoting equality and universal literacy for Tanzanians to effect change in society that would lead to equitable development independent of external influences. He recognized that to achieve such independence, education needed to be used not only for political socialization, but also for economic development. His approach and writings were suffused with a commitment to cooperation and community, articulating a form of education that fostered equality and the common good. That was in contrast to individual economic wellbeing, which he saw as being propagated by colonial education:

> [Colonial education] emphasized and encouraged the individualistic instincts of mankind [sic], instead of his co-operative instincts. It led to the possession of individual material wealth being the major criterion of social merit and worth. This meant that colonial education induced attitudes of human inequality, and in practice underpinned the domination of the weak by the strong, especially in the economic field. (Nyerere, 1968c, p. 47)

From the late 1960s into the 1970s, various education acts established how these ideas were implemented. Nyerere (1968c) summarized the purposes of education for self-reliance:

> The education provided by Tanzania for the students of Tanzania must serve the purposes of Tanzania. ... It must encourage the development of a proud, independent and free citizenry which relies upon itself for its development, and which knows the advantages and problems of cooperation. It must ensure that the educated know themselves to be an integral part of the nation, and to recognize the responsibility to give greater service the greater the opportunities they have had. (p. 74)

Through the universalization of primary and the expansion of secondary schooling, as well as adult education, Nyerere aimed to achieve equality and unity, and ensure that all Tanzanians could contribute to society. Primary education was to be a 'complete education' aimed at preparing young Tanzanians to contribute to their communities; similarly, secondary education was not only to prepare students for higher education but also for life and service in their villages (Nyerere, 1968a, pp. 280–281). From 1962 to 1985, there was a very large increase in students completing primary education, though still only a small percentage went on to secondary schools. (See Table 5.1 for the completion rates of primary school students and their transition into secondary school from the 1960s to 2012.) For the goals of unifying the nation and achieving socialist ideals of community development, this progress in school participation was deemed a great success.

Nyerere's policies relate to Education for Self-Reliance also aimed to reshape curricular practices, values, and outcomes of education. Mosha (1990) summarizes the following objectives of ESR: changing the values and attitudes inherited from

Table 5.1 Students completing Standard 6/7 and continuing to secondary school – Mainland Tanzania, 1962-2012, by number and percentage for government and non-government schools

Year	Students completing Standard 6/7	Government secondary schools N	%	Non-government secondary schools N	%	Total N	%
1962	13,730	4,810	35.0	N/A	N/A	N/A	N/A
1965	29,367	5,942	20.2	2,329	7.9	8,271	28.2
1970	64,630	7,350	11.4	3,254	5.0	10,604	16.4
1975	137,559	8,680	6.3	5,786	4.2	14,466	10.5
1980	212,446	8,913	4.2	7,095	3.3	16,008	7.5
1985	429,194	10,881	2.5	12,625	2.9	23,506	5.5
1990	306,656	19,673	6.4	27,554	9.0	47,227	15.4
1995	386,584	28,412	7.3	28,002	7.2	56,414	14.6
2000	389,746	48,404	12.4	36,305	9.3	84,709	21.7
2001*	444,903	58,159	13.1	41,593	9.3	99,752	22.4
2005	493,946	196,391	39.8	46,968	9.5	243,359	49.3
2010	894,889	403,873	45.1	63,282	7.1	467,155	52.2
2011	973,812	457,321	47.0	65,058	6.7	522,379	53.6
2012	865,534	444,532	51.4	70,060	8.1	514,592	59.5

*Year PEDP was initiated, which reinforces free primary education for all

Sources: United Republic of Tanzania, Ministry of Education and Vocational Training (MoEVT). *Basic Education Statistics in Tanzania (BEST)*, 2013a. Dar es Salaam, Tanzania: MoEVT

colonialism; promoting scientific and technical skills; fostering support for secondary schools by integrating students into the life and work of the community; promoting democratic rights, a sense of belonging, and the value of work; and creating a socialist society based on equality, dignity, and work. To achieve these goals, ESR policies changed the content of school curricula that had previously been about Britain and Europe to content reflecting the history and cultures of Tanzania and sub-Saharan Africa. Nyerere also pronounced Swahili as the language of instruction at the primary level in an effort to foster national unity and identity.[3] These curricular changes ensured that most Tanzanians became literate in Swahili and learned attitudes to overcome class, ethnic, and religious differences and to unify the nation (Cooksey, 1986). A new civics curriculum was immediately implemented that included political education and activities from Standard 3 onward. In addition, primary students were given character assessments on dimensions such as their appreciation of work, and dedication and cooperative behaviors (Cooksey, 1986). Nyerere's aim of changing colonial attitudes, in which only an elite group was educated and able to lead the country and work in 'white collar' work, was necessary to foster development oriented toward Tanzanian's needs and strengths.

Education was integral to developing skills for work in and for the development of Tanzanian communities. Nyerere (1968c) eschewed an individualistic and material wealth development approach, as well as integration into a global economy. He stated:

> Alongside this change in the approach of the curriculum [referencing knowledge relevant for work in Tanzania] there must be a parallel and integrated change in the way our schools are run, so as to make them and their inhabitants a real part of our society and our economy. Schools must, in fact, become communities – and communities which practise the precept of self-reliance. ... This means that all schools, but especially secondary schools and other forms of higher education, must contribute to their own upkeep; they must be economic communities as well as social and educational communities. Each school should have, as an integral part of it, a farm or workshop which provides the food eaten by the community, and makes some contribution to the total national income. (p. 64)

Within the context of decolonization and nation building in Tanzania, self-reliance has a particular material meaning of freeing Tanzanians from a colonial economy and external government aid. It also reflects a psychological meaning in the way that Tanzanians should make decisions for themselves that support their own community and nation. Self-reliance had changing meanings over time, referring not only to national independence, but also that of villages and regions – places that could not necessarily depend on state or external support or aid. In a 1984 interview, Nyerere discussed his idea of self-reliance and noted how it started from his critique of Members of Parliament who demanded money all the time (El Saadawi, 2010). He suggested that not only must the nation work to be independent of foreign aid, but that villages and regions also needed to find ways to support themselves. This meaning can also be seen in ESR, where communities were expected to partially fund secondary schools rather than to be fully supported by the national government.

The main thrust of changing attitudes toward work, self-reliance in communities, and the country's development occurred at the secondary level, where the curriculum was diversified to include formal education subjects, agriculture, commerce, technical studies, and domestic science. Knowledge, skills, and livelihoods were to be developed, particularly in agricultural areas, so the country could feed itself without international imports or aid. Cooksey (1986) refers to this approach as the 'diversification and vocationalization' of schooling that aimed to promote skills and local jobs (p. 193). It also promoted a spirit of service to the community. To achieve both vocationalization and integration of schools into the life of the community, students did practical work on farms and in small businesses in an effort to earn money and contribute toward 25% of the secondary school operations (Cooksey, 1986). Involving students in income-generating activities in the community had several diverse aims – academic, ideological, and economic.

While Nyerere's approach to secondary education was considered by many within and outside Tanzania as an ideal for Tanzanian development (King, 1984; Cooksey, 1986; Samoff, 1987), the vocationalization of the curriculum fell short in several ways (Cooksey, 1986; Mosha, 1990). First, there was a shortage of equipment and materials for students to actually learn required techniques for agricultural and scientific production, such as how to test soil. Because they learned didactically, they could not actually apply the theories when they went out to farm or work. Second, by the early 1980s, most reports suggested that schools were nowhere near able to resource the required 25% of their budget from such community work. Third, because government funding was used to address the increase in primary school enrollment, the irony was that secondary schools, particularly their vocationalization, were supported through millions of dollars in loans from the World Bank (Cooksey, 1986) – in direct contrast to Nyerere's dictum of self-reliance. Finally, from an economic efficiency perspective, vocationalization was not successful because there were so few students who were attending secondary schools, thus making the per-pupil costs, particularly for some technical areas, very high.[4] In effect, the diverse set of academic, political, and economic goals of ESR were difficult to achieve, and the secondary school system was in real need of reform to address the growing demands as more students completed primary school.

One of the unintended consequences of Nyerere's policies – ones that emphasized primary and adult education over secondary, and that limited secondary schooling to achieving socialist planning goals as well as community development – was that private schools burgeoned. Those who completed primary school had little access to government secondary schools, and the upper classes, especially, invested in private education.[5] As seen in Table 5.1 above, primary school completion (Standard 6/7) declined slightly and stagnated from 1985 to 1995, and the percentage of students continuing to secondary was higher for non-government than government schools. These changes in secondary school participation were due in part to economic decline, a reduction in foreign aid, and the initiation of structural adjustment policies that decreased government investment in social services, especially education (Vavrus, 2003). These policies opened the door for private education to fill the demand that was not addressed by government schools (Samoff, 1987). Many Tanzanians felt that increased government financing for secondary education was needed to further achieve the desired goals of self-reliance and equality (Cooksey, 1986; Samoff, 1987).

Some of the challenges ESR aimed to address persist today, and some Tanzanians still harken back to many of its ideals to address these problems. ESR gave greater attention to a balance between theoretical and practical knowledge and the expansion of scientific and technical knowledge. Secondary education continues to be highly theoretical and abstract, oriented toward testing and, in turn, producing an elite few who pass the exams and go onto higher levels of education (Vavrus and Bartlett, 2013). An emphasis on practical knowledge, including vocational/technical skills and entrepreneurship, while contested, are deemed necessary to address unemployment problems in the changing labor market (King, 2001). While practical knowledge and skills for self-employment are advocated, they may not be the main value that ESR espoused as important for Tanzanian development. Chachage (2010) argues that the value of ESR was in its emancipatory approach to education for and by the community, and he believes this still has relevance for Tanzanian's education system today. He writes how Nyerere, near the end of his life in 1998, reflected on Education for Self-Reliance and its relevance for the purposes of education as a social and community endeavor today. It is helpful to quote Nyerere at length to understand his evolving discursive meanings of ESR:

> '[O]ur education, especially our higher education, should be socially responsible. Education for Self-Reliance is not Education for Selfishness. Yes, it is for Self-Reliance of the individual, but it is also for the Self-Reliance of our country. I believe that the community has a responsibility to educate its members. The need for individuals to contribute directly to their own education and the education of their children cannot absolve the community as a whole, represented by local and central government, from its duty to assist every Tanzanian to receive a good education. But a poor country like Tanzania cannot afford to educate the selfish. It invests in education in the belief that such investment is good for both the individual concerned and for the community as a whole. In the language of yesterday: Education for Self-Reliance ... should also be Education for Service. Not all of us will have the same concept of community, but all of us have a need to belong ... [T]hose of us who have been lucky enough to receive a good education have a duty also to help improve the well-being of the community to which we belong. (p. 164)

ESR was and is valued, in part, for its emphasis on social development and community, not only individual skills and employment secured through education. As a socialist project, then, it was deemed successful in producing a population with a basic education that had a mindset for community development and national unity. It was however, less successful in producing enough highly skilled people to work in formal employment, in part because it policies were unable to support adequate and relevant secondary education.

Changing ideas of development, education, and economy in Tanzania

Much was to change by the mid 1980s as the government was in economic and political crisis, affected by an international economic recession, poor government planning and spending, and costs accrued during the war in Uganda (Vavrus and Moshi, 2009). In 1985, the government shifted to the leadership of Ali Hassan Mwinyi, who engaged with the IMF and international donors in a different way than Nyerere. Nyerere had resisted a capitalist economy, specifically the IMF and the World Bank, with their structural adjustment programs of privatization and fiscal reduction of government sectors and services that resulted in user fees for social services, including education. Even though Tanzania had been granted debt relief by some international donors in the early 1980s, the country's economy was characterized by significant shortage of foreign exchange, high inflation rates, large budget deficits, and a falling standard of living (Lipumba, 1990; Dijkstra, 2008). During this time, a socialist regime of governing and the discourse of equality and self-reliance gave way to hegemonic economic policies of the IMF, including privatization, decentralization, and a discourse of individual freedoms (Samoff, 1987). The influence of the IMF on development and governing policies continued when, in 2000, Tanzania received the status of a heavily indebted poor country (HIPC) and was required to prepare Poverty Reduction Strategy Plans (PRSPs) that served as a guide and benchmark to a range of reforms, including ones addressing basic education (Vavrus and Moshi, 2009). It was during this time that policies and discourses of neoliberalism, liberalism, and socialism encountered each other with great intensity. Policy documents increasingly aligned with the global and hegemonic discourses of development agencies, but local practices, daily life, and some technologies of governing still drew on Nyerere's *Ujamaa* ideals.

These macro-level policy changes in the late 1980s produced gradual, though notable, shifts in education policies and practices.[6] The Education Act of 1978, which established ESR, was amended in 1995 with a new Education and Training Policy that set out another vision for education (URT, 1995). This new vision followed the macro-economic policies that emphasized investment, liberalization, entrepreneurship, and self-reliance for development (p. xi). In conjunction with the neoliberal discourse and policies that undergirded the new policy, self-reliance remained the guiding philosophy for development (p. ix). The policy incorporated these neoliberal rationalities in its aim to expand the provision of education 'through liberalization', and to 'broaden the base of financing through cost-sharing mechanisms including NGOs, parents, and end-users' (no page no.). It also explicitly recognized the need for entrepreneurship and self-employment, stating that vocational/technical education should particularly prepare young people for entrepreneurship. A new National Youth Policy (URT, 1996a) and a National Technical Education Policy (URT, 1996b) followed the Education and Training Policy, both of which aimed to address the problem of youth employment. (See Appendix A for a summary of key education acts, policies and their main goals.)

In 1998, the Government of Tanzania released the National Development Vision 2025 because it recognized the need for a new direction in line with reforms taken since 1986 and because prior development strategies were 'not in consonance with the principles of a market-led economy' (URT Planning Commission, n.d., p. ix). The discourse and ideas set out in the Vision lay the groundwork for subsequent education strategies and other development policies in the new millennium. The Vision opens with this statement:

> It is clear it will be a century dominated by those with advanced technological capacity, high productivity, ... and above all, a highly skilled manpower

imbued with initiative. If we are to be an active participant in the global developments of the twenty-first century, we must, as a Nation, find ways of improving and strengthening ourselves in all these areas. (URT Planning Commission, n.d., p. v)

It puts forward the importance of skilled and productive citizens and points to the role of being active participants in improving oneself and the nation so as not to be subjugated. The document repeatedly emphasizes developing a market-led economy in which the Tanzanian people creatively take initiative to 'harness market forces' (p. 10). In addition to calling for increased productivity through higher levels of skills and knowledge, the Vision calls for expanding Tanzanian cultural values through a 'developmental mindset' that includes fostering competition, self-reliance, and a culture of saving and investment to accumulate wealth and spur development. These statements show a shift away from education for community development, and particularly a socialist informed strategy, toward one of skills and participation in a global economy. At the same time, the Vision attempts to retain certain ideas and discourses, such as self-reliance and pride in national unity that have been nurtured since independence. It represents an approach to governing through technologies of the self by encouraging young people to develop a competitive mindset and to take an active role in their own development.

The Education Sector Development Programme (URT, MoEVT, 2000) was designed to operationalize the new Education and Training Policy, and drew on ideas set out in the National Development Vision. This document was also aligned with PRSP requirements and goals in order to secure donor funding for support of the education sector and, as such, it set out specific plans for improving primary and secondary education. In line with the international agenda of Education for All, it called for the achievement of universal primary education and the attainment of gender parity. The goals set out in the document were subsequently implemented through the Primary Education Development Program (PEDP) and the Secondary Education Development Programs (SEDP), funded by the World Bank. These initiatives built more schools and trained more teachers (Vavrus and Moshi, 2009), and resulted in a large increase from 2001 to 2010 in the number of students both completing primary school and attending secondary school, with the majority of these in government schools (see Table 5.1). However, progression to secondary education was based, until the Education Act of 2016, on passing primary-school leaving exams (Standard 7 exams), which kept participation rates in secondary education quite low. In addition to exams that limited enrollment, secondary education still had higher fees, causing further dropout of youths, particularly from lower-income households and rural areas. Despite these considerable efforts to increase secondary school participation, only 34% of all school-age children were enrolled in secondary school in 2013 (URT, MoEVT, 2013a).

In addition to participation rates in secondary school, much attention has been given to the quality of learning and students' pass rates, the latter of which have seen a steady decline since 2005 as more students entered secondary schools (See Table 5.2). For example, overall pass rates have declined from 78% in 2000 to 43% in 2012, and girls tend to have lower pass rates across all subject areas than boys. While enrollment and participation have increased, many Tanzanians do not complete a basic education (O-level certificate) that is needed to pursue further education or to enter the formal labor market.[7] Those who pass division I or II (best and second best) and can go on to government upper secondary schools (A-levels) are, however, still very few (see last column of Table 5.2). With many young people not continuing to higher education, there is a need for additional educational opportunities that provide relevant knowledge and skills for young people's futures.

In parallel with the formal secondary schools, students can also enroll in vocational education schools (Vocational Educational and Training Authority [VETA]), which offer certification from one to four years in different vocational and technical areas.[8] Those who enroll in VETA tend to be secondary-school leavers (71% in 2013), though a smaller percentage (23%) are primary-school leavers (Sekei et al., 2015). While the policies discussed above have emphasized increasing access to vocational/technical education and expanding the kinds of skills learned, only 2% of the secondary school-age population participates in VETA certified programs, though enrollment has doubled from 2008 to 2013, with slightly less than 50% being female students (URT MoEVT, 2013b, table 7.1). Participation in vocational and technical education is still minimal compared to the large number of youths seeking further education and training; on average, more than 600,000 youths annually are not able to continue their post-primary education (URT MoEVT, 2013b, p. vi). Training programs offered through private organizations and NGOs have proliferated as a means to address education and employment needs; however, some programs do not give a certification upon completion, and their cost and quality vary.

Table 5.2 Pass rates for Form 4 exam (end of Ordinary Level), 2000–2012

Year	Total no. of candidates	Percent passed	Percent passed in division I and II[1]
2000	47,389	78.4	9.8
2001	50,820	77.5	5.9
2005	85,292	89.3	11.7
2010	352,840	50.4	4.3
2011	339,330	53.6	3.5
2012	397,222	43.1	3.7

Sources: United Republic of Tanzania, Ministry of Education and Vocational Training (MoEVT). *Basic Education Statistics in Tanzania (BEST)*, 2010, 2012, 2013a. Dar es Salaam, Tanzania: MoEVT.

[1] Division I and II passes allow for students to continue their studies in government upper-secondary schools, or A-levels. Pass rates at Division III or IV allow students to continue studies in colleges and private schools, including teacher training and other areas of professional practice.

Being educated, at secondary school or in a VETA program, is by no means a guarantee of formal employment in Tanzania (as in many other countries, cf: Jeffrey et al., 2008; Mains, 2012); however, getting a secondary school certificate is important for securing a job in the formal labor market. This certificate is also a social marker of being an educated member of society. For those who complete higher levels of education and have the social networks to secure employment, they realize higher and more stable earnings and other benefits. But given low pass rates in secondary school exams, high dropout rates, and the low enrollment in VETA programs, a large population of youths is seeking alternatives to learning for and working in the labor market.

The formal labor market in Tanzania has grown since the late 1980s, from 5 million employed in 1990 to 22.3 million in 2014, but the informal sector[9] has also grown, comprising 8.7% of total employment in 1991 and 21.7% in 2014 (Mukyanuzi, 2003, p. 51; NBS, 2015). Youths comprise over 50% of the employable population in Tanzania, of which 84% of those aged 24–35 years are employed (NBS, 2015, p. 37). However, the majority (78%) are informally employed in agriculture, crafts, trades, and services in either the informal sector or in noncontract labor in the formal sector, which has unstable earnings and few social benefits, such as insurance and pension (Shamchiyeva et al., 2014, p. 4). Employment also has a gender imbalance, with the informal employment rates being nearly 90% for women and 70% for men (Shamchiyeva et al., 2014, p. 30) (see Figure 5.1). Of those who are unemployed, 50% are without work for longer than two years, and the transition for youths in Tanzania from school to work is

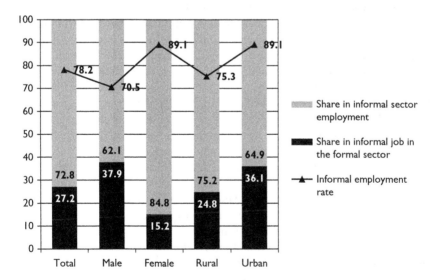

Figure 5.1 Youth informal employment rates by sex and area of residence
Source: Shamchiyeva, Kizu, and Kahyarara, 2014, p. 31

up to five years, longer than most countries in sub-Saharan Africa. Despite these labor market trends, most young people hope to work in the public and professional sector, which provides only 5% of jobs (Shamchiyeva et al., 2014).

Working in the informal economy has long been a prominent part of the Tanzanian economy, particularly as rural economies tend to be characterized by agricultural work and household microenterprises (NBS, 2014). Tripp (1997) notes that when real wages in the formal sector, particularly in urban areas, fell by 83% between 1974 and 1988, second jobs and micro- and small enterprises emerged as a way to supplement wages, and informal and small enterprises nearly doubled from 1985 to 1989 (Tripp, 1997, p. 24). The growth of the informal economy (and the lack of formal employment, particularly for youths) in Tanzania and throughout sub-Saharan Africa paved the way for new practices of entrepreneurialism. While the informal economy has often been regarded as outside state regulations and is either ignored or suppressed, the increasing participation in it has required new ways of conceptualizing and regulating it. Generally characterized by low-wage and low-skilled work and few social protections, the informal economy has become increasing regulated, entrepreneurial, and diversified. In addition, communities and trade groups provide their own norms and regulations for the relations and transactions that occur in the informal economy, offering forms of social protection and economic security. In this sense, the informal economy may be characterized as a moral economy (Tripp, 1997).

While Tripp (1997) shows the emergence of the informal economy in the 1980s in urban Tanzania, Mains (2012) argues that notions of reciprocity and exchange persist today, albeit in new forms, to support young men's livelihoods in Ethiopia. He shows how community social relations exist alongside economic activity that is part of a global capitalist economy. For instance, in his study, young men often migrated at some point to the US, and this migration allowed them to work in the formal labor sector or start their own enterprises from which they sent money back to their families in Ethiopia, thereby fulfilling their roles as independent working men who contribute to the wellbeing of their family. While these men worked in the formal sector, they often applied the norms of the informal economy by working together to start enterprises and by acting on principles of reciprocity, using their profits to give back to those who helped them either in their current work environment or back in Ethiopia.

While it is commonly practiced in the less-regulated informal and moral economic structures in Tanzania, entrepreneurship is increasingly included in policies for development in Tanzania. Since 1995 with the new Education and Training Policy that called for entrepreneurship to be included in education and training, various policies have emerged in the support of entrepreneurship as a method for economic development and job creation. Most notable is the development of the National Economic Empowerment Council (NEEC) in 2004, which established the Tanzanian Entrepreneurship Competitiveness Centre with a mission to foster skills development, create public and private partnerships, and support value chains at all levels. Recent policies and documents developed under the Economic Empowerment Policy (URT, 2004) have expounded upon how entrepreneurship as a mindset should be taught in order to achieve self-reliance and economic development. For example, the NEEC, working with ILO support and various governmental agencies, prepared the National Entrepreneurship Training Framework (NETF) (NEEC, 2013). It restates the Vision for Development 2025 and calls for an expanded developmental mindset as its rationale for infusing entrepreneurship education and training at all formal and non-formal education levels, from pre-primary to tertiary.

Strikingly, its rationale ties the aims of entrepreneurship to Nyerere's concept of self-reliance. It makes the argument that, as in 1967, the 'education system needs to be better aligned to the changing environment. Graduates must acquire employability skills' for both self-employment and salaried employment in a range of organizations (NEEC, 2013, p. 2). It goes on to argue that effective implementation of self-reliance then and entrepreneurship education and training now require a commitment to a mindset where youths '(i) take ownership and leadership of their learning and development, (ii) to start with whatever they have, even with very little, (iii) [to] work to learn and (iv) [to] get their hands dirty,' though they acknowledge this mindset was never fully embraced during Nyerere's period and, therefore, the policy failed (p. 2). It is unclear, then, why the authors of this framework assume that this mindset will be accepted in Tanzania today and that it will necessarily foster development, particularly for those who have limited resources and opportunities to expand their enterprise beyond the informal sector.

The NETF (NEEC, 2013) also lays out the objectives related to two sets of competencies, 1) enterprising tendencies and 2) business creation and development, or the former referring to mindset and lifeskills, and the latter to the outcomes of enterprise creation. At the primary and secondary levels, the objective is to build 'an entrepreneurial character in the student as well as motivation towards the entrepreneurial career'. The framework acknowledges that some, particularly those with only vocational level education, will primarily achieve owning and managing a microenterprise, while those with higher education levels should create and expand formal businesses. This distinction resembles the difference in target groups and outcomes that we also saw in entrepreneurship education programs discussed in Chapter 4. Notably, the framework gives substantial focus to expanding business into international sectors or markets, with little attention on how international markets, trade, and finances affect business development for even small enterprises. While much work remains to integrate this framework into all levels of education, there is a clear effort to incorporate these ideas into vocational education and training in Tanzania. For instance, as of 2013, a vocational and technical course on entrepreneurship is now available.

Despite efforts to include *ujasiriamali* (entrepreneurship) in the education system, there is much ambiguity in the interpretations and enactments of entrepreneurship. Even within the NETF, a tension exists in the values that entrepreneurship should foster, or the kind of good that is achieved and the purpose of such work for Tanzanians, the communities, and the country. The NETF states in its introduction that entrepreneurship is '[a] way of thinking, reasoning, and acting that results in the creation, enhancement, realization, and renewal of value', but the kinds of value are not defined. Later, it adds that 'value' is the process of change for individuals, communities, and the society, suggesting social change and transformation; but it also purports that entrepreneurship is to foster economic value in the pursuit of profit (p. 5). Thus, value is used loosely to refer to both social contributions of an entrepreneurial mindset and the economic outcomes of enterprise development.

Since the 2000s, entrepreneurship has become more formalized in economic, education, and youth policies in Tanzania. The practices of entrepreneurship in the informal economy that are still common to many Tanzanians differ from ones that aim to engage in a global economy and foster economic growth, as is the goal of many of the entrepreneurship policies. For instance, the Swahili term for entrepreneurship, *ujasiriamali*, is distinct from the common term of *biashara midogo midogo*, often used to refer to a household enterprise or small business in the informal economy, and these terms reference different goals and practices. While the new policies draw on affinities with *Ujamaa*, such as self-reliance and independence, the meanings differ from that of Nyerere's anti-colonial and nation-building discourse, which called for Tanzanians to be self-reliant from a capitalist economy and foreign aid. In the new uses of self-reliance, the emphasis seems to be more individualistic[10] and capitalistic. In this way, neoliberal discourses have permeated economic and educational policies in Tanzania. But this use of self-reliance in relation to entrepreneurship can also be read another way as global discourses of economic development encounter local and historically situated ones, as Tsing (2005) and Muehlebach (2012) remind us. From another perspective, entrepreneurship articulated with self-reliance can be an effort to foster cooperation and innovativeness among Tanzanians to work and develop their communities, rather than allowing international companies to use Tanzanian labor and extract the surplus. The multiple and changing meanings of self-reliance and economic development suggest that these ideas and practices of entrepreneurship education are polyvalent as they get enacted in local contexts (Ferguson, 2010). It is these polyvalent meanings that I explore in Chapter 6 by examining how international and local NGO staff implement their economically self-sufficient schools (ESS) program that aims to produce enterprising schools and students. Similarly, in Chapters 7 and 8, I examine how youths' lives and livelihoods illustrate the frictions between practices of reciprocity, solidarity and social development in a moral economy and those of profit, individual responsibility, and economic development as they learn to develop and enact their own entrepreneurial skills and enterprises.

Notes

1 This program of villagization, however, came under considerable critique for moving people to different localities, in a sense an infringement of human rights to live and work where one chooses. The actual practices of governing may not have lived up to the discourse of promoting human development.

2 These data refer to those attending school in Tanganyika (not including Zanzibar). In general, data related to school participation in this chapter refers to mainland Tanzania.
3 While Swahili had been used both in German missionary schools and in some British schools, English was also used in certain primary grades and in some schools. Nyerere called for a complete and thorough use of Swahili to foster literacy and national identity.
4 Psacharopoulos and Loxley (1984) undertook a large study of their financing of vocational education in Tanzania and found that inequities persisted across the different vocational areas, and that there were no real differences in work outcomes of those who studied agriculture versus other trades. Finally, they concluded that vocational studies were inadequate in Tanzania from a cost-effectiveness standpoint, particularly because so few students were entering the secondary level, thus making the cost per pupil high. While economic efficiency should not be the key determinant of the outcomes of vocationalization of secondary education in Tanzania, it does raise important questions related to economic sustainability of such programs even today.
5 I use private here because that was the term the government used up until 1995, and it referred to both for-profit schools and not-for-profit, religious schools. In the table, the term non-government is used because that captures more accurately the broad categories of schools, and it is the term used by the government since 1995. Private school was defined in The National Education Act of 1978, meaning 'a school wholly owned and maintained by a Person or body of Persons other than the Government or a local authority' (p. 7). In the Education Act of 1995, the term 'private' was changed to 'non-government school', with a slight change in definition: 'a school wholly owned and maintained by a person, body of persons or any Institution other than the government' (p. 3).
6 I analyzed the changing purposes, objectives, and content found in selected policies related to development, education and youth in Tanzania from particularly 1967 to 2013. These various policies are listed in Appendix A.
7 While some may be informally employed in the formal sector, most formal sector work with contracts and benefits requires an O-level certificate.
8 VETA certifies vocational programs for students who have not completed lower or upper secondary. There are also corresponding vocational and technical programs and certification following secondary completion.
9 According to the ILO (2012), the informal sector includes work in an enterprise that has 'informal characteristics', such lack as of formal business registration. Informal employment includes those who work in either the formal or informal sector without legal and social protections, such as young people working informally for a household with no contract or benefits (p. 2).
10 Self-reliance in Swahili, *kujitegemea*, has both a plural and singular reference. As a reflexive verb, it can mean independence for oneself or for a collective group. In this way, it can be semantically versatile in what it signifies. I am grateful to Emily Morris for her suggestion of this point.

References

Burgess, T. (2005). Introduction to youth and citizenship in East Africa. *Africa Today*, *51*(3), vii–xxiv.
Campbell, H. (2010). Julius Nyerere: Between state-centred and people-centred Pan-Africanism. In C. Chachage and A. Cassam (Eds.) *Africa's liberation: The legacy of Nyerere*, pp. 44–60. Kampala, Uganda: Pambazuka Press.

Chachage, C. (2010). Mwalimu and the state of education. In C. Chachage and A. Cassam (Eds.) *Africa's liberation: The legacy of Nyerere*, pp. 175–188. Kampala, Uganda: Pambazuka Press.

Cooksey, B. (1986) Policy and practice in Tanzanian secondary education since 1967. *International Journal of Educational Development, 6*(3), 183–202.

Dijkstra, A. (2008). *The impact of international debt relief.* London, UK: Routledge.

El Saadawi, N (2010). President Nyerere talks to *El Mussawar* (1984). In C. Chachage and A. Cassam (Eds.) *Africa's liberation: The legacy of Nyerere*, pp. 175–188. Kampala, Uganda: Pambazuka Press.

Ferguson, J. (2010). The uses of neoliberalism. *Antipode, 41*(s1), 166–184.

International Labour Organization. (ILO) (2012). *The youth employment crisis: Time for action*. Report prepared by youth for the Youth Employment Forum (Geneva, 23–25 May 2012). Geneva, Switzerland: ILO.

Jeffrey, C., Jeffery, P., and Jeffery, R. (2008). *Degrees without freedom? Education, masculinities, and unemployment in north India*. Stanford, CA: Stanford University Press.

King, K. (1984). *The end of educational self-reliance in Tanzania?* (Vol. 1). Edinburgh, Scotland: Centre of African Studies, Edinburgh University.

King, K. (2001). Africa's informal economies: Thirty years on. *SAIS review, 21*(1), 97–108.

Lipumba, N. H. 1990. Reflections on long-term development strategy in Tanzania. In *The Long-Term Perspective Study of Sub-Saharan Africa*. Washington D.C.: World Bank Group.

Mains, D. (2012). *Hope is cut: Youth, unemployment, and the future in urban Ethiopia*. Philadelphia, PA: Temple University Press.

Mbilinyi, M. (2010). Reflecting with Nyerere on people-centred leadership. In C. Chachage and A. Cassam (Eds.) *Africa's liberation: The legacy of Nyerere*, pp. 77–92. Kampala, Uganda: Pambazuka Press.

Mosha, H. J. (1990). Twenty years after education for self-reliance: A critical review. *International Journal of Educational Development, 10*(1), 59–67.

Muehlebach, A. (2012). *The moral neoliberal: Welfare and citizenship in Italy*. Chicago, IL: University of Chicago Press.

Mukyanuzi, F. (2003). *Where has all the education gone in Tanzania? Employment outcomes among secondary school and university leavers*. Dar es Salaam, Tanzania: DfID.

Mushi, P. A. K. (2009). *History and development of education in Tanzania*. Dar es Salaam, Tanzania: Dar Es Salaam University Press.

Nyerere, J. K. (1967). Education for Self-Reliance. *The Ecumenical Review, 19*(4), 382–403.

Nyerere, J. K. (1968a). *Freedom and socialism/Uhuru na Ujamaa: A selection from writings and speeches, 1965–1967*. Oxford, UK: Oxford University Press.

Nyerere, J. K. (1968b). *Freedom and socialism*. Nairobi, Kenya: Oxford University Press.

Nyerere, J. K. (1968c). *Ujamaa: Essays on socialism*. Oxford, UK: Oxford University Press.

Psacharopoulos, G. and Loxley, W. (1984). *Diversified secondary education and development: A report on the diversified secondary curriculum study*. Washington, DC: World Bank Group.

Samoff, J. (1987). School expansion in Tanzania: Private initiatives and public policy. *Comparative Education Review, 31*(3), 333–360.

Sekei, L. Altvater, A. Kisinda A. and Chuachua, R. (2015). *Mapping study on the vocational education, skills training and entrepreneurship in Tanzania*. Baar, Switzerland: Development Pioneers Consultants.

Shamchiyeva, L., Kizu, T. and Kahyarara, G. (2014). *Labor market transitions of young women and men in the United Republic of Tanzania*. Geneva, Switzerland: ILO.

The National Bureau of Statistics (NBS) [Tanzania]. (2014). *Basic demographic and socio-economic profile 2012*. Tanzania census. Retrieved from http://www.nbs.go.tz.

The National Bureau of Statistics (NBS) [Tanzania]. (2015). *Tanzania mainland integrated labour force survey: Analytical report 2014*. Dar es Salaam, Tanzania: NBS.

The National Economic Empowerment Council (NEEC) [Tanzania]. (2013). *National Entrepreneurship Training Framework (NETF)*. Dar es Salaam, Tanzania: The Prime Minister's Office.

Tripp, A. M. (1997). *Changing the rules: The politics of liberalization and the urban informal economy in Tanzania*. Berkeley, CA: University of California Press.

Tsing, A. L. (2005). *Friction: An ethnography of global connection*. Princeton, NJ: Princeton University Press.

United Republic of Tanzania (URT). (1995). *Education and Training Policy*. Dar es Salaam, Tanzania: Ministry of Education and Culture.

United Republic of Tanzania (URT). (1996a). *National Youth Policy*. Dar es Salaam, Tanzania: Ministry of Labour, Employment and Youth Development.

United Republic of Tanzania (URT). (1996b). *National Technical Education Policy*. Dar es Salaam, Tanzania: Ministry of Labour, Employment and Youth Development.

United Republic of Tanzania (URT). (2004). *National Economic Empowerment Policy*. Dar es Salaam, Tanzania: The Prime Minister's Office.

United Republic of Tanzania (URT), MOEVT. (2000). *Education Sector Development Plan*. Dar es Salaam, Tanzania: Ministry of Education and Vocational Training.

United Republic of Tanzania (URT), MoEVT, (2013a). *BEST 2013: Secondary education* [Excel format report]. Retrieved from http://www.moe.go.tz/index.php?option=com_docman&task=cat_view&gid=358&Itemid=619

United Republic of Tanzania (URT), MoEVT. (2013b). *BEST 2013: Primary education* [Excel format report]. Retrieved from http://www.moe.go.tz/index.php?option=com_docman&task=cat_view&gid=358&Itemid=619

United Republic of Tanzania (URT) Planning Commission (n.d.). *Tanzania Development Vision 2025*. Dar es Salaam, Tanzania: President's Office.

Vavrus, F. (2003). *Desire and decline: Schooling amid crisis in Tanzania* (Vol. 13). New York: Peter Lang Publishers.

Vavrus, F. and Bartlett, L. (2013). *Teaching in tension: International pedagogies, national policies and teachers' pedagogies in Tanzania*. Rotterdam, Netherlands: Sense Publisher.

Vavrus, F. and Moshi, G. (2009). The cost of a 'free' primary education in Tanzania. *International Critical Childhood Policy Studies Journal, 2*(1), 31–42.

Chapter 6

Educating for Self-sufficiency
Schools, Markets, and Social Good[1]

Understanding entrepreneurship education and training programs, the discourses they use and the effects they have on youths requires a close examination of NGOs, their staff and practices as they take shape in the in-between spaces of international agencies who fund them and local economic and social practices where they implement their programs. NGOs operate at the interstices of international agencies and local communities, often mediating global development discourses through the state and communities, or what Kamat (2004) calls 'implement[ing] the global commitment to "bottom-up" development' (p. 155). Other scholars have argued NGOs provide an 'alternative space' that offers 'parallel discursive arenas where members of subordinated social groups invent and circulate counterdiscourses (Fraser, 1997, p. 81). Qualitative and ethnographic studies have shown that NGOs are a contested space where meanings of rights, participation, and empowerment are negotiated among actors at many levels (Englund, 2006; Sharma, 2008; DeJaeghere and Pellowski Wiger, 2013; Sharma et al., 2013). NGOs are diverse and complex institutions. Some are strongly associated with international funding and discourses; others are more connected to local concerns and practices. The NGOs in this study employ universalizing ideas and norms about entrepreneurship education that are moved from one place to another. Additionally their local staff reinterpret the purposes and meanings of entrepreneurship education as they negotiate its implementation and desired outcomes in local schools and communities. The staff wield power to enact their programs because they have funding from an international foundation. At the same time, the staff need to understand and respond to the concerns of the youths who participate in their program. This chapter examines NGO and school actors' discourses of entrepreneurship education to understand how they utilize neo/liberal ideas that might depoliticize inequalities at the same time that they are inspired by alternative and local practices that call for redistribution and justice (Sharma, 2008).

NGOs play a critical role in providing secondary education for those who do not have easy access to schooling after the primary level in many countries in sub-Saharan Africa. In Tanzania, non-government schools, which include those run by or affiliated with NGOs, churches, and for-profit institutions, comprise nearly one-fourth of all schools (BEST, 2013). In effect, NGOs have moved into the education space to provide learning for all children, often those who do not qualify for government secondary schools. While NGO and government schools are similar, there are distinct differences. NGO schools are non-profits committed to providing an education for all children, but they often do require students to pay tuition fees. They also follow the government curriculum, but they introduce new forms of teaching and learning – in this case, ones directed at entrepreneurial skills and mindset. In this way, NGO schools are situated within state policies for education, and they bring in global practices supported by international agencies.

In this chapter, I examine how *Parka*, an international NGO funded by an international foundation, implements an economically self-sufficient schools (ESS) model in Tanzania. *Parka* is among a number of NGOs working in entrepreneurship education and training in Tanzania. Its economically self-sufficient school model is found in five NGO schools[2] in central and southern Tanzania, and its entrepreneurship education curriculum is being taught in extra-curricular programs in more than 60 government schools in the same regions. The ESS program is particularly interesting as it has many parallels with Nyerere's (1967) Education for Self-Reliance (ESR) program in secondary schools. ESS is designed to help schools become financially independent by having them develop businesses to contribute to the operating budget, while simultaneously teaching students technical skills and entrepreneurship through these businesses. To understand how ESS is influencing and reshaping the purposes and practices of education for citizenship, the following questions guided this analysis: How do NGO actors and school staff frame the purposes and practices of entrepreneurship education? And, how do such purposes and practices reshape the role of schools in fostering citizens for a changing Tanzanian society?

Drawing on this case of ESS, I explore the program's goals and values as it is implemented in Tanzanian secondary schools that serve young people who are socially and economically marginalized. I examine the contradictions of this education model: on the one hand, it provides the right to an education for young people who have been excluded from schooling and teaches them knowledge and skills to 'get out of poverty'.[3] On the other hand, it requires schools to market products and themselves in order to finance at least part of the schools' operating costs. I show how *Parka* and school staff also face the challenge of introducing a pedagogical approach that international and NGO actors regard as necessary to improve the quality of education, but is often resisted by some parents and students as not being 'academic enough'. In implementing the ESS model, the NGO schools are reshaping pedagogy that is overly theoretical, based on rote learning, and irrelevant for students' lives and livelihoods. The NGO staff and school teachers face some resistance to this 'vocationalization' of schooling, though most families and students eventually see its value as students complete their education and pursue their livelihoods (Cooksey, 1986; King, 2001; King and Martin, 2002). Finally, I analyze how staff make sense of a self-sufficient school in relation to ideas of self-reliance, and the frictions that result in doing so through an education model that engages in a capitalist economy. The data illustrate how the schools are vulnerable to a volatile global economy that constrains their ability to be wholly self-supporting. At the same time, through their use of businesses and by producing for markets, ESS schools result in an important social good: supporting marginalized youths to complete their secondary degree and pursue further education or livelihoods.

The economically self-sufficient school model

Parka and its ESS model utilize the discourse of self-reliance, with affinities to that of Nyerere's ESR (see Chapter 4), in efforts to 'free' schools from the contingencies of external donor funding. They do this through the ownership of school businesses that produce and sell products in the local community. The schools also teach skills related to these businesses so that students might use them toward future self-employment and better livelihoods. In many ways, Tanzania seemed like an appropriate place for this model to be adapted. The country has a large number of NGO-funded and managed schools, greater demand for secondary school participation, and growing policy concerns about the quality of education and the need for skills in a changing labor force.

Parka was originally founded in the late 1980s as a micro-finance and entrepreneurship training organization to address poverty in rural regions of a country in the Global South, ruled at the time by a dictatorship. In the 1990s and early 2000s, *Parka* developed its economically self-sufficient schools model by starting its own vocational school in an effort to bring training and finance together to improve the 'lives of the poor'. The model has been expanded to other schools and countries since then. As a micro-finance and entrepreneurship education organization, it is affiliated with international agencies that promote and financially support these efforts. In addition to the ESS model, *Parka* has also developed a program of financial education and business development that is closely aligned with the Junior Achievement Young Enterprise program of starting a mini-company,[4] which *Parka* implements in public schools in Tanzania and elsewhere. The ESS model and financial education programs are heavily influenced by an international discourse about entrepreneurship education and the purpose of skills development for use in the global capitalist economy, an approach for job creation that I discussed in Chapter 4. Still, NGO schools implementing ESS espouse a commitment to educating young people who have been marginalized by the education system (e.g., indigenous groups, rural communities, and children from poor families). *Parka*'s approach brings together two seemingly different roles for schools: making profits in the consumer market and redistributing income to support the education of those who cannot afford it.

In Tanzania, *Parka* collaborates with NGO[5] – or privately managed – schools that desire to decrease their dependence on external donor funding or decrease their reliance on families' tuition payments. The schools serve youths who had been unable to continue to secondary school due in part to low results on their primary leaving exams or their inability to pay secondary school fees. These NGO schools are also distinct from those who implemented Nyerere's ESR, which were government schools that were to serve the development of the community. This study focuses on two formal schools. Sasema is a formal secondary boarding school that enrolls only girls who had previously been out-of-school; Usawa is a co-ed vocational/technical education boarding school focusing on traditionally male-dominated trades, such as masonry, carpentry, and agriculture.[6] At Sasema, the staff and teachers have integrated the entrepreneurship and financial education curriculum within existing curricula, such as commerce and business studies, and in extracurricular activities, such as after-school clubs. At Usawa, the curriculum complements existing subjects on business and entrepreneurship, as well as technical and vocational areas. Similar to other VETA schools, students are required to study didactic (theory) units as well as to do 'practicals' – applying their knowledge and skills in specific trades and vocational work. Students also complete an internship. Different from many VETA schools, the ESS model develops businesses, or what they call 'didactic production units', on campus for students to learn and practice their skills while producing goods. At both schools, the businesses are designed for learning and producing. However, the model ultimately requires them to make a profit so they can contribute to the financial operations of the school. The goal is to reach near 100% of operating costs, though the goals vary by schools and their financial and marketing plan.

While the formal and VETA schools have distinct curricula, they share some common features of the ESS model: Staff and teachers from Sasema and Usawa worked with *Parka* to develop a business plan that would enable self-sufficiency within seven to ten years; *Parka* staff provided technical consultation to set up a financial system to track all business and school accounting; and *Parka* staff consulted and provided teachers (and other staff and students) with training on business skills and entrepreneurship. The training included workshops on their entrepreneurship education curriculum; starting a business, producing and selling goods; and financial management of the businesses. *Parka* also assisted teachers with integrating curriculum and pedagogical practices into the formal and VETA curriculum, and they helped the schools and teachers establish an extracurricular club that teaches financial education and business development and helps students start microenterprises. So both Sasema and Usawa operate larger-scale school businesses in which students learn and work, and they develop microenterprises that are completely student managed where they learn more about financial education and entrepreneurship.

Below, I draw on interviews conducted with *Parka*'s national and international staff; school staff, including directors of schools who represent the NGOs that fund the schools and who are usually non-nationals; academic directors and teachers (usually nationals, though a few international staff); and community members, including business owners, financial service providers, and educational officers over a five-year period (2011–2016). I focus particularly on how the ESS model was implemented over time, the challenges the schools faced, and the adaptations school and NGO staff made in order to participate in the markets and make a profit. In analyzing the interview data, I examine the competing purposes related to education, skills and business development that the NGO and school staff and teachers had to negotiate. I illustrate how national and international *Parka* staff and school staff aligned in their aims of achieving self-sufficiency, but they also differed in the ways the model was enacted and reshaped in the schools. I also reveal the contradictions of using market-based mechanisms to redistribute income and achieve equity goals in education, or the frictions that result when neo/liberal discourses of entrepreneurship education and practices encounter local idea(l)s and practices of equality and self-reliance. In this analysis, then, I consider the 'strange conjunction' (Ferguson, 2010) of ideas of *Ujamaa* and community development that persist in Tanzania today and participation in a capitalist economy, meanings that are brought together in the idea of self-reliance in this ESS program.

Marketization of schools and students

Both *Parka* and these NGO schools, Sasema and Usawa, are committed to providing a secondary education for young girls and boys who typically would not be able to go to school because they could not pay the related fees. The schools, mostly through external donations and some funding from *Parka*, support nearly all the school costs, including teachers' salaries, students' room and board, and other services they offer so that students generally do not have to pay, or pay only a very small amount of fees. As private boarding schools without government support, and in an effort to not depend on donor aid, the ESS model provides an alternative source of funding through producing and selling products from on-campus businesses. The businesses need to be profitable so they can increasingly support the schools' operating costs. This means that the schools' ability to cover fees for more students, or offer new classes with additional teachers, is contingent on the market viability and profit of their businesses. Therefore, success is measured not only by student learning outcomes but also by profitability. In addition, the ESS model depends on students learning skills and applying them (successfully) in the work of the businesses. *Parka* and the school staff and teachers believed that the model is necessary to provide an education for young people so they can lead a 'better life', as Ms. Justine Cordoba, who oversaw the program implementation in Tanzania, stated:

> The overarching goal of the program is for these low-income youth attending our partner schools to overcome poverty, and to do so by entrepreneurial activities that teach them to learn how to do and actually involve them in practical activities, but also in activities that allow them to earn and to save money. That is the most important goal of our program … We want the

youth to have access to quality education. We want the youth to overcome poverty through this program so that that they can really lead decent lives upon graduation – to be able to achieve financial independence and be successful in life, both personally and professionally. (*Parka* program coordinator, Ms. Cordoba, 2014)[7]

To achieve this goal, the schools' operations and students' learning were intricately linked with production and markets. The discourse of preparing students with skills for a capitalist market permeated school planning, curriculum, pedagogy, and the daily interactions between teachers, students, and the community. Sasema and Usawa began implementing this model with *Parka* by developing a school business plan that included identifying local market needs, demand and supply of certain goods, and competition of other businesses. They then started businesses that operated on the school premises to produce goods for the local market, integrating all aspects of managing the businesses, from planning and buying to production and selling, into the school curriculum. Sasema and Usawa both initially began businesses based in agricultural production, such as raising chickens for their eggs and meat. Vegetables and cow's milk were other products for which Usawa saw a local demand. Sasema also began growing organic vegetables, mostly to provide nutritious school meals. Other types of businesses undertaken at Usawa included carpentry and masonry, both because Usawa is a VETA school and these are on the VETA curricula, and its region in southern Tanzania was growing so construction was in demand in the local economy. Sasema has worked on developing hotel and conference services, and feed and water services (for local farmers), but they have not fully implemented these ideas.

Learning about how to manage businesses was critical for school staff and students. *Parka* staff taught teachers and students about the production, care, costs, and marketing of products. Enthusiasm for the general idea and the businesses grew among students and school staff as they learned how to market and sell their products and began to earn money. Mr. Herbert Foster, an international staff member who serves as the country director for *Parka*, explained how they conducted training for Sasema students and staff in the first year of setting up the model in the Tanzanian schools:

> We talked about the market – the simple form of how to sell commercially – and they learned how to sell in a market. They also learned about the cost of materials and how to cost materials. It was a small activity to see if the girls could leave the school and could do this. They could, in reality, take [the costs] into account, and when they knew this they were very excited. They learned they could make a difference. (*Parka* country director, Mr. Foster, 2012)

'Make a difference' here referred to making a profit – earning above and beyond their costs and recognizing that they could make money from their efforts, for the school and ultimately for themselves. *Parka* staff, however, reminded them

98 Educating for Self-sufficiency

that just producing and selling was not sufficient for becoming economically self-sufficient. Mr. Leonardo Chacha, an international staff member who served for a short time in Tanzania as the program director, stated emphatically, 'The school's businesses need to complete the production cycle by selling their goods and making a profit'. The school enterprises needed to 'add value to simple production processes'. For example, it was not enough for students to simply learn how to produce milk; they needed to make products such as cheese or yogurt that either created a new market or filled a demand in the consumer market.

Each year, Sasema and Usawa staff and *Parka* staff reassessed their business strategy, considering profits or losses, whether to start another enterprise, and how they could better market their goods. *Parka* staff generally regarded business management, and ultimately the making of a profit, as a technical matter. That is, if the schools had the right inputs, such as managers, and processes in place including information on costs and profits, they would succeed. Ms. Cordoba stated it this way:

> We need to use that information to see how the business is actually doing, what are the weak spots, what do we need to do, and what can we do to improve the performance of our businesses. ... We know our model is a market-driven model. In order for this education to be really useful for our students in the future, we need our businesses to be completely market-driven and market-oriented. (*Parka* program coordinator, Ms. Cordoba, 2014)

But the challenge was more than technical. Over the five years, the research team observed other challenges of combining education with business efforts. First, business management was new for many of the school staff, and particularly teachers, so the school administration sought to hire personnel who could both teach business commerce (a subject offered in both academic tracks and VETA schools) and manage the businesses' finances. But both Sasema and Usawa struggled to hire qualified teachers and production managers at a cost by which they could still make a profit. Second, when the students were marketing their products, such as eggs, chickens, and even small goods like sweets from their business club enterprises, they faced challenges to show to community members that this would subsidize their education. For many in the community, the role of education, particularly in a formal school like Sasema, was to produce educated youths, not products. Some community members could not see how producing and selling goods fostered their formal learning. Others regarded education as something provided by the government or for those who could afford to pay. Usawa's school director, Mr. Bakari Evans, who had taught in a business college and was brought in to manage the school more effectively, told me that the community believes the school is subsidized, by either the government or donors. Therefore, the community thinks the school businesses should be selling goods at a cheaper price, 'which is in conflict with the sustainability model. The businesses have to be run professionally. We have to compete in the market like any other businesses if we are to achieve self-sufficiency'. Finally, the schools had to market themselves in terms of the quality of learning they produced, as well as the products they sold. It was a challenge to integrate these distinct efforts in a way that both students were academically successful and the community saw the schools as successful.

The challenge of how to market their schools, both to local communities through sale of products they produced and to parents and a broader set of communities (both outside their geographic area and to donor communities) through the quality of education, continued to affect school decisions. By the fourth year, the director of Sasema, Ms. Patricia Dean, who is employed by the international NGO that supports the school and participates in the daily management of the school finances, fundraising and operations, was seeking complementary ways to support their budget. Ms. Dean said the school faced a dilemma in seeking to be cost-effective and self-sufficient. One option was to have businesses that produced income above and beyond what they received from student fees, which presently comprised a very small portion of the budget. Another option was to enroll more fee-paying students. She recognized the contradiction of having a larger fee-paying group when the school was committed to educating those who could not afford secondary school. In addition to the markets for their commercial products, which seemed unstable and uncertain, she faced challenges in the education market because families would chose a private school based on students' academic performance in their O-level exams and the subsequent opportunities that would result from their doing well while at the school. Yet the students' performance on these exams was not yet outstanding.[8]

> We're still a small school. To become more cost-effective, we need to be bigger. But how can we attract paying students when we've got poor performance? How can we bring our costs down unless we get more students? We have enough infrastructure now where we can get students, so the only thing holding us back is operating costs … So we're going to work on marketing and getting people to know our school and crafting our message about why our performance may be not stronger. (Sasema school director, Ms. Dean, 2015)

These forms of engaging in a capitalist market, either with commercial products or with fee-paying students/families, are different attempts to achieve the same goal: redistributing income to ensure the education of more young people in Tanzania. Perhaps, though, it is easier for the community to understand the role of schools as teaching and learning rather than making and selling consumer products.

The (initial) attraction of the ESS model for these schools was that they did not have to depend on government or donor funds, which are notoriously insecure and unstable. Making a profit from businesses, however, is also insecure and unstable; furthermore, making a profit is an unconventional school practice in these communities. Compounding the uncertainty is a challenging economic environment. In a time of highly flexible markets, where demand and profit, particularly for agricultural products, are dependent on global economic trade and aid, this form of financial support is fraught with risks. Mr. Chacha captured these risks, noting that choosing a business is like 'trial and error': if a business is not successful, the school needs to end it and open a different one. Changing a business enterprise for a school is no small act, in part because operating businesses is not the 'usual business' of schools. They need staff with management, financial, and production expertise to make these decisions. In addition, hundreds of young people's lives, as well as teachers, are dependent on the success or failure of the business in that proceeds help pay tuitions, salaries, and general operating costs. When businesses were not profitable, staff were laid off and students had to pay higher fees. Given this quandary of how to support financially these secondary school students, we need to ask which values were learned through this model of operating businesses and participating in the consumer market, and how this entrepreneurship education affected the daily life of teachers and students.

Learning by doing (skills) and being an entrepreneur

Implementing the ESS model, and its 'learning by doing' pedagogy, has both positively and negatively affected daily life at school for students and teachers. On the positive side, everyone – community members, teachers, and students – extol the importance of developing entrepreneurial skills useful for employment in the local labor market. Many faulted the highly theoretical nature of schooling as a reason graduates do not pass exams and do not become employed. Thus, the skills and competencies students learn through working with school businesses are particularly attractive, especially to local businesses and the community. Ms. Cordoba explained the importance of their model this way: 'Education must go beyond what is mandated by the MOE (Ministry of Education). Students need skills to be really employable after graduation' (*Parka* program coordinator). When discussing the goals and practices of ESS in their schools, teachers and community members often invoked Nyerere's ESR and the ways in which secondary schools, in particular, were to link their instruction with community needs, including agricultural production. Many staff felt that this history gave the ESS model legitimacy. But the ESS model is also different than ESR in the community and market it engages, though they both draw upon a similar pedagogical approach of learning by doing.

In this pedagogical approach that permeated school life, students related their knowledge of different subjects to the businesses and they solved real-life problems. For example, Ms. Albert, a science teacher, told us how when teaching about cell and embryonic development, they used their experience with the chickens, of fertilizing eggs, developing embryos, and then hatching baby chicks to make the lesson more meaningful and concrete. In another example of learning to solve problems, when the chickens caught a disease and began to die, teachers and students worked together to consider the factors that may have caused the disease, and what they could do to address the underlying causes. Students were also learning how to manage finances of the businesses and to market their skills so they could obtain their desired livelihoods. They recognized that their own educational and economic futures depended on learning this practical knowledge and solving these problems. Mr. Daniel Msoga, a local staff member who worked on integrating the ESS model into all the schools, commented:

> [The students] feel like [this learning experience] will make them become independent because it helps them to become confident. Yesterday, I was at a school and I met a guy who was trained in marketing and he was telling me – he's about to finish this year – he can't wait to go out because he knows how to market himself. He's ready. He's not afraid of anything. (*Parka* ESS coordinator, Mr. Msoga, 2015)

Staff, teachers and students felt that they were not only learning how to produce agricultural or other products, but they were engaging with the labor and consumer markets in new ways. They were learning business and marketing skills, applying their technical and content skills to real situations, and employing new attitudes of confidence, competition, and creativity.

Through the financial education, business development, and entrepreneurship that the school staff taught, students were learning specific business skills. Business clubs were set up to model a small business, and members had different roles, such as the financial officer. They worked together to decide on the type of business product they would make, how they would market and sell it, and what they would do with the profit. The teachers who facilitated the business clubs initially emphasized the technical knowledge of how to create a business and a product, and how to sell it to make a profit. Nearly all the teachers and staff asserted that the business clubs generated a lot of excitement among students, helping to motivate and persuade other teachers and parents of its educational value. These extracurricular clubs have expanded to many government and private schools in the region over the five years of this study, suggesting interest in the idea and the value they offer. But students did not only learn technical and business skills. They also learned entrepreneurial skills of risk-taking in new markets, leadership of their enterprise, communication with consumers, and commitment to their work.

The business clubs had been set up from the first year at Sasema and over the years, the teachers and students improved upon their curricula and practices for managing their business, working together, and making decisions. The students decided how to reward members of the club based on their participation, such that when the club dissolved at the end of the school year, one person could be allocated a greater portion of earnings than another. Earning money from their work served as extrinsic motivation, and in an environment where most of these students were in need of money to pay for even basic needs, how this material reward shaped the ethos and actions of the group cannot be overlooked. For example, disciplinary actions were also taken, such as not allowing a student to earn from the profits if others regarded her as not adequately participating. This ethos of differentially distributing funds did not necessarily align with the ethos of the school to redistribute profits to benefit those in need, or its ethos to ensure that every student could have the necessary material means to get an education. Merit and competition became driving motivators that were at times in conflict with an ethos of solidarity and support for all. Mr. George Lawrence, a teacher at Sasema, suggested that the groups learned and exhibited leadership and discipline through their decision-making and participation in these groups: 'Some members are so committed and they are self-driven, and we feel it is important to reward them.' But the students' actions could also be read in another way – that these students learned entrepreneurial characteristics that put business or their own interests above other social interests.

Students learned how to run small business, such as selling 'bites' or snacks in the school canteen, or raising rabbits. If they made a profit, it was distributed from the clubs to students themselves. Depending on the business and the group, some students told us they might make enough money to help pay for school fees or buy necessities for school. Over time, this purpose evolved as the schools increasingly felt a need for more funds, and taking some of the profit from all enterprises seemed necessary. The model for students' small businesses was adapted to allocate some earnings (usually 40% or less) to the schools; school and *Parka* staff regarded this as a fair practice as the school provided staff and other physical resources, such as the canteen, for the businesses. This adaptation was implemented at both the ESS schools and government schools that only had a club. At the end of each academic year, when the clubs liquidated a portion of the earnings it was given to the school for use of their facilities and for teachers' salaries. In this way, the small businesses were valued by school staff and teachers not only for the learning they fostered, but the earnings they made.

When these clubs first started, the focus was on learning the basics of producing goods and selling them. As these clubs matured, teachers and students paid more attention to how to increase their profits. During the fourth year of the evaluation, Mr. Lawrence, who led the business clubs for Sasema, noted:

> The learning and doing business has to be more creative, more innovative, and add value. So we are seeking other alternatives beyond selling snacks … [W]e are thinking of trying to [start a] processing activity … [W]e were looking at locally available inputs which are cheap and around their community, and they could add value to those. And when they add value, they could [make much more money]. (Sasema teacher, Mr. Lawrence, 2015)

Staff and teachers at both schools put considerable energy and time into finding more profitable alternatives. They considered products with higher profit margins, greater demand, and lower costs. Each year brought new experimentation of products that, they hoped, would be interesting for students and also make a profit for the school. Sasema invited the government Small Industry and Development Organization (SIDO) to conduct training for their students so they could learn how to package other products, such as honey, that they could resell quickly, with the aim of earning a profit. But the educational value of packaging honey that was already prepared and bought in bulk was considerably less than what they learned through raising vegetables or chickens. This search for alternative commercial products and making a profit illustrates that the school staff and students were learning that the stakes were high and risks were great. To respond to these risks, they were learning to be innovative, adaptive, and competitive. But being competitive in the markets and adaptive was not always positive; it had negative effects. If businesses did not make a profit, they needed to change, as had to happen with the chicken business at Sasema (see next section). When the business (and the school) incurred a loss, the effects on staff and students were detrimental, including cutting teachers who were integral to running the business. Losing teachers also resulted in an inconsistent and interrupted education for students.

The ESS model also faced some resistance for vocationalizing education, at least at the formal academic school. While the new pedagogies and business clubs were generally valued, some parents and students resisted learning skills and producing products for school enterprises. They and their families perceived a secondary education as an academic endeavor preparing them for 'white collar' work and higher education, not for agricultural production. Some community members also challenged the value of these experiences. For example, when Sasema first began producing eggs and selling them at the local market, local government officials forbade the girls to sell eggs, even though those students had their teachers' support. Town officials were concerned that selling products in the market was 'not a good use of the girls' times' (Sasema school director, Ms. Dean). Teachers had varying interpretations of this interference by the local government. Some said having girls sell products in the local market raised concerns about their safety. Also, community members might misunderstand, seeing the girls not as 'students' but rather as handlers for local enterprises; the assumption would be that they were not educated and did not have other opportunities but to sell. The girls told us that when they explained to customers and community members what they were learning and doing, and how the money supported their school, most understood their efforts. *Parka* staff also said some parents and school staff were initially concerned that once students learned to start and manage a business, those students would drop out of school to work.

> At first parents were concerned the students would leave the school ... but now the attitude of parents and teachers has changed, as well as students.

The students proved they could do it and that changed the teachers' [attitudes]. Parents were afraid, but we exposed them to the business so they [could see that the purpose was to help them] achieve skills, not so they [would] leave the school. (*Parka* Program director, Mr. Chacha, 2014)

Still, 'being educated' was not regarded as compatible with selling in the local market or having an enterprise, and this perception had some factual basis. As Ms. Dean told us, 'There is a past history in the country with self-sustaining schools, that I think it was ... in many cases successful, but it got pushed to the limit where students were farming the fields of the teachers or head teacher' (Sasema school director). For all the nostalgia about Nyerere's ESR, the vestiges of the colonial system and its education of an elite still hold. In addition, the memory persisted of how the self-sufficient secondary schools of the past had gone too far in promoting work rather than learning.

Over time, and particularly as students completed their studies, the students and community members came to value these skills. Ms. Dean told us early in this project that acquiring skills and experience in running a microenterprise is a necessary 'back-up' option for some of the students who might not fare well on their O-level exams, which would limit their options when pursuing further education. Indeed, when the first class that had been involved in the businesses completed their exams, many began small income-generating activities or group enterprises as a way to earn an income that could help pay for fees for their continuing education. A few did not pass the exams, and therefore, their knowledge and experience in running a microenterprise was necessary for their livelihood. Both the students and the teachers felt that the entrepreneurial learning experience gave them an advantage over others who also pursued a secondary education and did not pass the exams. For students at Usawa, their experiences of working in school businesses gave them an advantage over most other VETA schools. This school had the necessary equipment, tools, and inputs (seeds, chickens, etc.) by which to learn and practice their trade, whereas so many VETA schools in Tanzania teach these trades in the absence of experiential learning and sufficient inputs. The local VETA officer commented that Usawa was a 'real model' for what all VETA schools should be doing. Most students in these schools also had several opportunities to work with local employers, or to start their own enterprises upon completion of their studies. Whereas so many young Tanzanians, even when they pursue secondary school but they do not do well on the exams, feel they have few options, these young women and men told us of different alternatives they could and did pursue (DeJaeghere et al., 2016).

Beyond the businesses and technical skills students were learning in these schools, this entrepreneurship education also instilled a particular mindset and values: those of competitiveness, innovativeness, flexibility, and capitalism. These skills and attitudes were used to form enterprising individuals and to make young people responsible for getting themselves out of poverty, one of *Parka*'s goals. Mr. Foster who served the role of sharing the idea, philosophy and practice of

ESS from its origins, summarized the values they are teaching in their model in this way: 'To be an entrepreneur is to "own your life" – not just to have your own business. With the right attitudes, [youths] can succeed' (*Parka* country director). But getting out of poverty and succeeding, particularly as an individual entrepreneur, was yet to be seen. It was also, in many ways, uncertain. Many youths we talked to after completing their schooling had started microenterprises, but they met many challenges of selling their products and making a profit. They had to be innovative and flexible, using multiple strategies to survive. Youths in these schools also carried the burden of being responsible for the lives of the many family members who expected much from them as educated young people.[9]

Learning responsibility meant more than taking care of themselves and their family. Students were also partially responsible for the self-sufficiency of the school. Without students' contributions to the businesses, the school could not survive financially. Their work was not only to help the school make a profit; the business profits were used to subsidize their and other (future) students' education. It is in this purpose of supporting marginalized youths' education that teachers were enacting – and students were learning – other values, not only of the enterprising self but also those of solidarity and reciprocity. Teachers and students were committed to and supportive of others' needs in an environment in which they faced many material and social uncertainties. Even the value they were learning of making a profit, when coupled with the values of solidarity and redistribution, was used to alter unequal economic relations in their community to support the education of those who could not afford to pay.

Being self-sufficient is an indicator of a successful graduate and also an indicator of the success of the schools, both in economic and social terms. But how can schools become self-sufficient? What would the staff need to do to achieve it? *Parka* and school staff and teachers had to contend with the contradiction of achieving a social good – educating young people – through an economic mechanism of selling and earning in an uncertain consumer market.

Managing schools for economic self-sufficiency and self-reliance

To achieve economic self-sufficiency, the school staff, teachers, and even students had to be increasingly responsible for the financial management of the businesses. This required improving their financial knowledge and analyses and implementing new management techniques, such that a main purpose of their work became making a profit. In the first year of the project, when Sasema and Usawa developed their businesses and projected budgets, *Parka* staff believed that success required more than just understanding how to budget and track the businesses. Rather, every teacher and administrator had to understand the purpose of the business and take ownership of the financial aspects. Mr. Foster, who worked with the schools to set up their financial management systems, explained:

> A budget isn't only a responsibility of the general manager or the accountant; ... the budget is the responsibility of all. All have to put their best effort to increase their incomes and to be very rational with their spending ... Because in a self-sufficient school, when you want to complete an action, you need to consider how it is affecting your money ... This is a crucial moment, the moment in which the worker [is] converted into a part of the bigger educational business. (*Parka* country director, Mr. Foster, 2012)

Therefore, in the ESS model, teachers do not simply work for the school and educate young people; they are integral in making the school 'work' as a business to pay its teachers.

School administrative staff told us that this responsibility was not always realized, possibly because teachers saw their primary responsibility as instructing students and not as ensuring the school's fiscal viability. Only those teachers directly working in, or responsible for, the businesses were most attuned to the management and how to integrate the business into learning, but they did not always consider the profit or loss of their work. Mr. Lawrence, a business and commerce teacher who facilitated the business clubs, commented on how the business and learning visions had evolved. 'Initially, the way the structure was laid, we expected the business department would be independent and the school [classes] run independently. Now I see they are matched and you can't distinguish the school and the business'. He saw this as a positive integration of the businesses into classroom teaching. When new teachers are hired, he said, they understood that part of their teaching responsibilities was to integrate knowledge and skills of the businesses into their classes. However, the responsibility for financial success and earning a profit came about more slowly and required additional management techniques.

Usawa school experienced the opposite problem to that of Sasema school regarding the tension between business management and teaching: teachers were often overly involved in the enterprise and were not effectively teaching the 'theory' classes. Students were also concerned about learning academic subjects and passing VETA exams. Many teachers left Usawa because, as school management surmised, they were not committed to the school and its role in teaching and producing. Other times they left to pursue their trade outside the school, thus taking students, customers, and the resultant profit with them.[10]

To address the need for better financial management, *Parka* staff focused on training teachers to monitor and manage the profit and loss of the businesses. Mr. Chacha explained:

> [The schools] usually have the minimum in terms of accounting and financial procedures. Some are new to this idea, to having the school run businesses.

> So we need to do a lot of work on this issue. Also, [we need to] make sure that, as much as possible, we are integrating the students and the teachers into these businesses so that the capacity really stays at the school. So that is why it is not only important to do projections and to draw budgets, but it is just as important to track the actual performance of these different businesses and analyze [them]. (*Parka* program director, Mr. Chacha, 2014)

This tracking of performance occurred through monthly income statement check-ins, where expenses and profit were recorded for each production unit. Mr. Foster felt that with this process and checking, profits would be possible.

> I look forward to each department having its own accounts, showing income and expenditures at each department level so that each can know where they are making losses and profits. And what kind of ... inputs they need ... to avoid mixing accounting and some depending on those who are making profit. So every month I am given a monthly income statement ... If all that is clearly worked out, the departments will not be [incurring] heavy losses. (*Parka* country director, Mr. Foster, 2015)

But even with knowledge of budgets and data that tracked expenses, profits were elusive. While some businesses were profitable, such as the carpentry at Usawa, others, such as selling eggs, were not. Ms. Dean's staff lamented how problems accrued in multiple areas for Sasema school. The chickens suffered from diseases, which resulted in a loss. The school had a good production manager for the chicken business, but then had to release him because it was not profitable to pay his salary. At Usawa, theft of animals, such as chickens and pigs, and lumber cut into profits; the business managers/teachers did not stay long. Costs were high and profits were low. In 2015, Sasema gave the chicken business one last chance to make a profit:

> We should be raking in the money with our production, but the feed [for chickens] is so expensive ... It's just demoralizing. I really thought this is the time we should be making money. The price [of eggs] is lower now than what we were getting a year ago [or] a year and a half ago. There's a lot of competition in the market. (Sasema director, Ms. Dean, 2015)

Sasema finally shut down the chicken business. When it was originally conceived, the school expected it to provide $25,000 dollars of the school's budget. This amount was not enough for total self-sufficiency, but it was enough to cover some of the staff/school costs. Instead, the business, and thus the school, lost about $10,000 per year. But beyond the costs of staff or low consumer prices, the business plan never really took into account the challenge of agricultural markets being linked to national and international policy and trade. In this case, the cost of feed had risen sharply while the price of eggs had declined, even while inflation was increasing and pushing up other food prices in Tanzania. Being a school, and not an agricultural business, resulted in multiple disadvantages.[11] The vocational school, Usawa, which might seem to have an advantage because the businesses were more related to their teaching and they could hire technical staff/teachers to both run businesses and teach students, also struggled with earning profits from some businesses, such as their milk enterprise. According to the school director, Mr. Evans, they made only a little profit because the one company they sold to had a monopoly in the area, which meant the school had no choice but to sell their milk for just a narrow profit margin.

Still, the NGO and school staff were hopeful, trying new mechanisms to achieve profits from business that could support their school budget. *Parka* staff and school management increasingly agreed that all school staff needed to be responsible for the financial wellbeing of their school. Ms. Dean told us, 'I need people to take up – take it up and run with it and take ownership over it, instead of me being the one who minds. I want them to mind, to care'. Initially, *Parka* staff and the school management had conceived of this model as one that teachers would buy into and support because they believed in what it did for the school, and in turn, the teachers and students. The NGO director, Mr. Fischbein, explained it this way in the first year of the project:

> The pressure [to succeed and make a profit] comes through setting of goals. So when they have specific [financial] goals that is when they become an entrepreneur. ... We don't have to give them incentives and pay them extra to manage this model; ... the school can manage it. (*Parka* Director, Mr. Fischbein, 2012)

Gradually, *Parka* and school staff began to talk about tying teachers' compensation to profits, and this was a new management practice both schools were now considering.

> Yesterday in the staffing meeting, one of the teachers ... said they need more incentives. A few years ago, this would have upset me and made me think, 'What's wrong?' But I understand that's what other schools do, and I realize that people here are motivated in different ways ... We have implemented ... a bonus program. This year we will give it [out] at the end of the year. We look at production, what you are able to do. We know the income from your department, and we can gauge what bonus you qualify for, based on what you are able to do. (Sasema school director, Ms. Dean, 2015)

In both schools, the teachers were paid as well as teachers in government schools,[12] so the directors did not see the problem of staff commitment as one of salary. However, the teaching staff have commented that they worked many more hours than their counterparts in government schools, in part because they were teaching young people who had not been slated to go to secondary school.

They also have to work harder and put in extra hours to help these students learn the required curriculum, as well as to teach them the additional entrepreneurship and business skills. This incentive technique may increase the income of some teachers, and it may, in some cases, also improve the economic viability of the schools, but that is to be seen. More certain is that these schools, with their mission to educate young people who cannot pay school fees, are caught in the tension of ensuring a social good of education through a financial mechanism of donor funds or the consumer market.

These two schools likely will not achieve 100% economic self-sufficiency any time soon, though some businesses may make profits and support the school, at least some of the time. They will have to continue to rely on donor support and student fees to make up the difference. They are operating in an education market where, paradoxically, education is a right and a social good, but secondary schools are not fully funded by the government and achieving this good is often left to those who can afford to pay. Still, the young women and men at these schools, their families, and the community value the formal, vocational, and entrepreneurship education they are getting. Furthermore, they see that many students are finishing school, acquiring skills they can use to earn and live by, and pursuing further education and meaningful livelihoods. However, it will be difficult for these NGO schools to garner the financial support for education, either directly from parents or indirectly from the consumer market, and funds from the government and international donors also seem precarious.

Reflections on frictions between ESS and self-reliance

Becoming economically self-sufficient through a market mechanism is a paradox for both the schools and the students because running a business for the consumer market can lead to economic loss and *more* insecurity, in part because the communities are under-resourced and markets are volatile. Usawa and Sasema, and other schools implementing the ESS model, are trading insecure financial means from donors with the fickleness of the consumer market. In addition to the challenges for the schools to achieve economic self-sufficiency, students' self-reliance is contingent on completing their education and learning valued skills, which can be a precarious endeavor when schools have to change their courses and pedagogy to match the market's demands for their products, and do not always have sufficient financial means to educate students well. For example, Usawa encountered a loss of both teachers and students. Some teachers left because they sought greater earnings elsewhere; some students dropped out, possibly because they were not learning or could not pay the fees. Students who stayed largely felt they were unable to learn the subjects well during these times of transitions, and blamed their low exam scores on poor teaching. These changes caused great uncertainty for both the academic and financial viability of the school.

The staff of *Parka* and the two schools articulated a commitment to ensuring the education of these young people and to fostering their future livelihoods, but their commitment was not easily achieved and schools had to adapt increasingly neoliberal practices to manage their businesses. Most staff seemed to conjoin this commitment of a right to education and reducing educational inequalities with practices of competition, profit maximization, and economic efficiency that can, at times, cause greater inequalities. Staff aimed to implement ESS so that profits could be redistributed toward a social good: the education of young people who would otherwise not be educated. But as shown above, sometimes these profits were elusive, and the schools turned to other mechanisms, such as fee-paying students. The two new management practices that the schools have now begun to use – incentives and a two-tiered system of students (paying and non-paying) – may exacerbate inequalities, but they are implementing these in an effort to increase profits and provide for the education of more young people. In this way, their discourse and practices are neo/liberal, linking the claiming of rights and reduction of inequalities with capitalistic market mechanisms.

Finally, the conjunction of ESS with local discourses of self-reliance also produced shifts in the NGO goals and practices of the program and the schools. *Parka* has adapted its approach and goals, stating that its model is not only about self-sufficiency, but also about teaching and learning the skills needed for youth's future livelihoods. Sasema and Usawa school staff and teachers generally believed in the value of the school businesses as a means to improve students' learning and their future opportunities. The ESS model has shifted schools' pedagogical approaches in small ways through the skills and attitudes that teachers now impart, and students' future opportunities have changed. Most young women and men who complete their education from these school may be slightly better off economically than they were before, or their families were. Even when these young people may not secure a place in higher levels of education, they have found ways to make themselves more self-reliant. In this way, implementing ESS has been valuable even more so than for the profit and financial sustainability it would have hopefully yielded.

In the encounter between the underlying rationalities of profit and consumer market participation and those of self-reliance and solidarity, new ways of educating young people toward their future livelihoods and citizenship have emerged. NGOs have a role to play in upholding principles of a social good and fostering solidarity and equality. But they are challenged to do so without strong social policies and financial support, from either the state or other forms of governing. Entrepreneurship education, and this model of economically self-sufficient schools, is a technical solution for addressing economic problems (e.g., insufficient funding for education, unemployment of secondary school graduates) through the capitalist market. But in small ways, staff and students also reshape and use it to serve social purposes by redistributing income to address inequalities and to create better future opportunities for youths. The next two chapters turn to the effects of such entrepreneurship education and training on youths in Tanzania.

Notes

1 This chapter is derived in part from an article published in *Comparative Education* on 18 June 2013, available online: http://www.tandfonline.com/10.1080/03050068. 2013.798514. The analysis in this chapter, however, presents different conclusions because the longitudinal data revealed how the discourse of the NGO model was reshaped over time, different from the way it was discussed and implemented in the first year of the project.
2 These NGO schools are a combination of church-affiliated schools and non-profit NGO supported schools. In all cases, they require external funding from religious institutions, donors and individuals to support the schooling of students, and they require, in some cases, a payment of fees from students' families.
3 *Parka* uses the term *getting out of poverty* as their goal. I use this terms in quotations because I aim to problematize that the challenges facing these youths are purely economical, and that we can solve them through economic means.
4 Despite all the support for entrepreneurship education among youths in policy discourse and, to some extent, in research studies showing certain effects on skills and attitudes, the Junior Achievement program has been critiqued for not achieving intended results of becoming an entrepreneur (Osterbeek et al., 2008). It has also been critiqued for its commercialization of schools (Sukarieh and Tannock, 2009).
5 These NGO schools are affiliated with small, private NGO organizations based in the US and Europe. They are not supported by large NGOs, such as CARE or Save the Children, but these NGOs have had considerable bilateral donor funding from the US and European countries.
6 *Parka* implements the ESS model in five NGO schools in Tanzania, a combination of formal and VETA curricula. For this chapter, however, I focus on the implementation of the model in two schools.
7 All names are pseudonyms. In addition, I provide the general position the staff and teachers held and the year of the interview, which helps situate how their ideas regarding entrepreneurship education and training changed over time.
8 The school's first graduating class performed better than the national average on O-level secondary exams. Still, two students did not pass at all, and most passed at low levels, which allowed them to pursue further studies in some areas, such as teacher training or community development work, but not to continue on to A-levels in government schools. Exam scores are public in Tanzania, and schools are ranked based on that metric.
9 Our Year 4 report of the evaluation shows how youths were becoming more independent and also supporting their families; it also shows the precariousness of their livelihood situations (See Pellowski Wiger et al., 2015).
10 In the Year 3 report of the project evaluation, we report on the loss of teaching staff and the challenges the school faced in hiring teachers who were committed and able to teach both theory and practice (Willemsen, Krause, Jaafar, and Pellowski Wiger, with Chapman and DeJaeghere, 2014).
11 See, for example, Mbilinyi (2012), who argues that agribusiness, funded in part by international donors such as USAID, has negatively affected small landholders in Tanzania. The USAID programs have resulted in decreased access to and increased cost of supplies, such as seeds and fertilizer, particularly for small farmers and businesses.
12 Their salaries may have been nearly equivalent or better, but staff noted that they did not receive the equivalent social benefits that are given to government teachers, who receive reimbursement for travel and house, as well as pensions.

References

Cooksey, B. (1986). Policy and practice in Tanzanian secondary education since 1967. *International Journal of Educational Development*, 6(3), 183–202.

DeJaeghere, J., and Pellowski Wiger, N. (2013). Gender discourses in an NGO education project: Openings for transformation toward gender equality in Bangladesh. *International Journal of Educational Development*, 33(6), 557–565.

DeJaeghere, J., Pellowski Wiger, N. and Willemsen, L. (2016). Broadening educational outcomes: Social relations, skills development and employability for youth. *Comparative Education Review*, 60(3), 457–479.

Englund, H. (2006). *Prisoners of freedom: Human rights and the African poor.* Berkeley, CA: University of California Press.

Ferguson, J. (2010). The uses of neoliberalism. *Antipode*, 41(s1), 166–184.

Fraser, N. (1997). *Justice interruptus: Critical reflections on the 'postsocialist' condition.* New York, NY: Routledge.

Kamat, S. (2004). The privatization of public interest: Theorizing NGO discourse in a neoliberal era. *Review of International Political Economy*, 11(1), 155–176.

King, K. (2001). Africa's informal economies: Thirty years on. *SAIS review*, 21(1), 97–108.

King, K. and Martin, C. (2002). The vocational school fallacy revisited: education, aspiration and work in Ghana 1959–2000. *International Journal of Educational Development*, 22(1), 5–26.

Mbilinyi, M. (2012). Struggles over land and livelihoods in African agriculture. *Development*, 55(3), 390–392.

Nyerere, J. K. (1967). Education for Self-reliance. *The Ecumenical Review*, 19(4), 382–403.

Oosterbeek, H. and van Praag, M. and IJsselstein, A., (2008). *The impact of entrepreneurship education on entrepreneurship competencies and intentions: An evaluation of the Junior Achievement Student Mini-Company Program.* Available at SSRN: https://ssrn.com/abstract=1118251 or http://dx.doi.org/10.2139/ssrn.1118251

Pellowski Wiger, N., DeJaeghere, J. and Chapman, D. (2015). *Year 4 cross-site report for the Learn, Earn and Save Initiative.* Minneapolis, MN: University of Minnesota, Department of Organizational Leadership, Policy, and Development.

Sharma, A. (2008). *Logics of empowerment: Development, gender, and governance in neoliberal India.* Minneapolis, MN: University of Minnesota Press.

Sharma, P., Verma, G. and Arur, A. (2013). Negotiating meanings of gender justice: Critical reflections on dialogs and debates in a non-governmental organization (NGO). *International Journal of Educational Development*, 33(6), 576–584.

Sukarieh, M. and Tannock, S. (2009). Putting school commercialism in context: A global history of junior achievement worldwide. *Journal of Education Policy*, 24(6), 769–786.

United Republic of Tanzania (URT), MoEVT, (2013). *BEST 2013: Secondary education* [Excel format report]. Retrieved from http://www.moe.go.tz/index.php?option=com_docman&task=cat_view&gid=358&Itemid=619

Willemsen, L. W., Krause, B., Jaafar, A. and Pellowski Wiger, N., with Chapman, D., & DeJaeghere, J. (2014). *The MasterCard Foundation Learn, Earn, and Save Initiative: Year 3 synthesis report.* Minneapolis: University of Minnesota, Department of Organizational Leadership, Policy, and Development.

Chapter 7

Becoming Entrepreneurial Citizens
Economic Development and Social Relations

> The community regards me as the person with technical skills ... They [also] regard me as the community change agent, one that can bring development in the community.
> —Sudi, mechanic, 23 years old, 2014

Dominant approaches to entrepreneurship education and training, as discussed in Chapter 3, represent quintessential attributes of neo/liberal governmentality. As a technology of governing, entrepreneurship education and training promotes private ownership/property, profits, and economic growth; as a technology of the self, it trains young people to be responsible, claim their rights, take initiative, get out of poverty, and become risk-takers in an insecure economic environment. But these neo/liberal practices also take many different forms and have unexpected and contradictory effects, particularly as they meet the social, political, and economic contexts within Tanzania. Motala and Vally (2014) argue that analyses of education and employment initiatives need to be historicized in economic and social relations to understand the effects they may have. To do so, we need to understand how the informal economy emerged and works today in Tanzania as it relates to norms and practices of a moral economy. For instance, Tripp's (1997) analysis describes the emergence of the urban informal economy[1] in Tanzania during the 1980s, suggesting that rather than the interests of the capitalist market shaping economic activity, a moral economy of community interests, reciprocity, and mutuality operates to ensure everyone's survival.[2] Furthermore, she argues that participation in the informal economy was a strategy that counterintuitively pressured the state into greater claims on rights, including wage policies and social benefits, and shifted social relations in society around inclusion (Tripp, 1997, p. 127). The economic liberalization of a socialist political economy, she contends, had contradictory effects, exacerbating economic and social inequality while at the same time opening up debates about who was included and excluded from society.

Others have explored the contradictory effects of macroeconomic policies and labor market changes in Tanzania on microenterprises and entrepreneurs, such as Lyons, Brown, and Msoka's (2014) study of 'doing business reforms' and its generally negative effects on microenterprises. In this study, I explore the micro-level practices, relations, and forms of citizen subjectivity that take shape for youths who participate in entrepreneurship education and training. I aim to answer the following questions: Does participation in an entrepreneurship training program[3] produce the enterprising citizen and, if so, what does this mean in these communities? How do NGO staff and youths reshape entrepreneurship skills and mindsets within their local material and social contexts? And, how does a socially embedded or moral economy affect the meanings, goals, and outcomes of this entrepreneurship training program? I examine these questions through an analysis of *Apprentice*'s non-formal entrepreneurship training program for youths who have not completed secondary education in Tanzania, and therefore have limited access to the formal labor market.

In this chapter, I examine the 'strange conjunction' (Ferguson, 2010) of neo/liberal approaches to entrepreneurship and local discourses of a moral economy in the implementation of *Apprentice*'s entrepreneurship training program. On the one hand, these youths had been excluded from participating in many aspects of social and economic life because they were not regarded as educated. They also did not have 'work membership', a sort of recognition and inclusion based on being employed or participating in wage labor (Ferguson, 2013). The *Apprentice* program was ethically committed to training these youths and fostering opportunities for their future livelihoods – a sort of liberal orientation to ensuring their rights and alleviating poverty. On the other hand, the program goals were to support primarily self-employment through youths investing their own earnings in these microenterprises. It did not provide 'handouts' of a grant or loan to achieve this. In this way, it aimed to 'responsibilize' these youths to take control of their own lives and livelihoods. But the program also encountered and, in turn, adapted its approach to social and economic relations that existed in these communities, such as the youths working together and sharing their resources to support each other and their families, including making loans to each other. It is these encounters of neo/liberal and local ways of thinking related to entrepreneurship that I detail in this chapter, by analyzing the frictions that occur between the ideas and practices of responsible individuals and community wellbeing, as well as those of profits and reciprocity. I use the term *entrepreneurial citizen* to capture the connections, contradictions, and possibilities between economic and social relations, as well as the double meanings that arise when different discourses of entrepreneurship education meet.

Entrepreneurship education and training programs in sub-Saharan African countries, as I discuss in Chapter 1, are situated within discourses and practices of a global economy and those of local and moral economies, or embedded non-economic and economic relations (Tripp, 1997; Mains, 2012; Ferguson, 2013). I start by exploring how social relations in a moral economy shape ideas of work, entrepreneurship, livelihoods, and wellbeing in these contexts. I then briefly describe the social and economic context of the Kagera region, the communities where *Apprentice* is being implemented and where these youths live and work.

To understand how this program utilizes discursive meanings of skills, enterprise, and economic development, as well as the practices it uses to foster social relations and wellbeing, I describe *Apprentice*'s training aims, curriculum, and pedagogical practices. Using survey data from more than 700 program participants and qualitative interview data from 31 youths,[4] I identify unintended and, at times, contradictory effects of this entrepreneurship training on youths to show which skills are learned and valued, how young people create enterprises and for what purposes, and, finally, how these youths seek economic and social value through their labor.[5]

Entrepreneurship in a moral economy

The outcomes of entrepreneurship training, usually those of self-employment and improving income through starting an enterprise,[6] are contested and uncertain, particularly for marginalized youths. Most programs assume that if they get the technical aspects of adequate technical and business training, financial knowledge and management, and incentives to start an enterprise 'right' that enterprise development and improved income will result (see, for example, Valerio, et al., 2014). Another perspective suggests that there are other forms of economy, beyond the capitalist and 'free' market, at work in Tanzania and other countries in sub-Saharan Africa, that utilize different principles and practices for enterprise development and earnings (Tripp, 1997; Mains, 2012; Ferguson, 2013). For instance, the expansion of household and microenterprises in the informal economy in Tanzania during the 1980s did not emerge as a result of policies or initiatives aimed at addressing economic growth or unemployment. Rather they endogenously developed as a result of economic and social conflict and decline, and as part of social practices in communities. In addition, this enterprise development did not necessarily represent autonomous entrepreneurs who were creating value added products for the global economy and promoting national economic development. In contrast, Tripp (1997) asserts that these microenterprises operated to address financial needs of families and social needs of communities. They sought to be self-reliant and to support the survival of others. 'Even with increased market activity, the moral-economy rationales have not given way to the more market-oriented ones' (Tripp, 1997, p. 127). She does not claim that those who started microenterprises operated within pure moral economy principles; there may be self-interest and reciprocity, competition and mutuality. Still, a moral economy perspective helps explain conflicting rationales that are at work, in this case in the adaptation of neoliberal and socialist discourses and practices that existed at that time in Tanzania. From this perspective, entrepreneurship training programs need to consider non-economic relations and desired outcomes alongside economic relations that are more disembedded from society.

Mains' (2012) more recent analysis of social relations, labor markets and entrepreneurship in Ethiopia is also relevant. He argues that 'social relationship rather than the logic of the market' guide young Ethiopian men's engagement with neoliberal capitalism (loc. 2584). For example, he details that the social practice of gift-giving places young men in a network of relations that could either support them financially or help ensure access to different forms of labor and earnings. These social relations shifted over time, as Ethiopia's macro-economy faced inflation, and he notes that such social practices no longer sufficed for sustaining a livelihood. To respond to these economic changes, Mains shows that many young men found ways to engage in entrepreneurial work in the informal economy, 'providing the sharpest rebuttal to the pessimism that is often directed toward Africa'. He argues that entrepreneurial work offers possibilities for improved livelihoods and self-sufficiency that is not about 'economic success', but rather about how these men 'grow their families instead of their businesses' (loc. 2697). He draws on Gibson-Graham (2006) who call for a construction of 'diverse economies' composed of a myriad of contingent forms of economic and cultural activity instead of a monolithic notion of a capitalist economy (loc. 1616). From this perspective, not all microenterprise labor represents a neoliberal discourse; nor are its goals oriented toward economic development. In a surprising contrast to common assumptions about neoliberal entrepreneurialism and individualism, Mains (2012) posits that such entrepreneurial work opens up possibilities and hope – forms of social and psychological wellbeing – for these men to be recognized by others as members of society.

Ferguson (2013, 2015), writing about southern African societies (in South Africa, Zambia, Namibia), also offers an analysis of how social relations and social policies aimed at addressing inequalities coexist alongside neoliberal discourses, policies, and practices. In his 2013 article, Ferguson aims to understand how personhood (or being a valued member of society and community) and welfare are achieved in a context of labor surplus, where becoming a part of society requires engaging in recognized waged labor, or what he calls 'work membership'. He argues that the capitalist economy has thrown off many workers, making them seemingly 'independent', but then these workers seek other forms of 'dependencies'. He places this concept of 'dependency' within historical and social contexts of southern Africa, arguing that dependency may not be the antithesis of autonomy and independence, as it is often positioned by neoliberal governance. Ferguson asserts:

> [I]n a social system put together around competition for followers, it was actually the existence of possibilities for hierarchical affiliation that created the most important forms of free choice. Where many such possibilities for affiliation existed, dependents could enjoy considerable agency. (2013, p. 226)

Dependency, as part of social relations and networks in sub-Saharan African societies, has particular relevance for young people in *Apprentice*'s informal training program. They are engaged in apprenticeships that help them learn a set of skills (and a trade), possibly earn an income, and develop a set of relationships by which they might gain more choice, opportunity, and even a sense of membership or inclusion in society.

Ferguson (2013) does not suggest that we should valorize this dependency; rather, he explains how it is related to a particular social system and set of (a)social inequalities. He specifically uses the term *asocial* rather than *social*: *social* implies a membership and set of relations in 'a morally binding group', or social relations exemplified by equality, whereas *asocial* represents the lived experiences of those experiencing inequality. The goals of independence and autonomy sought through entrepreneurship training programs may not necessarily improve economic outcomes for youths if they do not account for asocial inequalities or attend to the social relations and needs of youths. Ferguson suggests 'a social policy ... that takes maximizing independence and autonomy as its ultimate goal may not be able to address the crisis of personhood that ... is at the heart of southern Africa's contemporary predicament' (p. 238). This crisis of personhood is a result of people not being valued and included in their communities unless they are producing, specifically producing a surplus. From this perspective, entrepreneurship education and other work/livelihood programs cannot address this crisis by producing more workers per se, but by producing new kinds of social relations. How, then, might entrepreneurship training programs foster not only economic outcomes but also greater recognition and social inclusion when they meet the social relations and material realities that produce both solidarity and inequalities in Tanzanian communities? Before detailing the ways the *Apprentice* entrepreneurship training program is reshaped in rural Tanzania, I first provide a brief context of economic and social relations in Kagera region, where it is being implemented.

Economic and social development in Kagera region

Apprentice implements its non-formal entrepreneurship training program in the regions around Lake Victoria. Kagera lies in northwestern Tanzania, bordering Uganda, Rwanda, and Burundi, and is dominated by the Haya people in the north and Sukuma and other groups in the south. It has long had considerable 'autonomy' due to its isolation from the main cities of Tanzania and its distinct cultural/colonial history. While 90% of the population resides in rural areas, it has a history of international influence on economic and social life, including the colonial and missionary development of schools. The main cash crop has long been coffee, from colonial times when even small landowners exported coffee, and the main food crop is bananas. Both of these crops are subject to disease and price fluctuations, and are generally now regarded as not economically viable. As such, those households that primarily farm these crops tend to be the poorest (De Weerdt, 2010). It is also the region first and most affected by the HIV/AIDS epidemic in the 1980s, which has resulted in many orphaned children and the loss of income earners. Families and youths in Kagera, then, are faced with considerable economic and social challenges to their lives and livelihoods.

Education participation is generally lower in Kagera than other regions of Tanzania, though there is a history of missionary schools among the Haya in the north. In 2013, 84% (82% girls and 85% boys) of primary school-age children were in school, whereas other regions generally have enrollments rates in the ninetieth percentile (URT, MoEVT, 2013b, p. T2.8). In addition to lower participation rates, only 34% of these students pass the school-leaving exam (Standard VII), with girls passing at a lower rate (30%) than boys (35%) (URT, MoEVT, 2013a, chart T2.18). As a large percentage (more than 60%) of primary leavers do not continue to secondary school, additional education and training provided by vocational and technical schools is needed. Kagera has more than 39 Vocation and Education Training (VET) institutes that enroll youths, though in 2012 only 5,838 students enrolled. Female enrollment in these institutes is also lower than the national average: approximately 38% of students in Kagera compared to 45% overall (URT, MoEVT, 2013b, chart 7.3). These education participation rates suggest there is a large group of young people who are considered not 'educated' because they have not completed a basic education, and they are unable to be employed in a stable contract in the formal labor market. These are the youths that *Apprentice* aims to train and support. Other NGOs in the region offer various training and education opportunities, but local development officials told us that most programs, other than the one in this study, do not target non-completers of secondary school.

Economically, Kagera is a poor region; it has the lowest per capita gross domestic product in the country, and 29% percent of all households live below the basic needs poverty line (from URT, 2002, in Kessy, 2005, p. 1). In colonial times up until the 1980s, when the economy declined, the majority of the landholders, shareholders, and some 'peasants' engaged in coffee production, selling on the global market (Smith, 1989). Today, the economy and social life still revolve around agriculture and fishing, with approximately 95% of households engaged in food crop and subsistence agriculture, such as growing vegetables and bananas or raising cattle, and some cash-crop production, such as coffee. In addition, less than 10% of households are employed in their own non-agricultural business, and 5% of the population is employed in a growing industrial sector of mining, manufacturing, gas, and construction (NBS, 2014, pp. 113, 120). The growth in the industrial sector also increases options for labor in trades, goods and services to these sectors, such as an increasing need for transport or welding and electrical services. *Apprentice* identified training in trades in these related areas as viable enterprise options for youth today.

Social relations, or a moral economy, also play a critical role in economic transactions and wealth accumulation in Kagera. In a longitudinal study of rural villages in the region (comparing 1993 to 2004 data), De Weerdt (2010) examined why some households, particularly those that were not assumed to move 'out of poverty' given their initial assets, did improve, while others that were predicted to do so did not improve. He found households – farmers and traders – that improved their wealth and assets, in addition to having diversified earning activities, had strong social networks of people both within and outside the villages allowing them to trade and move food crops across the country. They often worked with apprentices as couriers between farmers and traders. Those whose income and assets grew did not depend on physical capital, but rather the continued trust of their *tajiri* (rich benefactor/boss). A *tajiri* benefits from the apprentice's knowledge of local markets; and the apprentice, with additional material support from the *tajiri*, often enters into the trade him/herself. Those who had fewer social networks often ended up in mining or fishing, both of which are less secure earning sectors (De Weerdt, 2010). These social networks and supports were less common for women, particularly those who were widowed or divorced as most were not able to claim inheritance rights through the husband's family, thus leaving them more vulnerable to poverty.

In sum, there is considerable demand for education and skills training in the region, as it is related to upward economic mobility and improved household welfare (De Weerdt, 2010). Few formal employment opportunities exist in the region and training in other trades and services, such as construction, and production and selling of food and other basic needs, is important for a large youth population to foster their livelihoods. However, earnings in the informal sector remain highly unstable and diversification seems necessary. Even with skills training, young people still need to be embedded in social networks that help them utilize their skills in the community. It is within this context that *Apprentice*'s non-formal training program began in 2011.

Apprentice's non-formal entrepreneurship training program

Apprentice's skills development and entrepreneurship training has an explicit goal of fostering enterprise development for youths. The program was created on the belief that skills and a trade offer young people an alternative to current livelihoods of subsistence agriculture or fishing in the region. With few formal employment opportunities and without a secondary school certificate, young men and women's most viable opportunities in these rural communities are to acquire technical and vocational skills and then to start their own enterprises. These resultant enterprises, *Apprentice* believes, will bring value to their families and the community.

Apprentice's program offers an integrated model of skills development: life, technical, entrepreneurial, and financial literacy skills. It is explicitly designed as a 'learning group' in which 20–30 youths learn a trade and related skills together over the course of nine months. NGO staff noted that these groups are critical for learning from each other and for mutual support. Young people are grouped, sometimes separately and sometimes mixed, by trade/training area, based on initial career guidance. Program facilitators, who are hired from the community, conduct simultaneous training in technical skills, entrepreneurship and business development, and life skills. Youths also participate in an apprenticeship with a community enterprise specializing in the trade area. The technical training areas/ trades for the youths we interviewed included knitting/embroidery/tailoring and cooking (for women); and carpentry, welding, masonry, and mechanics (for men). Most trades could be certified through Vocational Education and Training Association (VETA), so youths who passed the exam could get a certificate, thus giving them some symbolic capital as an 'educated' or 'skilled' person.[7] However, many of them did not complete the exam, and thus received only a certificate of attendance from *Apprentice*, which other employers in small enterprises and customers in the community have acknowledged as a valued credential.

The entrepreneurship training module complements the technical skills training so that youths can learn characteristics, values, and practices of being an entrepreneur; develop business ideas and plan start-ups; and learn to manage a business in their trade.[8] During their learning sessions, the youths self-assess their entrepreneurial motivation as well as entrepreneurial personality traits, and then develop a personal plan of action so they can learn to 'behave and conduct [themselves] as an entrepreneur in whatever [they] are doing' (Entrepreneurship Training Module, Tanzania). An *Apprentice* program staff noted that the purpose of this training is to get them to 'think like an entrepreneur', which includes teaching concrete business skills as well as non-cognitive skills, such as effective communication, leadership, and creativity. While the training content emphasizes the individual entrepreneur, it also includes the group dynamics necessary for being a successful entrepreneur/business owner in the community. Learning groups discuss the importance of pooling finances, bringing together resources, and buying and selling together, an adaptation of a cooperative model. Training facilitators tended to emphasize individual business plans and development; however, more recently the program staff began a series of training sessions to foster group businesses and networks in similar trade areas (*Apprentice* Senior Facilitator Staff, Ms. Luisa Jona, 2015, 2016). The training curriculum also stresses financial education and having the youths learn how to keep records for their business; however, there is little mention of profit or global value chains in the curriculum. NGO staff and community facilitators emphasized earning money to support themselves and their family, placing importance on community needs, and using enterprises to serve the community.

Life skills, or as one trainer called it 'learning how to live in the community and plan their future', is a key component of the training. These 'skills' cover health, HIV/AIDs, and family planning – skills deemed particularly necessary for out-of-school youths who might not have received this type of education during their schooling. The life skills curriculum aimed to responsibilize youths who are regarded as potentially engaging in risky behavior. For example, youths were taught to not only protect their own health, but also the health of their entire community. In addition, they learned how to access health care and to claim their rights to such care in the community. Many of these topics and skills are found throughout life skill curriculum in Tanzania, and in many international agencies' programs. But these life skills were also attentive to specific issues these youths faced in 'learning how to live in the community' and negotiating social constraints to their future opportunities. For example, community members told us that when young women did not have connections for employment, a male boss might demand a sexual favor; likewise, young men might be expected to pay a monetary bribe. Trainers used these life skills discussions to help youths negotiate these asocial inequalities in ways that might reshape not only their economic opportunities, but also their social relations in the community. For instance, young women told us how they worked together or with an adult woman, such as going to interviews together or working near each other when they had customers, so as to minimize the sexual pressures they would otherwise receive.

Local trade experts who own or work in a small business provided the required apprenticeships. They also offered ongoing mentoring and, at times, material support for youths' entrepreneurship goals. So these apprenticeships encompassed more than just the acquisition of technical skills; many youths also came away with a valuable relationship with an adult who cared about them and their contributions to the community. They assisted with the youths' transition from the training program by employing them full-time, connecting them with another business, or helping them develop their own enterprise. These trade experts also benefitted monetarily and socially by having young people work in their business; they were often able to increase their tenders or number of customers, and *Apprentice* gave them tools or other goods as compensation.

Over the five years of this study, *Apprentice* adapted its program to address changing market demands and youths' interests. It has also increased its involvement of community members as facilitators in order to foster positive relationships with youths. *Apprentice*'s model as it was taught, learned, and enacted was further reinterpreted and reshaped by local actors and youths. The next sections draw on survey data from youths and interview data from *Apprentice* staff and the select group of youths to discuss the kind of skills youths learned, how youth labored and developed enterprises and for which purposes, and the value of this training for youths and the community. The survey data allowed us to examine the immediate effects of the program, while the longitudinal interview data provide an understanding of the youths' livelihoods and wellbeing over time.

Learning skills and developing social relations for livelihoods

Learning skills was a primary reason that young men and women enrolled in *Apprentice*'s non-formal training. They believed the program would help them secure more reliable work and earnings, something they had not been able to achieve after leaving primary school. A dominant discourse, both globally and in Tanzanian society, is that young people are not learning the skills they need to work in a changing labor market. These youths not only had not acquired certain technical or employability skills, but they were also not employable – in the formal labor market, at least – because they lacked a secondary school certification. As stated earlier, this certificate is a social signifier of an educated, and presumably skilled, person, and important for most formal labor market jobs. None of the youths who enrolled in the program were studying in a formal school at the time, although nearly one-quarter of those we interviewed had studied up to Form 4 (the last year of O-levels) but did not pass the O-level leaving exam. The majority (67%) had completed only up to Standard 7, or the last year of primary school, and did not pass the primary school leaving exam. Of the 712 youths we surveyed, only 14% had ever worked for pay prior to enrolling; less than a quarter had started a household enterprise or another small enterprise (see also Chapter 4). Given their educational and employment challenges, these participants were seeking additional skills from *Apprentice* with the hope of having some alternative livelihood.

Perhaps because their prior schooling was highly academic, it was not a surprise that the survey and interview data following the training showed an increase in employability-related knowledge and skills. In an analysis of youths who completed *Apprentice*'s training, they reported statistically significant higher responses for their skills, knowledge and attitudes compared with those who had not yet started (see also, Krause et al., 2016). Their attitudes, motivations, and behaviors toward work and their future lives positively increased over the course of the nine-month program. They were more confident in their skills and stated that they knew how to find employment. In general, their satisfaction with their life increased considerably. Relationships with other peers and adults were also important, and the support they felt from them also increased over the course of the training[9] (see Table 7.1; changes to business and financial skills are reported and discussed in Chapter 8). For example, below we can see that women and men who completed the program (compared with those who hadn't started) reported a 60% and 69%, respectively, higher rating on a four-point scale of whether they had skills employers were looking for.[10] In general, women reported a greater change in their knowledge, skills, and attitudes than men, except for those questions related to work skills and having adults help them when needed.

While youths learned much during the training about finding employment, taking action toward their goals, and starting their own enterprise, doing so immediately after the program was challenging. In the first year post-training, most young people continued to apprentice with their trade expert. This relationship of earning from them – often at a lower wage than they would have if they had their own enterprise – could be considered a 'dependency', as Ferguson (2013) describes it. Despite not providing the economic benefits they desired, they continued the apprenticeship to gain more skills and develop relationships for future opportunities. In a few cases, this apprentice relationship inhibited their wellbeing and livelihoods, so they sought alternatives to this work and social relationship.[11] By the fourth year, most youth were on a path to starting their own enterprises, either alone or with others.

Table 7.1 Difference between participants' views and non-participants' views on their employability knowledge, skills and relationships, by female and male[1]

Change in knowledge, skill, or attitude from training	Female, % difference/ non-treatment mean	Male, % difference/ non-treatment mean
Have skills employers are looking for	60 (2.00)	69 (1.87)
Know how to find employment in the community	76 (2.65)	49 (2.02)
Confident in work skills	47 (2.45)	50 (2.43)
Satisfied with your life	46 (2.20)	36 (2.09)
Take action to achieve goals	47 (2.50)	20 (2.87)
Set goals for self	23 (2.91)	17 (3.19)
Know adults are available for them when they need	14 (2.74)	16 (2.64)
Adults willing to help you in practical ways	Not sign. Change	14 (2.38)
Peers are willing to listen when they have a problem	23 (2.85)	10 (2.90)

N = 434
Source: Krause, McCarthy and Chapman, 2016

[1] This analysis, reported in Krause, McCarthy, & Chapman (2016), is based on a propensity score matching test in which all scores of participants at the start of the program are matched with those who have not started/not yet participated in the program. The analysis uses two cohorts of youths, thus the sample size here is smaller than that reported for other analyses of the survey. The percentage change reflects the effects of the program in changing youths' responses to these questions, compared to the mean of the non-treatment groups, not the percentage of youths who changed.

Despite all they seemed to learn during the program, the technical and entrepreneurship/business skills the youths had learned were insufficient for the development of livelihoods. Four years after graduation, 86% of participants said they needed additional education or training, particularly skills in related or different trades, to sustain their livelihoods. For example, Goma, who had completed Standard 7 and at age 19 years, enrolled in the *Apprentice* program to learn knitting. She then started her own small enterprise and later pursued additional training in embroidery with a trainer, since selling knitted uniforms for school children, her main customers, was seasonal. Others participated in agricultural training to learn about farming techniques and products they could grow at home as a supplement to their microenterprise.[12] Goma and others sought out these additional knowledge and skills, sometimes in certified programs but more often in non-formal training courses, in part to diversify and stabilize their earnings and in part to be recognized as an educated or skilled person in the community.

Being a person with skills is one thing. With technical and life skills, these youths were able earn money to ensure their future livelihood in the face of uncertainty. It is, however, a different attribute to be a *skilled person*, which confers greater trustworthiness, recognition, and value in a community. These youths felt they had also acquired the necessary social relations in the community to elevate their status. They developed relationships with adult community members not only for economic benefit, but also out of a desire to become involved in their community. At the beginning of the program, nearly a third of the youths stated that adults were not willing to help them in practical ways or were not available when they needed them. Youths were conscious that the community often regarded them as idle, partaking in illicit behavior and not contributing to the community. Sudi, an orphan who had completed Standard 7, and then started the program at age 20 years to train as a mechanic, captured how young men are commonly viewed:

> [I]f the community doesn't know you, they see you like those other youth I am talking about [those who are idle, stealing, etc.] when you yourself are different. You could go and ask for work, like if someone is building a house, [but] they may not hire you because they have grouped you with all the other youth. ... [They think,] if I give him work, he will run away and steal. So this costs us, because people don't have faith in us youth even though we aren't like *those* youth. (Sudi, mechanic 24 years old, 2015)

Over the course of their training and thereafter, both female and male students increasingly felt that adults were available, cared about their problems, and/or supported them in practical ways. Employers and community members changed their perceptions of these young people, developing trust in them and including them in the community. And increasingly, the young men and women felt valued. Sudi contrasted his relationship with the community before and after his apprenticeship training:

> Last year, my community was looking at me as if they didn't understand me. But now they [value and respect] me because I can give advice to other youth, and they trust me and give me ... work. I am hard worker. I can also catalyze change or help in my community. (Sudi, mechanic, 24 years old, 2015)

Apprentice's training helped these youths to develop relationships with other adults as well as with their peers, and involved these young people in their community. They were developing the social relations they needed to improve their livelihoods. For instance, a female business owner, Ms. Ruth Bembi, who apprenticed several young women, shared how she mentored them to navigate better the challenges women faced in relation to their enterprises or their lives. Starting a business and earning money were possible not only because they had the skills, but also because they had acquired the necessary social relations, which included the social power to access space, gain customers, and avoid extortion. Ms. Bembi explained how those without social connections would be asked to pay fees when they tried to secure a space for their enterprise: 'If you don't have money, you are given space in the back rooms, and no one knows you are there' (Tailoring community trainer, 2012). Here she refers to 'back rooms' as the physical space for less wealthy or less experienced business owners, who needed to 'pay their time in the pecking order'. The back rooms also metaphorically symbolize the mistreatment of poorer people and their exclusion from opportunities. By providing connections and support that enabled these young people's enterprises to develop, these local trade experts and community facilitators played an important role in disrupting some of the social inequalities young people faced.

Creating enterprises and supporting community development

Microenterprise development is a key aim of *Apprentice*'s training, as there are few industries and formal labor market jobs in the Kagera region. Youths also desired to be self-employed, as it was their most likely option given their education trajectory. While many youths have started enterprises after completing *Apprentice*'s program, those businesses were difficult to sustain, while a few provided for youths' basic needs. Two years after completing the training program, 337 youths (out of 865 enrollees at that time, or 39%) were self-employed, and less than one in five were working in the trade or area of their training, with nearly equivalent percentages for males and females.[13] A greater percentage of men working in masonry and women in knitting/tailoring had either their own enterprises or more stable work, in part because these trades were in greater demand in the growing region. While many of the graduates told us that being self-employed gave them more 'freedom', meaning they were not subjected to infrequent or uncertain payment or unfair labor conditions from a boss, youths with their own microenterprises nonetheless faced uncertain and unstable (seasonal) earnings even though they had customers. Many youths were dismayed at customers who failed to pay on time – or even at all. They quickly learned strategies, however, to negotiate payment and to seek out trusted customers, an important element of transacting in the informal economy where relationships matter and commensurability of transactions are negotiated in various ways (Gibson-Graham, 2006).

As one way to mitigate risks of unstable earnings or a lack of payment, most youths developed multiple earning strategies, combining their main trade with a small household enterprise or income-generating activity, such as selling small items or agricultural produce. Even those with more stable earnings found it necessary to have alternative revenue streams. Rashida, a young woman who had studied up to form 4 and then enrolled at age 20 years in the *Apprentice* program to learn to make sweaters explained her work:

> I'm trained in sweater making – that is, knitting and weaving. And most of the time I produce caps, socks, and sweaters. But since our work is seasonal, sometimes I find myself doing some other side activities ... like where I sell [vegetables] door to door. (Rashida, knitter, 21 years old, 2014)

In this way, these youths are enterprising; they are being innovative and creative in efforts to mitigate risk and to increase income, though their primary motivation is to meet basic needs. Rashida explained that even though she did not earn a lot of money selling vegetables, 'through my earnings I have the ability to pay for my personal expenses and also to assist my family members. Not because I have much money to do that, but at least to a certain extent I have the ability to do that'. She was responsible for two of her family members and sometimes had to pay for medicine and health care for her mother.

These youths mitigated risks and overcame challenges not only through their enterprising activities, but also through collaboration and reciprocity. They often worked together in groups to start enterprises, to obtain capital or loans, or to share their knowledge and resources. Working together was also was integral to being part of the community and minimizing risk. Jahi, a young man who was responsible for three family members explained how a group of young men in his trade helped each other:

> We *fundi*[14] have the practice of lending not cash, but items. For example, my friend came to borrow items from my workshop, like pipes, and after two days he will return it. So there is no interest/profit from this loan, but the person borrowing gets a profit from the work they are able to do. But even if you, as the person lending them the equipment, don't get any direct profit, you still help him as it could happen any day that you need help and he will help you. (Jahi, welder, 24 years old, 2015)

Jahi, similar to many youths, recognized that working together was not only important for achieving a profit, but also for ensuring long-term survival. *Apprentice* recognized the value in helping youths share resources. Through their savings and lending program, they supported youths to pool capital and keep interest and profits within the group and community. (This is discussed in more detail in Chapter 8.) In addition, *Apprentice* helped youths in similar trades to form cooperatives that would generate capital, bring in customers, and share profits (*Apprentice* Regional Facilitator, Ms. Luisa Jona, 2016). Cooperatives, or even group enterprises, also serve as a political mechanism to ensure greater social and economic protection from arbitrary fees or intermediaries who take a portion of their profits or charge extra on their inputs. Cooperatives have a long history in Nyerere's socialist development program, particularly in relation to collective agricultural production. Still, these group enterprises are different from those of the past because they bring together youths who have been excluded from established community groups, such as formal secondary schools or political parties. Cooperatives draw on community values of solidarity and reciprocity to ensure the development and wellbeing of the community.

In creating their group enterprises, youths focused on developing goods and services needed within the community, not the global market. For example, many youths worked in construction, building homes and schools for an expanding population, or in food production and sales to provide basic needs for the community. One of *Apprentice*'s staff, Ms. Luisa Jona, who coordinated the youth groups in one region, clarified that these jobs were not with large or international companies, but were locally owned enterprises, generating income that stayed in the community to benefit their families and community needs. While the region has a long history of engagement in the global capitalist market, through coffee production and, more recently, with mineral extraction, these microenterprises and cooperatives allow for labor and profit to be managed and used by those within the community. As Gibson-Graham (2006) point out, community economies are not isolated from the global economy, but they can engage in different strategies to use their profit or surplus, and to define what sort of 'good life' they aim to attain. These youths' enterprises not only served the needs of the individual and their families, but those of the larger community. Looking more deeply at the contours of these youths' livelihoods, we see how they saw this entrepreneurship training as fostering their inclusion in and being valued by the community.

Creating and being value(d)

Entrepreneurship presumably creates economic value for individuals who start and expand an enterprise, but starting even a microenterprise is contingent on social relations, which generates needed capital and customers. Enterprises not only have and create economic value; they are also deeply embedded in social relations in the community, or the moral economy (Booth, 1994; Tripp, 1997). Rashida, who was trying to expand her small enterprise, explained how getting even a small loan to buy yarn had been challenging before she gained the trust of a savings and lending group.

> I was just lonely [before I participated in *Apprentice*]. I had no other group members. But right now I have ... the [savings and lending] group. I can go there and these people actually ... trust me, not like before. Because before, you could join a group and maybe some people would not trust you. ... I've been able to get some earnings ... because I'm being trusted. I have the ability to go to someone and tell him or her to borrow [sic] me some money, not like before. (Rashida, knitter, 21 years old, 2014)

Society had labeled Rashida, and many of these youths as idle and untrustworthy, and excluded them from full participation in the community. However, this entrepreneurship training helped them acquired the status of a respected, trusted and skilled person – a *fundi*, as Rashida, Jahi, Sudi and many trained youths called themselves. These youths were reshaping what it meant to be a valued citizen in this community: not only a person with a formal secondary degree, but also a *fundi*, someone with respected skills and knowledge in a trade.

Apprentice's training offered an opportunity for these young men and women to *add value* to their lives, both economically and socially – or *being valued* in their community. While income generation is, of course, necessary and beneficial to these youths, the greater good seems to be their improved social standing. Jahi captured this value two years after he completed the program: 'I'm now viewed as a role model to some other youths in the street' (2013). He acknowledged that his training had 'changed [his] life'. The earnings from his welding have allowed him to rent his own room and buy a bike, material gains that are important to establishing himself in the community. He added that he hoped to soon 'have my own house, ... get married, ... and be able to send my children to school' (2013). When we met Jahi again in 2014, he had recently married and was saving to buy a plot of land. The money he earned and saved was used to invest in his family – his wife as well as his siblings and parents. Having one's own house and get married, as Mains (2012) also shows in his analysis of Ethiopian men, is an important transition to adulthood, particularly for men. These material and social markers allow these young people to be regarded as 'somebody' who is stable and can contribute to the community. Supporting and contributing to one's family and the community were also important markers for young women to be valued and included in the community. As Rashida recounted, 'Now, I am independent. I can also help my mother ... And there are now people who depend on me' (2015). Establishing one's own home, however, was not a common marker of social change for young women.

While some entrepreneurship training programs teach participants to engage in *value-added* enterprises that are part of a global value chain, *Apprentice* staff and youths regarded their learning and earning as also creating social value for their families and community. The survey asked the youths who completed the program about their values related to work, owning an enterprise, educating their children and helping their community. It also asked about the belief that money leads to a happier life (see Table 7.2). We found that after completing the program, more men and women valued helping the community (70% and 67%, respectively) and ensuring the education of their children (89% and 86%, respectively).[15] Fewer men (72% decreased from 75%) regarded earning money as leading to a happier life after completing the program. The importance they placed on contributing to the community and their families continued to be adamantly expressed in interviews in subsequent years.

Table 7.2 Change in values that women and men hold, percentage before and after program

	Females		Males	
	Pre-program	Post-program	Pre-program	Post-program
Value helping your community	60%	67%	67%	70%
Value educating your children	82%	86%	89%	89%
Believe earning money leads to a happier life	67%	70%	75%	72%

N = 712
Source: DeJaeghere, Chapman and Pellowski Wiger and Learn, Earn, Save Project Team at University of Minnesota survey

The ways in which young men and women saw themselves contributing to their community changed over the years. Sudi, who expressed concern about how community members viewed youths as idle, later felt he was 'paying it back' and gaining respect: 'I have been able to support others. I am now supporting other youths, I have been able to teach them and train them. I can help other youths, meaning I am contributing to the community and they see me advancing my life' (Sudi, mechanic, 24 years old, 2015).

The youths also supported the community in monetary ways by paying business taxes and contributing to a social fund that aids others in times of need, such as paying for funeral expenses. Goma, who finally opened her own shop four years after completing the *Apprentice* program, proudly described how she contributed to the community and livelihoods of other youths:

> I pay the [municipal] license [for doing business] and make some community contributions and donations. So, for instance, when there is one ward leader whose mom died, I had to contribute [to the social fund]. Also there's one girl who couldn't pay her school fees, so her uncle came by to ask us to help. So I contributed to her fees. Also, there was a girl that I trained and I didn't earn any money from her. (Goma, tailor, 23 years old, 2015)

Many youths, including Rashida and Jahi, had hired and trained others to work with them, giving these youths opportunities for a livelihood that they may not otherwise have. Goma and other *Apprentice* youths tended not emphasize the profit they were making or the success of their enterprises; rather, they focused on how their earnings supported their families and how they, in turn, contributed to broader community needs. In this way, the values of solidarity and reciprocity were lived out through these youths' enterprising activities.

Adults in the community came to recognize and value these youths. Ms. Aretha Jacob, who owned several microenterprises and was a community-based trainer for *Apprentice* described the youths' newfound status: 'They feel themselves to be Tanzanians because they are working and getting money'. She met the youths on a weekly basis and saw the challenges they faced and changes in how they and others saw them. She added that when these youths were 'idle', they did not know who they were and did not claim this identity. With this training and their new status, 'they can go into politics … not to be elected, but to know his [sic] political rights, … to vote, … to participate in democratic activities'. For these youths, *Apprentice*'s training, while not intentionally aimed at fostering citizenship, altered social relationships in the community that had previously excluded them. Their social status changed, shifting both how these youths regarded themselves and how other adults and peers included them as people who belong and contribute. While entrepreneurship training is foremost about creating skilled workers, developing livelihoods, and fostering 'work membership', it ultimately became so much more by producing a generation of trusted and valued young people (Ferguson, 2013).

Reflections on the encounter of entrepreneurship with the local and moral economy

Most entrepreneurship education and training programs, as well as education policies focused on skills development and the transition to employment, emphasize working and earning – either starting an enterprise or being employed – as the desired and measured outcomes. The contradiction of these training programs is that they may not achieve these desired economic outcomes without engaging with and changing social and other inequalities that are intertwined with economic inequalities. Working and earning an income, particularly for the youths in *Apprentice*'s training, were embedded in '(a)social inequalities"; these included being unable to pay for and, therefore, participate in basic and further education; an inability to enter the formal labor force due to lack of educational certification; and other structural barriers that they encountered on a daily basis (Ferguson, 2013).

Changing these inequalities and fostering social inclusion do not necessarily happen by participating in skill development and entrepreneurship training programs. These programs must attend to the moral economy of social relations that both exclude and include (Booth, 1994). In effect, staff, community members, and youths either intentionally or inadvertently reshaped the goals and processes of entrepreneurship training in efforts to address some of these inequalities. In the encounter of a neo/liberal approach to entrepreneurship training – focused on individual entrepreneurs, their skills and capital, and their rights and responsibilities – with the moral economy of relationships, reciprocity, and solidarity, the program processes and outcomes had shifted for many of these youths.

The *Apprentice* staff, community facilitators, and trainers not only taught technical skills, they also mentored youths on important social and life skills, including creating connections with others in the community so adults got to know and see them in a different way. Teaching youths these life skills responsibilized them into being motivated and active in pursuing their economic wellbeing. But by being motivated, trustworthy, and responsible, these youths were also becoming respected members that contributed economically *and* socially to the community. Becoming entrepreneurial citizens also means the youths had to reciprocate by sharing their learning and earnings, and contributing to the wellbeing of others in their communities. In turn, they were included in their communities as valued members. For example, many youths shared resources and customers, and trained and hired other youths. Community members valued their skills and their trustworthiness. Organizations sought them out to train other young men and women. For these youths, *Apprentice*'s training did not just teach them to be entrepreneurial; rather, it helped them become respected *fundi* and community members.

Learning to become an entrepreneur and starting an enterprise are key aspects of these entrepreneurship training programs, and so, too, is financial education and inclusion important if youths are to start enterprises and sustain them as well. I now turn to the multiple and contradictory effects of financial education and inclusion on these youths' lives.

Notes

1 I use the term *informal economy*, rather than *informal sector* or *informal employment*, because I wish to distinguish between a global capitalist economy and an economy that operates according to community institutions and rules, much as Tripp's (1997) use of it. The informal economy in Tanzania has many elements of a moral economy.
2 I use the term *moral economy*, as discussed in Chapter 1, to signify how economic transactions and relations are embedded in social relations and non-economic institutions and norms, as Booth (1994), drawing on Polanyi (1944), suggests. Booth also states that a moral economy approach assumes that scarcity, surplus, and an economizing rationale are not universal (p. 655). Both Booth and Gibson-Graham (2006), while approaching this idea from different analyses, suggest that in order to understand economic relations, we need to consider what purposes they serve and the ways they define 'the good' they aim to achieve.
3 In this chapter, I usually refer only to entrepreneurship training, rather than entrepreneurship education and training, as *Apprentice* is a non-formal training program. I use *entrepreneurship education and training* when referring to a composite of approaches or programs.
4 As explained in Chapter 3, we collected interview data from 30 participants over four years, and then two years later from another 10 participants. We added the latter 10 because some of the original participants moved or were no longer available to participate in the interview. Therefore, we have 31 youths, 13 women and 18 men, for whom we have consistent interviews over the two- or four-year period.
5 I use *labor* as distinct from *work*, following Gibson-Graham's (2006) broader definition of different forms of labor – wage, unpaid, and alternative paid – to indicate the possibility for exploitation but also for alternative values in using one's capability to generate products and value.
6 Some entrepreneurship education and training programs also focus on entrepreneurial behaviors and attitudes for working in formal employment, or for others.
7 While an *educated* person is distinct from a *skilled* person in Tanzania, with the former most closely associated with completion of secondary school, both hold value in being a respected person. Nyerere's socialist program of *Ujamaa*, in effect, valued all who contributed to society through their knowledge and skills.
8 The curriculum uses the term *business*, though usually these youths will start a microenterprise, which may eventually be registered with the local municipality. The use of the term *business* may be an inappropriate translation in these materials, which are used for other Apprentice programs in other countries.
9 While youths in the program reported a higher rating of business and financial skills, this may be in part because these skills are more concrete and more easily measured. Responses to learning life skills and relations with adults and peers were also greater for those who went through the program compared to those who had not started, but the magnitude was less. However, the qualitative data suggest that these were critical for enabling them to work and earn and for improving their livelihoods. In addition, these changes were particularly notable for these Tanzanian youths in this program. Similar analyses were conducted for *Apprentice's* program with out-of-school youths in Uganda and found positive changes, but

not to this extent. These analyses were also conducted for youths participating in *Parka*'s entrepreneurship program at the secondary level; again, the extent of change was much less.
10 The propensity score analysis compares those who participated in the program with those who had not yet started. Responses to the questions were based on a four-point scale from 'not at all' to 'a lot'. The percentage change reported in the table reflects the average treatment effect for each question divided by the group mean for women and men. For example, women who participated in the program had a 60% higher response on their belief that they have the skills employers were looking (e.g., some or a lot) for than those who hadn't yet participated in the program.
11 For example, some youths told us that the local trade experts were not treating them well, such as not sharing any profit. Some youths left these apprenticeships and sought out other relationships or established their own enterprises. *Apprentice* also took action by not continuing apprenticeships with these community members.
12 Agriculture was not a training program initially offered, even though most people in the region engage in (subsistence) farming. Some youths may have been interested in pursuing this subject because the government recently initiated a youth fund for loans directed at groups who engage in agriculture production. Many youths were seeking loans for their enterprises, and few opportunities existed.
13 These data were collected by the NGO program. Staff met with youths on a quarterly basis to follow up on their training and livelihoods.
14 *Fundi* (pronounced FOON-dee) is a term used to refer to a skilled craftsperson or tradesperson in Tanzania. It is usually, according to our interviews with youths, an honorable technical title that reflects that a person has accomplished skills in a trade. Not all *fundi* are respected in the community, as they might engage in dishonest transactions.
15 I provide here the frequency of women and men who responded that they 'considerably or very much' value helping their community or educating their children. In our statistical analysis, we conducted non-parametric tests of difference over time in the mean scores for both men and women and these were statistically significant, at p value = .01 and .05, respectively.

References

Booth, W. J. (1994). On the idea of the moral economy. *American Political Science Review*, 88(03), 653–667.
De Weerdt, J. (2010). Moving out of poverty in Tanzania: Evidence from Kagera. *The Journal of Development Studies*, 46(2), 331–349.
Ferguson, J. (2010). The uses of neoliberalism. *Antipode*, 41(s1), 166–184.
Ferguson, J. (2013). Declarations of dependence: Labour, personhood, and welfare in southern Africa. *Journal of the Royal Anthropological Institute*, 19(2), 223–242.
Ferguson, J. (2015). *Give a man a fish: Reflections on the new politics of distribution*. Durham, NC: Duke University Press.
Gibson-Graham, J. K. (2006). *A postcapitalist politics*. Minneapolis, MN: University of Minnesota Press.
Kessy, F. (2005). *Rural income dynamics in Kagera region, Tanzania*. Washington DC: World Bank Group.
Krause, B. L., McCarthy, A. S. and Chapman, D. (2016). Fuelling financial literacy: Estimating the impact of youth entrepreneurship training in Tanzania. *Journal of Development Effectiveness*, 8(2), 234–256.

Lyons, M., Brown, A. and Msoka, M. (2014). Do micro enterprises benefit from the "Doing Business" reform?: The case of street vending in Tanzania. *Urban Studies*, *51*(8), 1593-1612.

Mains, D. (2012). *Hope is cut: Youth, unemployment, and the future in urban Ethiopia*. Philadelphia, PA: Temple University Press.

Motala, E. and Vally, S. (2014). 'No one to blame but themselves': Rethinking the relationship between education, skills and employment. In S. Vally and E. Motala (Eds.) *Education, economy and society*. Pretoria, South Africa: UNISA Press.

Polanyi, K. (1944). *The great transformation: The political and economic origins of our time*. Boston, MA: Beacon Press.

Smith, C. D. (1989). *Did colonialism capture the peasantry? A case study of the Kagera District, Tanzania* (No. 83). Nordic Africa Institute.

The National Bureau of Statistics (NBS) [Tanzania]. (2014). *Basic demographic and socio-economic profile 2012*. Tanzania census. Retrieved from http://www.nbs.go.tz.

Tripp, A. M. (1997). *Changing the rules: The politics of liberalization and the urban informal economy in Tanzania*. Berkeley, CA: University of California Press.

United Republic of Tanzania (URT), MoEVT, (2013a). *BEST 2013: Secondary education* [Excel format report]. Retrieved from http://www.moe.go.tz/index.php?option=com_docman&task=cat_view&gid=358&Itemid=619

United Republic of Tanzania (URT), MoEVT. (2013b). *BEST 2013: Primary education* [Excel format report]. Retrieved from http://www.moe.go.tz/index.php?option=com_docman&task=cat_view&gid=358&Itemid=619

Valerio, A., Parton, B. and Robb, A. (2014). *Entrepreneurship education and training programs around the world: Dimensions for success*. Washington, DC: World Bank Group. doi: 10.1596/978-1-4648-0202-7.

Chapter 8
Educating Youths as Financially Responsible and Inclusive Citizens

Sudi, like most youths in *Apprentice*'s entrepreneurship training program, told us that even when he had customers who requested orders, he did not have access to enough capital or loans to buy the equipment and supplies he needed to run his welding/repair shop. He exemplified program participants, whose concern about obtaining financial resources persisted from the beginning of their training to four years later, when they continued to struggle to produce and earn from their enterprises. Access to capital was a challenge because most worked in the informal economy, which meant they did not have the necessary paperwork – pay stubs, income history, and other proofs of employment – to secure bank loans. Most youths did not have enough collateral to secure a sizeable loan, so investors considered them as credit risks. Financial service providers (FSPs) and microfinance institutions (MFIs), particularly those that serve youths or have products, such as saving accounts and loans,[1] that are amenable to their needs are not abundant in these communities in the Kagera region. In addition, investors and FSPs charge youths and 'the poor' higher fees and interest rates. Some youths understand the risks and costs that come with borrowing from financial institutions, and avoid doing so.

Still, the international foundation and *Apprentice* were keen to foster the financial *inclusion* of these youths. Financial inclusion is a concept that explicitly ties together double meanings associated with different discourses (Ferguson, 2010; Muehlebach, 2012). It appeals to many optimistic development practitioners who assume that it democratizes global capital, trying to ensure that the 'bottom billion' have access to financial resources. From this perspective, NGOs and international agencies work with financial service providers to create more youth-friendly products, ones that are more accessible and suited to their financial needs.[2] More pessimistic critics of microfinance and development argue that when financial inclusion programs engage the poor in financial markets as consumers of services and goods of global capitalist financial institutions, the result is greater vulnerability due to high interest rates and fees. Roy (2010) characterizes this theme of financial inclusion as bringing together market principles with a social good: It is about using 'business [and financial] principles to solve social problems like poverty' (p. 207). Roy argues that microfinance is driven by a double promise: 'it extends opportunities to the "non-banked" poor and it can yield profits for investors' (p. 208). Given this double promise, questions need to be asked of programs that serve youths living in conditions of poverty: How can participants in youth programs access financial services and the products that serve their needs? What purposes does this capital serve, and for whom? And who is making a profit from their savings and lending?

Microfinance, whether administered as a formal lending program through an MFI or informally through group savings and lending programs, is a particular technology of power and of self. It is a technology of power through the access to capital from a diverse array of institutions, including private banks and international and local MFIs that are regulated by government rules and international practices of financing, including investor risks and profits. These institutions also impose severe consequences for borrowers who do not follow their regulations for securing loans or repaying them, either by denying them loans or charging higher interest rates. But the poor often feel compelled to engage with these financial markets because of the pervasive discourse that says in order to be entrepreneurial and economically contributing citizens in society, they need capital from financial institutions. Microfinance is also a technology of the self in that these programs increasingly require participants to learn how to manage money and to conduct themselves responsibly in order to repay the loan. An underlying assumption of microfinance programs and financial education is that poor people do not know how save money or act responsibly, but if they can learn to do both, their lives will be improved. The World Bank (2009) states it this way: '[T]hose who are less financially literate are more likely to have problems with debt, are less likely to save, are more like to engage in high-cost credit, and are less likely to plan for the future' (p. 3). One of the paradoxes of this assumption is that instead of providing loans or directly increasing income through grants, financial education aims to help people better manage the money they have, but they often have very little (Van Rooyen et al., 2012). This paradox, as I show, occurs in *Apprentice*'s program, as the financial education component was designed to help young people manage their money, assuming they would slowly increase it, but it did not directly provide loans or cash transfers.

Connecting youths to financial services is one component of *Apprentice*'s program, but equally important is giving them a financial education.[3] They need to learn about savings options, such as bank accounts, mobile money,[4] and group mechanisms (described later in the chapter), as well as 'the value of savings', as the staff said repeatedly. Young people, they believed, need to have goals and to know for what purposes they are saving. Once they know how to save, the program model assumes, they would be able to increase their capital and have access to more through MFI or bank loans. Getting loans is often contingent on youths showing that they have an operating business, that they are earning, and that they have a certain amount of savings. In short, they need to show investors they are not a credit risk.

Apprentice's program of financial education was based on a group approach. Once these 20–30 youths developed the skills to monitor their savings and lending, and they accrued some capital, *Apprentice* linked them with MFIs in an effort to help them secure more capital. The group model relies on mutual trust, reciprocity, and solidarity to help each other out through their collective loans. If these three values did not exist, the group could not function well. In this way, financial education was an encounter between two schools of thought: neoliberal rationalities of securing a livelihood through responsibility and participation in the financial market; and local and historically situated discourses of self-reliance, reciprocity, and solidarity among young people in the group.

In this chapter I consider again the 'strange conjunction' (Ferguson, 2010) of neo/liberal ideas represented in the concepts of being financially responsible and financially included. In the *Apprentice* model of financial education, I show how the neo/liberal ideas of capital, markets, and financial inclusion encounter ideas of exchange, reciprocity, and social wellbeing for youths in these communities. In my analysis of interviews with youths in this program, I ask: what does it mean for these young people to be financially responsible? Is their financial responsibility primarily to ensure the profit of the lending institution or the wellbeing of their families and communities? What does financial inclusion look like in the financial market in their communities, and how do these young people and the NGO staff reshape how they are included? Finally, for what purposes are they engaged in the financial market – to foster enterprise and economic development or to redistribute wealth and promote human development? I ask these questions not to position financial education programs as necessarily beneficial or detrimental, but rather to examine the different discourses of financial inclusion that encounter each other and the specific local meanings and effects that they have on the livelihoods of Tanzanian youths.

To answer these questions, I describe the aims and pedagogy of *Apprentice*'s group savings and lending mechanism, Kichumi,[5] that is used to teach and practice financial education. Drawing on quantitative data collected from over 700 youth participants and qualitative interviews from 31 of them, I show the double meanings of learning to be financially responsible, of being financially included, and of using financial resources for development.

Financial education in contexts of poverty

Financial education comes in varied forms and programs. In low-income contexts, some form of financial education, usually financial literacy, is included as part of microfinance programs. Increasingly, youths and the poor are the targets of financial education, delivered through formal education, savings and lending programs, or entrepreneurship education. Financial education taught through these various programs usually has the general goal of 'empowering consumers to take action to improve their financial well-being' (World Bank, 2009, p. vii). This goal assumes that by being knowledgeable, or by empowering disempowered consumers, these disadvantaged groups will have fair and equitable access to financial resources from which they can choose. It also assumes that by participating in the market of financial services products, such as obtaining loans, this injection of capital necessarily improves one's financial wellbeing. These assumptions are challenged by those who criticize the underlying purposes and rationale of microfinance, and also by findings from empirical studies on the outcomes of microfinance programs.

Critics argue that these financial institutions, which are ostensibly designed to help the poor save money and to lend them money, actually take advantage of people with little money and power; what is really being served are the interests of global financial institutions and their investors (Fernando, 2006; Roy, 2010; Yunus and Weber, 2011). Roy (2010), in her book *Poverty Capital,* shows that financial institutions (international banks) are increasingly in partnership with smaller, bottom-up NGO-run MFIs and making a profit from them through fees and interest. She suggests that not only are the recipients of micro-lending being integrated into global capital markets in which they have little power, but so are the NGOs and other organizations that run MFIs. This was not the intent or the approach of the early work by Muhammad Yunus, a pioneer in microfinance. Roy argues that Yunus' approach to microfinance was to speak against financial institutions and to give rights of financial resources through a bottom-up or community-group initiative. Roy and other critics argue that microfinance, as practiced by many institutions, is less about extending capital access on reasonable terms to the poor than it is about making a profit for investors.

Financial education operates on the premise that if individuals acquire skills to manage, save, and invest their money, and if they have knowledge about the financial options available to them, they will make good choices and lift themselves out of poverty. But the empirical data on the varied outcomes of microfinance programs show otherwise. Van Rooyen et al. (2012), in a systematic review of various microfinance studies (of both micro-credit and savings programs) in sub-Saharan Africa, detail the contradictory evidence and note the shortcomings of what we can know about these financial education and microfinance programs. Most studies measure the impact of success only on limited financial outcomes, such as income levels or asset accumulation. In examining these outcomes, the evidence for improved income, or getting out of poverty, is mixed. For instance, in one study of micro-savings among women, Dupas and Robinson (2009) found that while women invested more in their businesses, there was no evidence of greater profit levels. The oft-cited controversial study by Banerjee et al. (2013), conducted in the slums of Hyderabad, India, makes an even stronger argument that micro-credit, even after being made available to households for three to four years, did not increase household consumption (a measure of wealth), nor did it increase the profits of small enterprises. The other commonly assessed metrics are non-financial: health, food security, education, women's empowerment, and job creation. The results for education, empowerment, and job creation are not so conclusive, though they are more certain for health and food security. Notably for purposes of this book, the studies reviewed by Van Rooyen et al. did not show convincing evidence of the impact of micro-credit on job creation, particularly over the longer-term (three years). They suggest that micro-credit programs should be used only after individuals/households have increased their financial income (p. 2, 258).

Missing from these studies, and from the debates about financial education and microfinance, is whether and how such programs draw on and affect social cohesion or, for the purposes of this book, social relations. Van Rooyen et al. (2012) note that none of the studies assess this, even though many of the programs took place in group lending or savings schemes. They add that non-formal community group schemes were not included in these studies, though many government and NGO programs now use them. This gap is important when considering *Apprentice*'s program, as it uses a group format for learning and participating in savings and lending, and it is similar to other community group schemes used in Tanzania, such as village saving and lending associations (VSLAs) and saving and credit cooperatives (SACCOs).[6]

Studies of financial education among youths in low-income countries are fewer, but they parallel the findings of the many studies of microfinance and financial education (Oseifuah, 2010; Berry et al., 2014; Financial Sector Deepening Trust, 2014). According to Berry et al. (2014) in a study of financial education in schools in Ghana, the most common outcomes of youth financial education – not unexpectedly – include an increase in financial literacy knowledge and starting a savings account, but this study did not find other non-financial outcomes. Most studies approach financial education from the perspective of the outcomes achieved, rather than aiming to understand the purposes of financial education or how youths regard their needs for being financially included in their contexts. Critics of microfinance contest these purposes because they are regarded as being ideologically linked to a global capitalist market. Both the empirical evidence and the ideological arguments related to the purposes and outcomes of microfinance and financial education remain divided, and even less is known about youths' outcomes. Rather than framing this analysis from one side or the other, I explore the different rationalities and practices of financial education that NGO staff and youth participants use and reshape in this *Apprentice* program in Tanzania. I start by describing the *Apprentice* savings and lending groups, Kichumi.

Savings and lending groups

A central component of the *Apprentice*'s entrepreneurship training program is Kichumi, which teaches young people about group-based savings and lending so they can acquire the financial resources and behaviors needed for their enterprises. Unlike many microfinance programs, *Apprentice* does not provide financial credit or loans. Kichumi is both in line with the local communities' practices of group social funds, and parallels other NGO and government finance initiatives, such as VLSAs and SACCOs. However, few of these community group mechanisms for savings and lending, including the social fund, include youths who have not completed a secondary education or who are not working. Sekei et al. (2015) report that only 1% of the youth population gets credit from banks or MFIs whereas between 2% and 3% of adults get loans from banks and MFIs, respectively (p. 9). Less than 5% of youths under 24 years old are involved in SACCOs or similar community groups, compared to 12% of the adult population (p. 10). Therefore, Kichumi offers an alternative for these youths, who have very few options to access other forms of savings and lending.

Kichumi is like other community-based savings and lending groups with one important difference: adult community facilitators are mentors to these youths. These advisers come from various backgrounds: Some have considerable experience in savings and loan mechanisms in neighboring villages, while others have a history of community organizing and development. Community facilitators are instrumental in teaching and mentoring the youths beyond what is contained in the curriculum.

About 20–30 youths participate in each Kichumi group. All members contribute weekly to a savings fund, and can withdraw their money at a later date or when the group dissolves. Members can take out a micro-loan from the accumulated savings and pay it back, with interest, on an agreed upon scheduled disbursement, usually monthly. Running each Kichumi group is a community facilitator who works with the group to facilitate other training courses for the youths, so he or she is known to the youths and manages the group's finances for 12 months. Thereafter, the group decides how to continue the management. The facilitator is paid a stipend out of a training fund to which each member contributes a small amount. Everyone also contributes to a third pool: a social fund. It is dispersed in cases of group or individual needs, such as group events or an individual's medical emergency. The given amount is not a loan, but rather a social benefit facilitated by the group members.

The Kichumi curriculum starts with how to form a savings and lending group, such as what qualities to look for in fellow members and leadership, and what rules and guidelines would help it run smoothly. The trainers gave considerable attention to ensuring that everyone knew how to participate in the savings and lending processes. Members select people to serve as chairperson, secretary, and treasurer. There are also money counters, which serve the purposes of verification and accountability. The most significant portion of the curriculum is directed at learning about and contributing to the savings fund. The group agrees on the amount each person has to contribute, often initially only 500 or 1000 Tanzanian shillings (about US$0.25–$0.50); the amount to be loaned (5,000–20,000 TZS, or about US$2–9); the interest charged (usually 10% per month); and how to address infractions, such as not contributing monthly or not repaying on time. The curriculum also stresses financial knowledge, such as how to calculate interest payments and compounded interest, as well as different ways that interest accrues. For some youths, this required more math literacy than they may have had. Thus, the leaders had to be literate, skilled in math, and trustworthy. All group members were to learn how to track their own savings.

Besides the mechanics of saving and lending, Kichumi facilitators also teach the youths goals and attitudes toward money. Participants discuss the reasons for saving money and avoiding buying frivolous items. Saving is seen as a moral obligation, a prerequisite for being a self-reliant individual and someone who contributes to the social and economic development of the community and nation. Relatedly, the curriculum presents borrowing as a grave matter. The training manual states that it should be 'embark[ed] on with care', and portrays financial institutions somewhat negatively, such as how difficult they are to access and how they charge excessive fees. Conversely, non-institutional group lending is described more positively as a way to invest in each other. Everyone has equal access to the savings fund for loans, and the interest is used for the group's benefit. Trust and solidarity are central values when forming the group and in maintaining it over time. There is also considerable discussion of transparency, accountability, and integrity in efforts to ensure loan repayments and to prevent any misuses of funds. These values relate to their relationships with each other as well as their community.

Learning to be financially responsible

Being financially responsible has a double meaning for these youths: economically responsible for their own livelihoods and fostering 'responsible solidarity' in the community (Miller and Rose, 2008). From the perspective of *Apprentice* and many of the youths, being responsible meant saving small amounts of money and not spending frivolously so that they could accumulate, bit by bit, to overcome their poverty. To do this, the program curriculum and the NGO staff/community facilitators taught them how to track their expenses and to budget for an enterprise and also their personal needs. The youths set goals for their enterprise and themselves, and then tried to achieve their goals through their work and savings.

When Sudi, Rashida, and other young women and men started *Apprentice*'s program, less than a quarter of them had been earning any money. More than a third had never saved any money, and only a few (4%) had some form of savings account. Over the course of the training and participation in Kichumi, they were beginning to save small amounts of money. While it was a requirement to participate in the group, some youths were not able to save every week, while others saved money they received from their parents, siblings, or others in their household. Savings usually meant putting aside a small amount so they could pay for their needs and daily expenses, such as food and transport. They hoped that by saving little by little, they would be able to have enough money to buy basic supplies for a small enterprise upon completing the program. But because most of them were not working and were not able to earn, their accumulated savings were very little. Aisha, who was married and had a child, and was studying cooking and hospitality, explained how she was learning about and doing savings in this program.

> Right now I'm saving very little. But I'd like to save more in the future, ... when I start working. At least an amount of 5,000 TZS per month [equivalent to US$2–3]. Because right now I'm saving 1,000 TZS per month ... 500 in the middle of the month and 500 at the end of the month. (Aisha, cook, 21 years old, 2012)

The following year, Aisha secured a job cooking in a hotel, was earning a regular monthly salary, and was putting money in her group's saving fund. Over the four years of our study, she continued in this work, earning, saving, and supporting her parents and young child. She told us that she usually saved 40,000–50,000 TZS [US$25] per month, a considerable increase, but she did not save it in a bank nor did she take out any loans. Despite her years of savings, she did not feel she could yet invest in the materials she needed to start her own restaurant, her long-term future goal.

For Aisha and others, their financial education and savings and lending group certainly had an effect, similar to other studies, of increasing youths' financial literacy. We asked the youths questions about what they knew about finances before and after their participation in the program, and then we compared what they said about the knowledge at the end of the program with those who had not yet participated in the program. We found that those youths who participated in Kichumi had a positive and significant increase in their financial knowledge (see also Krause et al., 2016). Furthermore, young women reported a greater increase in their financial knowledge than men, though young men's reported knowledge increased significantly over the course of the program compared to those that did not participate. For example, young women and men who participated in the program reported much greater knowledge of how to apply for a saving accounts than those who did not (112% and 87% respectively) (see Table 8.1).[7]

These skills served to responsibilize these youths, teaching them to conduct their lives so they could get out of poverty by having a budget and following it strictly so they could save bit by bit. These young men and women had learned to be frugal and careful so they could cover daily expenses. They also learned how to manage requests from family members and peers who wanted money, which they saw as distinct from those who needed financial support. David, a young man with a child who also supports his mother, captured this attitude of frugality: 'I try to balance ... so that whenever I save money it means I have to leave [unable to buy] some other things ... [I] minimize my expenses' (David, auto mechanic, 24 years old, 2014). David told us he generally saved 50,000 TZS [US$25] per month, but he also used his earnings to support others' education, basic needs and health care. So even when they had a budget, their spending and savings were always contingent on their earnings, which for most youths continued to be variable and unpredictable, even though they now had greater financial knowledge, skills, and attitudes.

Table 8.1 Difference between participants' views and non-participants' views on their financial knowledge and skills, by female and male [1]

Change in knowledge, skill, or attitude	Female % difference/ non treatment mean	Male % difference/ non treatment mean
Group savings helped to learn how to save	119 (1.63)	106 (1.74)
Know how to apply for a savings account	112 (1.16)	87 (1.44)
Know how to develop a business plan	84 (1.6)	62 (1.83)
Know how to track expenses	81 (1.9)	46 (2.26)
Know how to create a personal budget	61 (1.95)	48 (2.30)

N = 434
Source: Krause, McCarthy and Chapman, 2016

[1] This analysis, reported in Krause et al. (2016), is based on a propensity score matching test in which all scores of participants at the start of the program are matched with those who have not started/not yet participated in the program. The sample of participants, 434, is a portion of the total in our surveys as it only includes the first two years and cohorts. The percentage change reflects the effects of the program in changing youth's responses to these questions, compared to the mean of the non-treatment groups, not the percentage of youths who changed. The percentages reported here are slightly different from those reported in Krause et al. I use percentages based on an original analysis of nearest neighbor matching of demographic variables; Krause et al. reanalyzed these data and used a different matching method, Epanechnikov kernel, that included social support and value items in the matching.

Learning how to use one's earnings to pay for basic needs and to invest in one's future livelihood is an important process for youths' social development and economic self-reliance, as many of *Apprentice*'s participants stated. Their responsibilities for becoming an adult were complicated by the expectation that both young men and women had to create their own work and use their own resources and earnings to establish an enterprise that was expected to ensure their livelihood and often that of other family members. Being financially responsible in these communities meant that these youths were expected to contribute to their larger family's education and health care needs. As they began their training, nearly 1 in 5 (N = 712) had children (usually women), and nearly half were responsible for other dependents, such as parents, siblings or extended family members (men reported having more dependents) (see also Chapter 4 for demographics of participants). Similarly, half had only one person in their household earning an income. Siti, who was married, had a child, and was also responsible for others in her family, explained how her earnings, which were intermittent from tailoring, were used for her basic needs.

> The other goal that I have is to be self-sufficient in my needs. You know, I have a child, so when she gets sick or when I may get sick, I should have money for covering those expenses. And also whenever I want something, let's say I want to buy clothes for myself or for my child I don't need to ask anybody …. So I have plans of being independent and self-sufficient in things and buying things, whatever I want … So I also save money in community groups [for loans in emergency situations, she clarified], and also I have a safe where I save money at home for emergencies. (Siti, embroidery and tailoring, 22 years old, 2014)

When we saw Siti again in 2015, she explained that she was saving, though still a small amount, to buy a sewing machine, but that money had to be used for 'other small problems, like illnesses' – indicating that her household needed her savings.

Similarly, Tambo, a carpenter, who supported his mother and another family member, noted how his savings were used for his mother's health care.

> This way [my savings] helps when you get a problem like, a family problem, if you get sick. You can be working, but you have not yet received your payment and you know that you have money in the bank even if I am sick or my mother is sick. I can go to the bank to get a small amount to pay for the medicine. This new way of saving has helped me personally and for my family. For example, I managed to support my mother when she was sick using my savings. (Tambo, carpenter, 23 years old, 2015)

Being responsible also meant contributing to the community when others were in need.

Faraji, a bike mechanic who ran his own enterprise, explained how he was not able to achieve his own goals because he had to pay for a trainee's funeral. Community members provide for the social welfare of many youths and their families in the absence of national social protections, such as insurance. He explained:

> What has happened to my goals? To some extent, some of my goals that I planned for were not accomplished. I don't know, maybe it was due to the death of my trainee. Since then my planned goals haven't moved forward. He died due to a motorbike accident when he was testing it. And with some issues with the family, and their lack of resources, I covered all expenses, including transporting the corpse. Before the death, I had planned to work toward my goals and to start a tomato business, but after the funeral I was set backwards and used all my savings. What was there for me to do? I had planned to rent a place to put my things in a storeroom [have a secure place for his motorcycle business]. But after the funeral, I used all the money. (Faraji, bike mechanic, 21 years old, 2015)

Learning to save and be responsible meant these youths not only took care of their own needs and used their knowledge to make a profit for themselves, they also contributed to and supported others in the community who were in need. While some young people characterized these needs as emergencies, these expenses were necessary because others did not have sufficient resources or benefits to cover their basic needs, such as health care. Becoming responsibilized meant that these emergencies were now being planned for and partially addressed, even if in a limited way, with these young men's and women's earnings. While social benefits, such as minimum wages and health care insurance, are ensured for many who have jobs in the formal labor market, the work of these young people in the informal economy required them to assume responsibility for their and others' social welfare. The community social fund serves an important purpose of reciprocity and solidarity, and these youths, who were once not a part of these relationships, now were. But one could also argue that the other side of community social care and solidarity is that it reduces the obligation of government to provide for health care, child care, and other social welfare.

Being financially included and creating alternatives

Financial inclusion in financial institutions is an important outcome for *Apprentice*'s program and for the donor. The question that *Apprentice* staff and youths struggled with is how and according to which rules should they engage, and what alternatives could they create. From early on in *Apprentice*'s program, the local community and national level staff began conversations with banks and MFIs (referred to more broadly as financial service providers, FSPs) serving the communities around Lake Victoria and in Kagera region. They invited FSPs to share with them and the youths information about their savings and lending products. In turn, the NGO staff shared with the FSPs the kinds of products youths in their program would need – smaller loans, lower interest rates, requirements of less collateral, and fewer administrative requirements for documents that these youths did not have. For example, Mr. Bakera, the country director, recounted that in order to secure a loan of 600,000 TZS (~US$250) at one bank, the applicant needed to have 200,000 TZS in savings as collateral. This amount of collateral was nearly impossible for any individual youth. MFIs offered more accessible loans, but few MFIs had offices in Kagera region, particularly when the project started. As MFIs are less regulated and their money is not secured, they also charge higher interest rates, up to 30%.

The financial market and products for youths were changing during the implementation of this program (2011–2016) in response to both government policies and regulations and to investors' interests. During the period of this project, loans for youths, and particularly poor youths in rural areas of Tanzania, were not very available, though the government provided options, at least in policy if not the actual funding, through a Youth Development Fund. Loans from this fund were regarded as not accessible. In fact, staff as well as national media questioned whether the funds would ever be distributed (Kitabu, 2015). At the same time, banks and MFIs were expanding. In Kagera, government microfinance and cooperatives – the National Microfinance Bank (NMB) and the Kagera Farmer's Cooperative Bank – seemed the most accessible to *Apprentice* and its youths. These institutions required a group deposit, such as 500,000 TZS in a savings account, and then borrowers could access a group loan of 1.5 million TZS (Program Coordinator, 2014). By the fourth year after these *Apprentice* youths had completed training and been struggling to work and develop their enterprises, a couple of groups finally obtained a loan from the local government through an international microfinance program to be used to invest in their enterprises. In addition, mobile money evolved to offer new products for depositing, accessing, and transferring cash, and for some forms of saving. These various alternatives seemed to be responding to the demands of youths: to make credit more available and at reasonable interest rates. In some ways, financial service providers were adapting to youths' needs, and youths were adapting to financial services' regulations.

With all these options, youths were diversifying and choosing how they saved. After participating in the training program, most youths began to use multiple forms of savings, including keeping money at home, in bank accounts, mobile money, and various local savings/lending groups. While more youths we interviewed opened bank accounts over the years, still less than half had an individual or group bank account (See Table 6). There was a greater increase over the years in young women opening a bank account; this was in part because many of these women held formal jobs (working at hotels), where employers automatically deposited their wages into an account. Fewer men reported working in formal work; most opened a bank account so they could access group or individual loans. Having bank accounts seems to suggest these youths were being financially included.

But they were also creating alternatives to engaging in the financial market with other mechanisms that fostered greater trust, reciprocity, and solidarity. Most commonly used were 'merry-go-rounds', a group savings and lending mechanism, like their Kichumi group, where a small group of people put the same amount into a kitty each month and members take turns benefitting from the lump sum each month. The group devises their own rules and procedures for saving, distributing and charging interest and they are not registered, unlike SACCOs, which follow government regulations for cooperatives.

The increase in the use of merry-go-rounds was particularly telling of who they trusted with their money, where they had relationships to join, and how they could access funds/loans more easily. Slightly more than a quarter of the respondents were involved in merry-go-rounds or SACCOs in 2014, a couple of years after completing their training, while more than half were involved with these community savings and lending groups in 2015. Both young men and women decreased their involvement in Kichumi, *Apprentice*'s group savings they had started during the training. More than half of the men continued to use this mechanism, while only a few women did, possibly because many of them had married and moved, and were no longer geographically close to these groups (see Table 8.2).

Many youths took the initiative to start or become involved in merry-go-round groups with friends from their training program, as well as with other peers and adults in their community or work setting. Adia, a young tailor who lives in a rural village without formal banks, was involved in a merry-go-round with a group of 33 women. She explained that everyone puts in 10,000–15,000 TZS (~US$7–10) per month, and each person takes turns getting the total amount.

Table 8.2 Use of different forms of savings, % of women and men, 2014 and 2015

Form of Savings	% of Women (2014)	% of Women (2015)	% of Men (2014)	% of Men (2015)
Bank account	13%	42%	29%	44%
Mobile money	53%	42%	62%	65%
Kichumi	47%	8%	71%	69%
Merry-go-round (or SACCOs)	27%	50%	29%	53%

N = 36 in 2014; N = 29 in 2015

Source: DeJaeghere, Chapman and Pellowski Wiger and Learn, Earn, Save Project Team at University of Minnesota survey

So far she had contributed 50,000 TZS. When it's her turn, she will receive 330,000 TZS (~US$230). One woman served as the leader, and she was responsible for collecting and distributing the money. This form of saving and lending was critical for Adia as she was married with a child and had several other family members for whom she was financially responsible.

One reason that young women and some men became involved in merry-go-round groups was they wanted access to a larger saving pool: the more members there are, the more money each person has access to. These groups also established their own rules, making it easier for the youths to decide what they could contribute and who could join. Finally, these groups tended to be among community members that had formed trust and reciprocity, such as within in a church or women's cooperative.

Being involved and investing in community merry-go-round savings and lending groups was a response to being excluded from other financial service providers. While financial inclusion is the trope used to reach out to youths and involve them in banking products, the fees, requirements, and interest rates excluded many. Youths' involvement in the merry-go-rounds was also a way to keep their money with trusted peers and adults and to circulate it among the community so that any profits from interest were reinvested in the group, not a bank or an MFI.[8] Mr. Jeremiah, the program coordinator, had tried over several years trying to figure out how the program could work with financial institutions, and concluded that the program and youths needed to do what was best for them:

> So I can say there are challenges in collaborating with financial service providers, and we are thinking of how we can help youth to create their own financial associations whereby they can start lending themselves money.
> (Mr. Jeremiah, program coordinator, 2014)

The purpose of financial education and financial inclusion was to enhance ways for youths to save toward their investment in their enterprises, and to get access to additional capital, as needed. Most youths in the *Apprentice* program, however, did not get loans from financial service providers but rather from community savings and lending groups, and a few groups received loans through youth funds allocated through the local government. After the training, youths engaged more often with financial service providers, particularly by opening savings accounts, usually with greater knowledge of how to do this. They also resisted engagement with bank mechanisms that they regarded as too costly – either savings accounts that had fees, or loans that had higher interest rates (relative to what they could get from family, friends or even their merry-go-rounds). Their increased engagement with merry-go-rounds suggests the importance of informal and flexible group mechanisms grounded in a community ethos and trust and that aimed to support others. Sudi captured how he and his group of friends succeeded in saving and lending in ways that supported them and the community:

> One thing we have done in our group is that we have advanced in saving ways. We used ... to use one person to keep money for us. But now we opened a bank account ... We understand what the procedure is and the regulations needed to open a bank account ... After that, we have saved 300,000 TZS [~US$210] to that bank account [so we can get a loan] ... Though we have saved a small amount of money, we want by the coming year to be able to help members, meaning that we will be the ones to help ourselves ... we will be giving ourselves loans with fair conditions. And also being in a group with a big friend base we can get a loan from other banks. And also through borrowing to each other and returning money with interest we will improve ourselves. (Sudi, mechanic, 23 years old, 2014)

Sudi and his friends show how they use their financial knowledge of engaging with financial institutions combined with alternative ways for saving and lending. They regard their approach as fair, and it fosters the development of the group and the community rather than providing profit, through interest, for the banks.

Investing in enterprises and human development

One of the aims of financial education and participation in the Kichumi group was to accumulate money to invest in starting or expanding microenterprises. The paradox of their learning to be financially responsible and being financially included (at least in the ways that they created through the Kichumi groups) meant that they had accumulated only small amounts of savings and loans that they usually used in the day-to day operations of their enterprises and for caring for their families and other community members. Most youths used savings and loans to buy needed equipment and materials for their enterprises, and over the years, some expanded their businesses by buying additional tools and machines. Still, they did not regard this investment necessarily for the purposes of profit; rather it provided for their and their families' needs and for others in their community. Saka, a young man who was not yet married but was financially

Table 8.3 Uses of earnings, % of women and men, 2014 and 2015

	Women (2014)	Women (2015)	Men (2014)	Men (2015)
Paying for self or others' education	40%	70%	48%	50%
Paying for community weddings/funerals (social fund)	67%	77%	86%	100%
Financially responsible for at least one dependent	57%	92%	70%	89%

N = 36 in 2014; N = 31 in 2015

Source: DeJaeghere, Chapman and Pellowski Wiger and Learn, Earn, Save Project Team at University of Minnesota survey

responsible for five family members, told us why he saved money: 'for three reasons, I saved to help my family, to help me with my work, and for myself' (Furniture maker, 24 years old, 2015), and these seemed to be his prioritization of his savings and investment. For most youths, their earnings, and the small savings they had from it, were increasingly distributed to support family and community members, paying for siblings' education and supporting community members' health care or other needs (see Table 8.3). For example, the percentage of women we interviewed who were responsible for paying school fees increased from 40% to 70% from 2014 to 2015; similarly 89% of men were financially responsible for at least one dependent in 2015 whereas 70% told us they were in 2014. The youths regarded these 'responsibilities' as taking care of everyone in the community, not necessarily as sacrificing their goals and interests.

In addition to using their earnings to contribute directly to family needs and the social good of the community, they invested in their enterprises in efforts that redistributed wealth. For example, Hope, a young woman who at 22 years old was responsible for four household members, including her mother, also involved other youths in her tailoring and embroidery enterprise. Training others gave her great satisfaction because, she said, she hoped that other young people could have the opportunities she had. She regarded her investment in her business as a way to expand and involve other trainees and other family members in learning and earning a livelihood. Other youths, such as Tambo, aimed to expand their businesses so that they could hire young people who did not have a means to earn money. Tambo captured this sentiment well:

> I need to have my own big workshop so that I can employ other youths. For example, ... I want to be able to employ my friends and fellow youth that [I] used to played games and card with. I would like find them, train them and employ them in order to improve our lives. (Tambo, carpenter, 23 years old, 2015)

Often the decision to expand and hire others was not based on a calculated analysis of projected earnings of the enterprise and the costs of additional personnel.

Instead, youths had an ethos of sharing their work and wealth because so many family members and peers in their community were unable to earn anything.

The youths also gained social status in the community as a trainer and employer, someone who was valued for the development they brought to the community. For example, Saka explained how his earnings and savings from making furniture went toward not only supporting his family, but also to help them to develop their enterprises:

> I built this house with my money, but it's for my parents ... [M]y family and my community, they depend on me. In my family, I am a person that is depended on and who is listened to for my ideas. For example, if there is something that happens and a solution is needed, they depend on me a lot for my ideas ... there are some things that I don't do anymore because I am helping them with money to start their own income generating activity, so they can manage their own expense. (Saka, furniture maker, 24 years old, 2015)

Here Saka's independence, in the sense of being an earner, also supported the 'dependency of responsible solidarity' by allowing others within his family and community to depend on him so they could improve their lives (Miller and Rose, 2008).

It was also very common for youths to give small loans to others who did not have access to financial services or community savings and lending groups. For example, Hope is part of a group of youths that pooled its savings to secure a loan from the municipality. An equal amount of the municipal loan was distributed to each member, with the intent that everyone would invest money in his or her own enterprise. Hope used part of the loan to expand her tailoring business, and also lent some to a young man who did not have access to financial services.

> He wanted to start up a used clothing business. He is like my close friend ... I decided to give him a loan because most of the youth are not trusted by financial service providers ... [T]he conditions were ... he must pay me back after two months and with interest. (Hope, tailor, 22 years old, 2015)

Most youths are conscientious about repaying loans, and young people who lent to their peers and family members were generally repaid. While some asked for a small amount of interest, others did not. A small amount of interest was regarded as acceptable by most in the community, as a form of accountability. But the ethos of sharing and caring for others was stronger than making a profit.

Reflections on the double meanings of financial responsibility and inclusion

Learning to be financially responsible for these youths meant that they were acquiring attitudes about saving, but also skills to monitor their savings, spending, and lending. These are necessary attitudes and skills for youths, but when taught so that they can take responsibility for getting out of poverty and ensuring their livelihood by using these skills, they become responsibilized. Responsibilization is the moral regulation of one's conduct through daily curricular practices that emphasize making individual choices to ensure one's own wellbeing without relying on state and community support structures (Peters, 2009). Responsibilization, from this neoliberal perspective, aims to 'replace the dependency of responsible solidarity' (Miller and Rose, 2008, p. 79). But being responsible in these communities also meant they were using their earnings and savings in ways that advanced the wellbeing of their families and community members. For these youths, they were reshaping these notions of responsibility within an ethics of dependency and responsible solidarity. In this way, these youths were re-embedding their financial and market knowledge into the social life of the community. This re-embedding occurred, however, in part because the informal economy remains dis-embedded from social welfare policies that provide insurance, health care, and other social benefits.

Financial inclusion also had its double and contradictory meanings for these youths. It meant gaining access to savings accounts and loans from banks and MFIs for the development of their enterprises. But most youths could not or did not want to utilize them, even after four years of working and saving, due to account fees, high interest rates, impractical requirements, or the mere fact that there was not a financial institution nearby. Thus, their best option was to become involved in a community savings and lending group. Community groups generally operated on an ethos of reciprocity and solidarity, and they kept the profits (interest) within the group and community. Thus, financial inclusion was reshaped to create community group mechanisms for most of their savings and lending, but that also allowed these youths to obtain some loans from banks through their community group. Savings and lending groups were an alternative to financial service providers in that the former had fair conditions and supported a greater number of young people in the community.

Finally, as Gibson-Graham (2006) remind us, communities engaged in diverse economies define the purposes for which they use their labor and surplus income. While some savings and loans were clearly used to improve the youths' own wellbeing, members also used them to redistribute their wealth to ensure the social wellbeing of others. Wellbeing – not profit per se – was the motivating factor for their labor, earnings, and savings. The re-embedding of their financial behaviors into the social life of the community, however, was not solely because they had an ideological or ethical stance that solidarity was the only way to achieve community development and the economic development of the nation. Rather, their material and social realities in which their economic and social wellbeing were not cared for by the state nor by businesses (such as banks) meant that they needed to foster social solidarity as well as ensure their own economic wellbeing.

Notes

1 Donors, financial institutions, and development discourse tend to use the term *financial products*. I use it here to show the discourse of these institutions. Generally, *products* refer to a range of ways in which youths could open a savings account or access credit.
2 This discourse and commitment to financial inclusion is pervasive throughout international agencies and donors. For example, the UN General Assembly in 2016 'focused on the importance of financial inclusion for youths, including youth entrepreneurs, and it was asserted that the energy and dynamism of young people will be integral in achieving the newly adopted 2030 SDGs. Fifty-four percent of youths between 15–24 don't have a bank account.' See https://cfi-blog.org/category/youth-and-financial-inclusion/ retrieved 21 April 2016.
3 I use the term *financial education* throughout this chapter as a broader term than *literacy*. While the program aimed to increase numeracy and literacy related to financial terms, ideas, and practices, it also used experiential practices to engage in savings and lending. In this way, education captures a broader notion of financial learning than literacy. In addition, some studies reviewed in this chapter implement financial literacy in non-formal settings, others in formal education. Thus, *education* captures both uses of the term.
4 Mobile money is the use of a mobile (cell) phone to transfer money between people or accounts, or to pay bills; it is also used to save and withdraw money from accounts. Different forms of mobile money have developed over the course of this project in Tanzania, including mechanisms to do short-term savings.
5 I use a pseudonym for *Apprentice*'s savings and lending group program.
6 Village savings and lending associations (VSLAs) are usually implemented through international or national NGO programs as an informal group. Merry-go-rounds, which are commonly used by youths and discussed later, are informal groups that operate as a type of VSLA. They are not formally registered or regulated and they are formed independently by community groups. In contrast, SACCOs (savings and credit cooperatives) are registered with the government and can be regulated as a cooperative if their savings and lending reach a certain threshold. They are a mechanism used by government to provide loans, such as the youth development fund.
7 These data are from a propensity score matching analysis, which compares those who participated in the program with those who had not yet started. Responses to the questions were based on a four-point scale from 'not at all' to 'a lot'. The percentage change reported in the table reflects the average treatment effect for each question divided by the group mean for women and men. For example, women who participated in the program had a 112% higher response regarding their knowledge of how to apply for a savings account (e.g., some or a lot) for than those who had not yet participated in the program (a little).
8 It is important to note that many in Muslim communities in Tanzania do not take out loans that require repayment of interest. Rather interest is to stay within and support the community. While this idea was not explicitly discussed in the *Kichumi* program, there are some participants who are Muslim and this idea is also broadly known in Tanzanian society.

References

Banerjee, A. V., Duflo, E., Glennerster, R. and Kinnan, C. (2013). *The miracle of microfinance? Evidence from a randomized evaluation*. Massachusetts Institute of Technology Working Paper Series.

Berry, J., Karlan, D. and Pradhan, M. (September 2014). *The impact of financial education for youth in Ghana*. National Bureau of Economic Research Working Paper 21068. Retrieved at http://www.nber.org/papers/w21068

Dupas, P. and Robinson, J. (2009). *Savings constraints and microenterprise development: Evidence from a field experiment in Kenya* (No. w14693). Nairobi, Kenya: National Bureau of Economic Research.

Ferguson, J. (2010). The uses of neoliberalism. *Antipode*, *41*(s1), 166–184.

Fernando, J. L. (Ed.). (2006). *Microfinance: Perils and prospects*. Cambridge, UK: Routledge.

Financial Sector Deepening Trust (FSDT) (2014). *FinScope 2013 Survey: Widening your financial future*. Dar es Salaam, Tanzania: Author.

Gibson-Graham, J. K. (2006). *A postcapitalistpPolitics*. Minneapolis, MN: University of Minnesota Press.

Kitabu, G. (2015). *Where has Tanzania Youth Fund gone?* IPP media.com. Retrieved at http://www.ippmedia.com/?l=76267

Krause, B. L. McCarthy, A. S. and Chapman, D. (2016). Fuelling financial literacy: estimating the impact of youth entrepreneurship training in Tanzania. *Journal of Development Effectiveness*, *8*(2), 234–256.

Miller, P. and Rose, N. (2008). *Governing the present: Administering economic, social and personal life*. Cambridge, UK: Polity.

Muehlebach, A. (2012). *The moral neoliberal: Welfare and citizenship in Italy*. Chicago, IL: University of Chicago Press.

Oseifuah, E. K. (2010). Financial literacy and youth entrepreneurship in South Africa. *African Journal of Economic Management*, *1*(2), 164–182.

Peters, M. (2009). Education, enterprise culture and the entrepreneurial self: A Foucauldian perspective. *The Journal of Educational Enquiry*, *2*(2), 58–71.

Roy, A. (2010). *Poverty capital: Microfinance and the making of development*. Cambridge, UK: Routledge.

Sekei, L., Altvater, A., Kisinda A. and Chuachua, R. (2015). *Mapping study on the vocational education, skills training and entrepreneurship in Tanzania*. Baar, Switzerland: Development Pioneers Consultants.

Van Rooyen, C., Stewart, R. and de Wet, T. (2012). The impact of microfinance in sub-Saharan Africa: A systematic review of the evidence. *World Development*, *40*(11), 2,249–2,262.

World Bank (2009). *The case for financial literacy in development countries*. Washington, DC: World Bank Group.

Yunus, M. and Weber, K. (2011). *Building social business: The new kind of capitalism that serves humanity's most pressing needs*. New York, NY: Public Affairs.

Chapter 9

Conclusions
Reframing Entrepreneurship Education

The encounter between neo/liberal and local discourses and practices of entrepreneurship education and training occurs in many spaces and sites of governing: donors and foundations, national governments, NGOs, schools, local businesses and financial institutions, and youths. Actors in these sites have different meanings that they give to entrepreneurship education's goals and practices. In Chapter 3, I discussed three different approaches utilized by international agencies, NGOs, and governments that assumed entrepreneurship education and training could foster economic development, alleviate poverty, and improve wellbeing. But the evidence that entrepreneurship education and training for youths can achieve these different development goals is mixed, and positive outcomes are largely contingent on addressing social-economic conditions in communities and societies that perpetuate inequalities. International agencies, NGO practitioners, and educators have much to learn about how entrepreneurship education and training gets reshaped and enacted in these local sites through this analysis of the frictions created as these different discourses and practices meet. While international agencies and NGOs give considerable attention to how their work is situated within national and local contexts and how they can improve implementation to achieve desired goals, less attention is given to how international, national, and local actors interpret and act upon the ideas of entrepreneurship education and training for the diverse development and wellbeing goals they each aim to achieve, and the kinds of society and citizens they aspire to produce.

In this analysis of the multiple interpretations, meanings, and enactments that diverse actors give to entrepreneurship education and training, I suggest that such youth programs need to move beyond a singular economic framing. A singular framing of economy, Gibson-Graham (2006) say, perpetuates what Polanyi (1944) called an economistic fallacy, or 'analyzing all economic systems through the theoretical gaze that presumes that the horizons of the economy are fully comprehended by a map that includes only market exchange and the calculative behavior couplet' (loc. 1668). Gibson-Graham argue that we need to use a language that allows for understanding social and moral economies – or embedded and diverse economies – where actors engage in behaviors of solidarity, stewardship, and obligation alongside those of exchange and earning a profit.

This analysis of different governing rationalities related to state, economy, and citizen in these sites in Tanzania allows for examining whether and how neoliberalism reorganizes social relations around the idea of the enterprise (McNay, 2009, p. 57), or whether alternative forms of governmentality reshape economic and social relations to serve society and a social good. Polanyi (1944) refers to this as the 'double movement' of capitalism. On the one hand, capitalism disembeds the economy from society and aims to create the self-regulating market, or a *market society*; on the other hand, it prompts efforts to recapture and re-embed the economy within social and political life, or a *society of the market*. Framing entrepreneurship education programs in the tensions between a disembedded and embedded economy, as I have done in Chapter 7 and 8 in the analysis of entrepreneurship in a moral economy, allows for examining alternative perspectives and outcomes that emerge.

The two entrepreneurship education and training models analyzed in these chapters showed three main frictions as the various actors aimed to make sense of and enact these programs toward diverse goals of economy, society and citizen. These frictions were related to multiple goals of entrepreneurship, double meanings of self-reliance, and double meanings of inclusion in markets and in society. As discussed in Chapters 6, 7, and 8, many of the NGO staff and youth participants identified the goals of development and the purpose of their labor in relation to Nyerere's idea of self-reliance, or *kujitegemea*, and local practices of reciprocity and solidarity. These purposes and practices encountered and reshaped ideas of profit, competition, and capital accumulation to serve social goals as well as individual wellbeing. Below, I discuss each of these frictions and the forms of an entrepreneurial citizen that emerged from them.

The first friction is characterized by the entrepreneurship program goal to create an economic citizen – the enterprising self whose actions and attitudes are oriented toward the capitalist market and ensures one's own economic wellbeing in an uncertain economy (Gordon, 1991) – and youths' goals of developing social relations and being included. In these two projects analyzed in this book, school life and the daily life of trainees were oriented toward the capitalist market (c.f. Chapters 6 and 7). Both *Parka* and *Apprentice*'s programs taught business skills and an entrepreneurial mindset, and youths learned how to use these skills to sell, to make a profit, and to think of themselves as the economic goods they produced. They started small enterprises (selling snacks, making sweaters, constructing houses), earned some money, and got access to financial products that helped them to invest in their enterprise. But their enterprises often incurred losses or had unstable earnings. Even when their labor resulted in profits and they were able to put money aside, they often had to use their savings to pay for medical expenses or siblings' education rather than reinvesting the money in their enterprises. Although these youths tried to access formal financial services, they continued to be excluded from most individual bank loans; thus, they formed groups to access both informal and formal loans within their communities (c.f. Chapter 8). The precariousness of engaging in the capitalist economy for their livelihood meant that they needed to develop relationships with other adults and peers to ensure their inclusion in the community so that they could benefit economically and socially. For example, in Chapter 7, I recounted how youths relied on each other for the materials they needed to do their labor, and in Chapter 8, I showed how they formed groups to invest their savings and distributed loans within the group at rates that were deemed fair. These entrepreneurship education and training programs did not result in a singular economic citizen. Rather, their social and economic inclusions were contingent on each other, and their social relationships in the community were necessary to secure their enterprises and enable their and their families' survival.

The second friction emerged in how youths learned an entrepreneurial mindset oriented toward individual empowerment and enacted it in a communal sense of self-reliance. The youths who participated in *Apprentice*'s program developed work and life skills aimed at fostering their economic empowerment (c.f. Chapter 7). These young men and women also acquired skills of budgeting, saving, and being frugal in an effort to improve – albeit minimally – their incomes and to become financially independent (c.f. Chapter 8). But their financial independence and empowerment did not serve them only individually. Influenced by Nyerere's socialist policies and as an alternative community practice, self-reliance for these youths also meant distributing knowledge and wealth so that others' wellbeing could be supported. For example, in discussions with teachers who were implementing *Parka*'s business club program, which uses the recently coined Swahili word *ujasiriamali* to mean entrepreneurship, they also referred to ideas from Nyerere's *kujitegemea* (self-reliance) as the goals and purposes for entrepreneurship. In this way, they interpreted an entrepreneurial mindset not as an individual enterprising endeavor, but as a collective effort for 'getting rid of ignorance and poverty, and building unity'[1]. While the self-reliance of Nyerere's time and place cannot be reenacted in this current political economy, it can potentially influence new forms of being and engaging in social and political life in Tanzanian communities today. For example, *Apprentice* had initially supported youths to develop an individual business plan for an enterprise; however, in realizing that they both desired and needed to work in groups – to access customers, generate capital, reduce losses, and support each other emotionally, socially, and financially – the program began providing instruction for the development of group enterprises, or cooperatives. Such cooperatives harken to Nyerere's communal development, but with different nuances in how they engage with the capitalist market and how they support the economic as well as social development of individuals, the group, and the community. In these ways, these youths' empowerment and self-reliance were not individual, but rather involved using their skills and knowledge collectively to mitigate structural inequalities and support others' development.

Finally, a third friction occurred between the NGO program practices that aimed to include youths in a capitalist market, functioning under norms of competition and profit, and other practices used by youths and some staff that drew on an ethos of solidarity and reciprocity to ensure the wellbeing of all.

NGO schools hoping to become self-sufficient increasingly employed financial incentives and management of profit and loss in efforts to be competitive and to earn a profit (Chapter 6). They were engaging in a capitalist market and employing capitalist management practices, but they also redistributed the profit toward paying students' fees to support the inclusion of those who had been excluded from schooling. Engaging in a capitalist economy for these youths also meant developing skills of business planning, budgeting, and managing finances to start their enterprises and to be financially included – meaning having access to financial resources that were necessary to start and operate their enterprise (c.f. Chapter 8). While these youths were included in the capitalist market as entrepreneurs, they often encountered barriers to their inclusion. For instance, the social norms of a 'work membership' – belonging through employment in formal labor (Ferguson, 2013) – and practices for obtaining loans from financial institutions were exclusionary. But these social relations and structures were not static, and the staff and youth participants attempted to change them. For instance, youths used their affiliation with the program and developed their new identity as *fundi* to change these relationships with adults in the community. This allowed the youths to be valued for what they contributed socially and economically to society. In turn, these youths also used their economic resources and social relations to assist family members, peers, and other community members to obtain health care, to invest in household enterprises, and to pursue further education. In this way, participation in the capitalist market was reshaped as a commitment to the community and social solidarity. This solidarity was not necessarily the same as Nyerere's socialist policies at the time when Tanzania was building a united national identity, but it carried a semblance of *Ujamaa* in being able to care for and ensure the wellbeing of other Tanzanians and not simply oneself.

In these frictions of enacting entrepreneurship, neo/liberal technologies of power and of self are dominant, but they are not ubiquitous. Alternative discourses and practices influenced how these youths were being made and making themselves as citizens in Tanzania. The ways that NGO staff and youths interpreted and reshaped ideas of entrepreneurship were related to the purposes they saw for such labor in society, and the sort of 'good life' for which their labor and surplus would be used (Gibson-Graham, 2006). In the analysis in this book, I have attempted to show that these youths' goals for 'a good life' is defined and influenced by discourses of reciprocity, solidarity, and social good. The logic of neo/liberal approaches is that entrepreneurial knowledge and skills will increase individual earnings, as well as fostering economic development through one's own initiative and creativity. A capability approach, as discussed in Chapter 4, as an alternative approach challenges this logic, suggesting that knowledge and skills do not necessarily get converted into greater financial means or economic development as measured through traditional savings and income measures, especially if there are constraining social, economic, and environmental conditions (Sen, 1999). The value of a capability approach lies not in defining a priori what wellbeing is for any individual, but rather discerning how individuals define what wellbeing means for them within their political, social, and economic contexts.

For these Tanzanian youths, wellbeing meant addressing the social and economic inequalities they faced in being educated and working in the labor market. Their livelihoods were also embedded in and contingent on social relations that would support their educational and work aspirations, and those of others with whom they lived. The logic of an alternative approach to development and wellbeing, grounded in Nyerere's concept of self-reliance and its vestiges in Tanzanian society today, is that education and training can foster social and economic development when it is used for collective – not individual – purposes, and that knowledge, skills, and financial means are shared and redistributed to others for everyone to survive and thrive.

The entrepreneurial citizen as a social-economic citizen

The double meanings that resulted from these three frictions did not produce a 'homo economicus' (Gordon, 1991), but rather new subjectivities emerged in the form of a social-economic citizen. Staff, youths, and the programs drew on adapted notions of *Ujamaa* and *kujitegemea*, conjoining family-social relations and self-reliance to represent both a social and an economic way of being. This ethos brings together social solidarity with economic justice, one in which everyone should be able to do more than just survive. Thriving economically where neoliberal policies have exacerbated inequalities requires working together, albeit differently than during Nyerere's period of governing.

In a similar analysis of double meanings when neoliberalism meets local practices, Muehlebach (2012) offers the concept of 'ethical citizenship' as it emerges within neoliberal regimes in Italy. The ethical citizen is a moral and affective citizen who is created through state-sponsored laws and programs, as well as civil society organizations, to rebuild community relationships that were once supported through the social welfare state. She argues that the making of ethical citizenship 'serves to both make and unmake the neoliberal project out of which it emerged' (p. 200). For instance, caring for community members may appear as charity, but Muehlebach shows how some citizens use care to fight for equality and rights in relation to the state (p. 198). Similarly, in this analysis of entrepreneurship education and training in Tanzania, I suggest that the various actors – NGO staff, school teachers, community facilitators, and the youths themselves – were engaged in making and being made as *social-economic citizens*, a struggle over reshaping and claiming forms of social and economic rights and challenging injustices.

This social-economic citizen is not the same as Marshall's (1964) liberal conception in which the state granted and protected social and economic rights, such as those of education and work; nor is it the likeness of the socialist citizen oriented toward the collective means of production and use of surplus by the state that Nyerere aimed to create through his socialist policy of *Ujamaa*. It is also not the 'enterprising-self' of neoliberalism, as proposed by Rose (1998). Socially, these Tanzanian youths were reclaiming rights, albeit through non-state mechanisms, to an education or training that gives them knowledge, skills, and a status as an educated or skilled person. But these rights were not achieved individually; they were claimed and enacted in the social life of their communities. Social citizenship also signals the social relations of reciprocity and responsibility they need in order to achieve their economic wellbeing as well as to support others' wellbeing. These youths gave and received emotional and financial support from peers, community, and family members to continue their education and to develop a means for labor.

As economic citizens, these youths were participating in markets and enterprising in ways that they had not done before their training. But in contrast to notions of labor and surplus in neoliberal economies, their labor involved producing and selling goods needed by the community and earning money that was reinvested into their families, the community, and at times, their and others' enterprises. Their earnings did not necessarily result in a large capital accumulation, and their surplus was usually not extracted from their own labor, as it would be if they worked for large businesses. They were participating in forms of community economies that also had elements of capitalist markets (Gibson-Graham, 2006).

As social-economic citizens, these youths were increasingly empowered – albeit still limited – to address barriers that inhibited their labor, and in turn, their and their families' wellbeing. After completing their education or training, some chose not to engage or stay in dangerous or abusive environments; for example, some women refused to work in sexually exploitative situations. But these youths did not labor and struggle for greater equality alone; they drew on existing and emerging relationships in the community, as discussed in Chapter 7 and 8. They created new relationships with peers and adults that helped them navigate social inequalities that have existed for them. For instance, they worked with peers to share materials and earn together so they could avoid exploitative trainers or intermediaries (see also Pellowski Wiger, 2016). But their degree of choice, participation, and social wellbeing still hinged on their economic participation and status. So, in this way, the social and the economic were contingently related.

Within the context of these entrepreneurship education and training projects, this social-economic citizenship that staff and community members were making, and these youths were remaking, did not wholly transform inequalities that the latter faced. The youth and project staff were not necessarily activists, participating in social or labor movements within their communities. But their actions and behaviors exposed inequalities and changed them in small ways. As examples, carpenters worked together to share knowledge about government regulations of lumber after one young man had to pay excessive fees to a local government official, and women joined forces to support each other from sexually exploitative employers or customers. In small and meaningful ways, these Tanzanian youths and, to some extent, the NGOs and schools were attempting to hold the state, businesses, and employers accountable for fair, equal, and just practices even while engaging in more individualized and economic practices of entrepreneurship.

African scholars have critiqued the bifurcated forms of citizenship that have emerged in postcolonial sub-Saharan African countries, disconnecting social and economic rights and wellbeing from political rights and identity (Ndegwa, 1998; Aminzade, 2013). Political projects, including education, that can bring together claims for and enactment of economic, social, and political inclusion are important to redress the long-standing inequalities that many youths face. While entrepreneurship education and training is most often designed and implemented as an economic project, and not necessarily political, it does offer possibilities for greater social, economic and political change because it locates youths in a different position vis-à-vis the economy and the state. In contexts of poverty, high unemployment, and social vulnerabilities for youths, entrepreneurship education and training is political in part because it challenges schools and vocational training programs to consider how education fosters economic and, relatedly, social inclusion for youths who are marginalized. Furthermore, entrepreneurship education and training can intensify youths' expectations of their economic and social participation in society, offering them opportunities to make greater claims on and contributions to society.

Implications for entrepreneurship education and training programs

While entrepreneurship education and training programs' main aims are to create enterprises, enable financial inclusion, and reduce unemployment, they produce other effects as they are reshaped in local contexts. What are the implications, then, for donors, NGOs, and the multitude of actors, including governments, now implementing such programs? The discourses and practices of entrepreneurship education, as well as vocational education and training and youth livelihoods, are dominated by the idea of preparing young people with skills primarily for a global and unstable capitalist market, which often means self-employment in the informal economy. McGrath and Powell (2015) argue that this perspective is the current orthodoxy but it does not have to remain so. The NGO staff struggled over the five years of this study to achieve diverse outcomes for these youths, and they sought to reframe their models and daily practices to see how they could achieve not only 'intended effects' of raising incomes and starting enterprises, but also of improving the overall wellbeing of these young people. These struggles over the meanings of becoming an entrepreneur affected how they implemented their programs, and they have implications for others in two particular ways: how to address material and social inequalities that affected their labor opportunities and livelihoods, and how to foster a mindset of entrepreneurialism that draws on social relations in these contexts.

Most donor and NGO entrepreneurship education and training initiatives do not necessarily include in their theory of change how to transform social inequalities that affect economic participation in society. Development organizations and staff too often assume that participation in the economy will change other social inequalities. These programs and their staff were continually faced with inequalities that surfaced and inhibited the best laid livelihood plans. These inequalities included sexual exploitation that affected women's access to employment, unjust prices or fees when establishing and registering an enterprise, and administrative regulations or fees in attempting to obtain financial services. The response to these '(a)social' inequalities (Ferguson, 2013) is often to provide training so youths learn how to negotiate or respond to these inequalities, but programs could do more to change these inequalities by working with employers, financial providers, and government policymakers. Rather than designing entrepreneurship education and training initiatives as primarily focused on the individual entrepreneur, these programs need to be engaged with a broader set of actors, situating their work within the social and economic life of communities and societies.

The NGO staff also struggled over what constituted an entrepreneurial mindset for these youths. For example, they considered – and future programs ought to consider – whether it is about risk-taking or mitigating certain risks that are already there for these youths? Is it about instilling the self-confidence to be somebody different than was imagined for an educated or skilled youth, or it is also about improving community recognition and acceptance of youth's alternative futures? Is it about increasing an income, or securing and stabilizing one's income to support oneself and others in a different way? These questions about the means and ends of entrepreneurship education and training require consideration, and a critique, of intended or expected outcomes. As Gibson-Graham (2006) argue, these questions engage in an analysis of the different kinds of economies (and societies) these actors want to achieve. Such questions also require consideration of the historically situated and contingent values that exist in these communities, and how entrepreneurship education and training encounters these values.

While my primary purpose in this book has been to show how dominant global and local governing discourses and practices of entrepreneurship education and training encountered each other and the contradictory effects that occurred, there is also an opportunity to consider how this analysis can more intentionally inform and shape the purposes, aims, and outcomes desired and measured of such programs. One way to reframe entrepreneurship education and training, as mentioned above, is through understanding the locally valued meanings of wellbeing. Wellbeing for these Tanzanian youths in these communities is situated in notions of self-reliance, reciprocity and solidarity, which include economic outcomes of earning sufficiently for oneself and others. The technical, business, and entrepreneurial skills and attitudes that these youths learned could not be used alone to obtain work or income; they also needed to be integrated with social relations in their communities to achieve these and other outcomes. As such, they need to be framed as social skills or capabilities. For example, technical skills, such as learning to sew, need to be combined with being affiliated with others or having the safety and security in order to use the technical skills to provide goods to a customer (DeJaeghere and Baxter, 2014). To achieve these notions of wellbeing and address related social inequalities, entrepreneurship education and training programs might focus on fostering not only these technical and entrepreneurial, but also what I refer to as *social relations or capabilities* (see also, DeJaeghere et al., 2016). Such an approach to framing entrepreneurship education and training attends to longer-term effects of producing citizens who are included in and contributing members of society, rather than the short-term outcomes of learning skills or increasing an income.

Reframing entrepreneurship education and skills in the global development agenda

This book has argued that entrepreneurship education and training are shaped by many different approaches to development, and local actors reshape it to achieve their understandings of and purposes for social and economic development. There is a need, therefore, to consider how entrepreneurship education is framed, and can be reframed, in the current international agenda: the Sustainable Development Goals (SDGs). Education in the new global agenda has been mostly defined as sets of concrete knowledge and skills – numeracy, literacy, technical/vocational, and non-cognitive. While the current agenda broadens the set of skills that represent a quality education, the assessments, such as literacy tests, used to measure the outcomes circumscribe the type of skills taught. These skill sets are also assumed to achieve the primary goal of employment, though the broader agenda is concerned with not only economic development, but also sustainable development. For example, Goal 4.4 specifically addresses learning technical and vocational skills for employment and entrepreneurship; Goal 8 includes promoting economic growth through productive employment and decent work, with references to youth and entrepreneurship (United Nations, 2015). Those involved in the SDG process have already included entrepreneurship education and training in this new agenda because it attends to technical and business skills and non-cognitive skills, such as resiliency, risk-taking, and self-confidence, all deemed necessary to improve the education–employment linkage. But as I have argued throughout this book, the outcomes and effects of entrepreneurship education and training are not only employment or economic development; rather, these economic outcomes are mediated by goals of social development and practices of moral and local economies.

The analysis in this book of entrepreneurship education and training practices and the, at times contradictory, effects of them, suggest three areas for further consideration in the SDG agenda: which skills are valued by individuals and communities, which outcomes produce sustainable development, and which partners achieve which outcomes. First, skills are not simply technical and instrumental as I argue above; they are 'contested social and political constructions' (McGrath and Powell, 2015, p. 278). They are not universally valued; academic, vocational, and entrepreneurial skills all hold different value for youths, their families, the community, and businesses, and what these different actors aim to achieve with these skills for their future livelihoods or wellbeing. Skills not only serve the individual outcome of earning; they also have social value and are used to foster social wellbeing. There is also an assumption in the global agenda that youths have a skills deficit, particularly non-cognitive skills, and that by teaching these skills young people will improve their livelihoods. Non-cognitive skills have received increasing attention in the global agenda as the next panacea for improving educational outcomes and livelihoods. Heckman et al. (2006) and others have argued that teaching young people to be resilient, to have grit, and to be self-confident improves their employment outcomes. But my analysis has complicated the understanding of non-cognitive skills as individually learned and held; rather, resiliency and self-esteem, among other skills, are fostered through social relations of care and affiliation with others (see also DeJaeghere et al., 2016). As I argue above, conceptualizing skills as social capabilities, formed in relation to the social and economic environment, goes some way to rethinking how we teach skills.

Second, education and skills are not only valued for enabling employment, increasing income, creating enterprises, and creating economic development. As discussed in this study, education and skills are valued for the respect they bring to young people and the social value they have in communities (see also McGrath and Powell, 2015). This perspective requires reframing the measured learning outcomes to go beyond employment or earning and to consider paid, unpaid, or alternatively paid labor (Gibson-Graham, 2006) and other meaningful contributions that youths' knowledge and skills make to others' wellbeing. Other outcomes for sustainable development might consider how knowledge, skills, and – in turn – labor are used to support and care for community members, such as teaching or employing others rather than increasing one's own income. These social outcomes can be understood, though difficult to measure, through affiliation, community solidarity and wellbeing.

Finally, achieving the SDGs relies on the need for partnerships among government, civil society and the private sector. To address the concerns of unemployment, economic development, and sustainability, the SDGs currently give considerable emphasis to the role of private sector stakeholders, such as businesses, in defining relevant knowledge and skills for the labor market and a changing global economy. But as I show in Chapters 6, 7, and 8, education and skills for both employment and sustainability need to be grounded in the social life of communities – the values, needs, and types of economies they have and desire. This also means that local and national NGOs play a critical role in shaping what entrepreneurship education and training should include and look like, both in the national agenda and in local programs. By including communities and national NGOs as a critical and heterogeneous set of stakeholders, a debate can be fostered that considers 'different kinds of economic subjects' for diverse economies and sustainability, rather than solely for the purposes of economic development in the global economy (Gibson-Graham, 2006, loc. 3764). In addition, because these skills are contested, it is critical that a diverse group of actors are included in debates about which skills should be learned for which purposes. These debates should include young people and their interests and needs within their communities, rather than being driven predominantly by those of employers and businesses. Debates about the kind of education, and skills for whom and what purposes (Tikly, 2015), must also take up questions of social and ethical commitments alongside those of economic development.

This study has recounted how diverse actors struggle with the goals and practices of educational programs, such as entrepreneurship education and training, used to ensure quality education and young people's future livelihoods. Staff and youths reshaped these programs in ways that are repurposed toward valued outcomes for their families and communities. In this way, neo/liberal technologies of governing that aim to create the enterprising self are neither universal nor singular in their effects. Entrepreneurship education and training programs meet alternative discourses and local social relations that reshape the entrepreneurial young person as a socio-economic citizen. The analysis presented in this book is not necessarily a negative or a positive story about the effects of entrepreneurship education and training on youths' lives and livelihoods. Rather, I aimed to present how entrepreneurship education and training programs, as technologies of power and of the self, are implemented in complex and, at times, contradictory ways to the planned outcomes it aimed to achieve for youths' livelihoods. In this encounter, NGOs and international agencies would do well by attending to these local discourses and adapting their models, desired outcomes, and program processes, rather than focusing only on the initially planned or desired outcomes.

* * *

During the first few years of this project, I thought I understood how these entrepreneurship education and training programs were being implemented to teach skills and start enterprises. But I was continually surprised. As Foucault (1988) said, when asked about the 'categories' that describe his work, 'If you knew when you began a book what you would say at the end, do you think that you would have the courage to write it?' (p. 9). Through time and continued analysis of many conversations, I saw more clearly the encounter of these different forms of governmentality – of the diverse meanings that the entrepreneurial citizen had for these young Tanzanians. These programs were not necessarily neoliberal; they were also not intentionally oriented toward social justice and change. But somewhere in the encounter of neo/liberal and alternative ideas that occurred in local practices, there emerged possibilities for social justice and change for young people who had been excluded from social and economic life.

This analysis reveals the possibilities, risks, and dangers of entrepreneurship education and training as a technology of governing, and how it gets reshaped for purposes of development. Similar to Sharma's (2008) warning of the risks that feminist NGOs face, and the 'dangerous'[2] outcomes that could be produced when attempting to implement empowerment programs for women, these NGOs and entrepreneurship projects also had risks and produced potentially dangerous outcomes. If international agencies, NGOs and governments do not attend to youths' voices and experiences of '(a)social inequalities' (Ferguson, 2013), they risk reproducing such inequalities and not realizing the outcomes they had worked so hard to achieve. By subjecting youths to ever-increasing economic pressures and the intractability of poverty, these programs can be dangerous to youths' lives and wellbeing. But these projects can also be dangerous to the state by changing youths' social and economic status quo – of being uneducated/undereducated, working for subsistence living, and living on the edge of vulnerability. An attempt to alter, even in small ways, the conjunction between these social and economic inequalities allows for possibilities of social and economic change within the state and these communities. The state and communities need to contend with these changes. Those in development ought to ask themselves, then, how entrepreneurship education and training can create possibilities for not only economic but also social change. How can entrepreneurship education and training programs go beyond limited and technical approaches of creating enterprises and increasing income, and head toward approaches that consider the kinds of labor that young people and communities value for their wellbeing?

Notes

1 I'm grateful to Emily Morris for her suggestion of this point based on interviews with teachers in 2016 for a related evaluation of *Parka*'s program.
2 I use quotes here to indicate a double meaning of dangerous. One in which the programs could have negative effects on youths' lives. Another in which it could disrupt the current political, economic, and social status quo, and thus they create dangerous changes for the state and others who benefit from these inequalities.

References

Aminzade, R. (2013). *Race, nation, and citizenship in postcolonial Africa: The case of Tanzania*. Cambridge, UK: Cambridge University Press.

DeJaeghere, J. and Baxter, A. (2014). Entrepreneurship education for youth in sub-Saharan Africa: A capabilities approach as an alternative framework to neoliberalism's individualizing risks. *Progress in Development Studies*, *14*(1), 61–76.

DeJaeghere, J., Pellowski Wiger, N. and Willemsen, L. (2016). Broadening educational outcomes: Social relations, skills development and employability for youth. *Comparative Education Review*, *60*(3), 457–479.

Ferguson, J. (2013). Declarations of dependence: Labour, personhood, and welfare in southern Africa. *Journal of the Royal Anthropological Institute*, *19*(2), 223–242.

Foucault, M. (1988). Technologies of the self. In M. Foucault, L. H. Martin, H. Gutman, and P. H. Hutton (Eds.) *Technologies of the self: A seminar with Michel Foucault* (pp. 16–49). Amherst, MA: University of Massachusetts Press.

Gibson-Graham, J. K. (2006). *A postcapitalist politics*. Minneapolis, MN: University of Minnesota Press.

Gordon, C. (1991). Governmental rationality: an introduction. In G. Burchell, C. Gordon, and P. Miller (Eds.), *The Foucault effect: Studies in governmentality* (pp. 1–52). Chicago, IL: University of Chicago Press.

Heckman, J. J., Stixrud, J. and Urzua, S. (2006). *The effects of cognitive and noncognitive abilities on labor market outcomes and social behavior* (No. w12006). National Bureau of Economic Research.

Marshall, T. H. (1964). *Class, citizenship and social development*. New York, NY: Praeger.

McGrath, S. and Powell, L. (2015). Vocational education and training for human development. In S. McGrath and Q. Gu (Eds.), *Routledge handbook for international education and development*, (pp. 276–288). Oxford, UK: Routledge.

McNay, L. (2009). Self as enterprise dilemmas of control and resistance in Foucault's The Birth of Biopolitics. *Theory, Culture & Society*, 26(6), 55–77.

Muehlebach, A. (2012). *The moral neoliberal: Welfare and citizenship in Italy*. Chicago, IL: University of Chicago Press.

Ndegwa, S. N. (1998). Citizenship amid economic and political change in Kenya. *Africa Today*, 45(3/4), 351–367.

Pellowski Wiger, N. (2016). Social capital, education, and earning: The important role of peer relationships for marginalized Tanzanian youth (Unpublished Doctoral dissertation). Minneapolis: University of Minnesota.

Polanyi, K. (1944). *The great transformation: The political and economic origins of our time*. Boston, MA: Beacon Press.

Rose, N. (1998). *Inventing ourselves: Psychology, power and personhood*. Cambridge, UK: Cambridge University Press.

Sen, A. (1999). *Development as freedom*. Oxford, UK: Oxford University Press.

Sharma, A. (2008). *Logics of empowerment: Development, gender, and governance in neoliberal India*. Minneapolis: University of Minnesota Press.

Tikly, L. (2015). What works, for whom, and in what circumstances? Towards a critical realist understanding of learning in international and comparative education. *International Journal of Educational Development*, 40, 237–249.

United Nations (2015). *Sustainable development goals*. Retrieved from: http://www.un.org/sustainabledevelopment/sustainable-development-goals/

Appendix

Selected Economic, Education, and Youth Policies 1961–2015

Policy or document	Year	Brief Description
UDSM established	1961	
Education Act of 1962	1962	First independent United Republic of Tanzania Education Act.
	1963	Discrimination on racial or religious basis abolished for schools; Kiswahili national language
Arusha Declaration	1967	Policy on Socialism and Self-Reliance
Education for Self-Reliance	1967	Set out principles for primary and secondary schools, including reforms to curriculum and focus on education for rural development
	1972	Diversified secondary education into vocational areas (commercial, agriculture, technical and home economics)
Small Industries Development Organization (SIDO)	1973	Parastatal organization mandated to plan, coordinate, promote and offer every form of services to SMEs, including entrepreneurship development
Universal Primary Education	1974	Promoted basic education through Primary 7 for all children
Folk Development Colleges established	1975	Support adult literacy, promote post primary training and continuing education
Education Act of 1978	1978	Legalized and implemented education for self-reliance
Presidential Commission on Education	1981	Review the current system and propose necessary changes toward year 2000
Privatisation Policy and Act	1993	Policy to shift from state to private entities
Education and Training Policy	1996	Outlines a new vision for education
Education Development Sector Plan	1996–2000	Objectives include improving quality of education, expanding enrolment and improving equity and efficiency in education management and provision, through Primary Education Development Program (PEDP) and Secondary Education Development Program (SEDP)

(Continued)

Policy or document	Year	Brief Description
National Youth Policy	1996	Identifies youth unemployment as a main problem and the need for youths to work in informal labor market (micro-enterprises)
National Technical Education Policy	1996	Guides the provision of technical education. National Council for Technical Education (NACTE) - 1997
Sustainable Industrial Development Policy (SIDP)	(1996–2020)	Identifies the role of private sector in industry, as well as the informal sector and entrepreneurship as necessary, particularly for youths, to contribute to economic activities
National Development Vision 2025	1998	New vision for competitive economy and to cope with challenges of development in the regional and global economy
The Tanzanian Education System for the 21st Century Task Force Report	2000	Aligns with global mandates related to Education for All
Primary Education Development Program	2001	Focuses on expanding enrollment, improving quality for achieving UPE (and in line with Education for All)
Secondary Education Development Program	2003 (2004–2009)	Aims to expand post-primary education, and particularly formal secondary education. Also includes a goal to prepare students for the world of work and to create better links with VETA.
Small and Medium Enterprises (SME) Development Policy	2003	Specific policy objective is to foster job creation and income generation through SMEs for purposes of economic growth and reduction of poverty
Economic Empowerment Policy	2004	Roadmap for the participation of the majority of the citizens of Tanzania in all sectors of the economy, and particularly acknowledges that the education system should create a foundation for entrepreneurship and skills development for competitive markets
National Economic Empower Act	2004	Established the National Economic Empowerment Council to oversee entrepreneurship education
"Doing Business" Reform	2004	Various reforms to foster investment in development of businesses, including micro-enterprises and better regulation of the informal economy
MKUKUTA I/PGRSP I	2005 (2005–10)	The National Strategy for Growth and Reduction of Poverty (NSGRP) or MKUKUTA, including goals of enhancing life-skills and entrepreneurship training for rural population

(Continued)

Policy or document	Year	Brief Description
National Youth Development Policy	2007	Identifies entrepreneurship skills training and an enabling environment for youth enterprise development
Curriculum for Advanced Secondary Education in Tanzania	2007	Includes business studies and entrepreneurship to be integrated into, Economics, Commerce and Accountancy (ECA)
Education Sector Development Plan (2008-2017)	2008	Implements the various policy strategies and the MKUKUTA targets
National Employment Policy	2008	Includes support for self-employment, informal sector and entrepreneurship
Kilimo Kwanza Policy (Agriculture First)	2009	Aims to reduce poverty through agricultural employment and entrepreneurship
MKUKUTA II/PGRSP II	2010	Strategies to promote skills and entrepreneurship for formal and informal employment, and a particular focus on fostering youth entrepreneurship in agriculture
Secondary Education Development Program	2010 (2010–2015)	Strategies to improve the enrollment and quality of secondary education and includes attention to reshaping vocational/technical programs in the future
National Strategy for Civic Education	2011	Identifies how general education can contribute to citizenship, including an emphasis on entrepreneurship education
National Entrepreneurship Training Framework (NETF)	2013	Sets out the competencies for employability skills and entrepreneurship to be integrated throughout pre-primary, basic, secondary and tertiary education
Entrepreneurship curriculum released	2013	VETA entrepreneurship curriculum
Small Industries Development Organization (SIDO)	2014–15	Strategic Plan to promote growth of private/public partnerships and SMEs, including support for entrepreneurship development

Index

Added to a page number 'n' denotes notes.

accountability 11, 13, 25, 149, 159
active participants 83
adult relationships 124, 155, 158
adulthood: transition to 128
advanced liberalism *see* neoliberalism
affiliation 31, 116, 156, 161, 162
African states: imposition of privatization on 9; inclusiveness as separate from development 28; *see also individual states*
African values 75
agency 35, 57, 116
agricultural production 61, 62, 63, 95, 97, 100, 101, 103, 118, 125
aid *see* donor aid
alternatives: choice of 34
Aminzade, R. 33, 35, 159
angel money 45
Apprentice 2, 3, 117; adaptiveness to socio-economic relations 114; apprenticeships 50; creating and being value(d) 127–9; creating enterprises and supporting community development 125–8; ethical commitment 114; financial education 3, 63, 119, 120, 135, 136, 140–4; financial inclusion and alternatives 134, 135, 144–7; frictions in 154–6; investing in enterprises and human development 147–9; Kagera region 114, 117–19; learning skills and developing social relations 116–17, 121–6; non-formal entrepreneurship training 119–21; post-training 122; reflections on encounter of entrepreneurship with the local and moral economy 130–1; savings and lending groups 138–40; *see also* comparative case study
apprenticeships 50
Arnot, M. 32
Arusha Declaration 75
Ashoka 60
(a)social inequalities 117, 121, 130, 160, 164
at-risk youth 30, 31, 47
attitudes 42, 44, 77–8, 105, 122, 149–50
autonomy 11, 30, 116, 117

bank accounts 135, 145
bank credit 137
Bannerjee, A. 49, 137
Bartlett, L. 56–7, 71
Baxter, A. 50
Berry, J. 138
biashara midogo midogo 88
botho 32
Botswana 31, 32
Brown, A. 113
budgeting 11, 155, 156
business clubs 61, 101–2, 103, 155
business development 1, 45, 87, 94, 95, 96, 101, 119
business failure 46, 49
business management 97, 98, 106
business plans 2, 95, 97, 107, 120, 155, 156
business skills 2, 42, 45, 122, 123, 160–1

Campbell, H. 74–5
capabilities 9, 161, 162
capability approach 43, 49, 50–1, 64, 156–7; good life 127, 156
capital: access to 134, 135

capital accumulation 154, 158
capitalism 104, 154
capitalist markets: entrepreneurship education and inclusion in 3; ESS engagement with 99; neoliberalism 9, 11; Pan-African socialism as resistance to 75; precariousness of engaging in 154–5; preparation for 97; wealth accumulation 83, 118–19; youth engagement in 156; *see also* global capitalist economy
care/caring 30, 120, 149, 157, 162
Chachage, C. 80–1
character assessments (student) 78
choice(s) 9, 10, 11, 12, 30, 33, 34, 137, 150, 158
citizen subjectivities 5, 27–8, 32, 33, 35, 36, *37*
citizen-subject divide 27, 28
citizenship: communal perspectives 28; entrepreneurship education and training 3, 129; ESS model and 93, 110; ethical 157; inclusive 28; indigenous conceptions 28; liberal 28, 157; neo/liberal discourses 23; Pan-Africanism 74; participatory 36; participation and enactment of 33; postcolonial 159; social 158; socialist 157–8; Sub-Saharan Africa 35
citizenship education 28, 29, 32, 35; civic education 7, 33, 35; civics curriculam 78
civic engagement 48
civil rights 31
civil society 10, 27, 32, 157
collateral 134, 144
collective agriculture 76, 126
colonialism: bisected relationship between rights and obligations 31; education 2, 76, 77, 104; ESR attempt to change attitudes and values of 77–8; illiberal governmentality 12; Kagera region under 118; Nyerere regime as an attempt to redress 75; political subjectivities 27; *Ujamaa* as an alternative to 74; *see also* postcolonialism
communitarianism 32, 33, 36
community 77; re-embedding of financial and market knowledge 150; supporting and contributing to 128, 129, 147, 148, 156, 158
community development 77, 80, 81, 83, 96, 125–8, 150
community economies 127, 158

community ethos 147
community facilitators 121, 125, 130, 139, 140, 157, 158
community members: caring for 157; perception of youth as idle 124, 127, 129; provision of social welfare 143; recognition of youth's newfound status 129; resistance to ESS model 103; youth relations with 124
community relationships 31, 86, 157
comparative case study, entrepreneurship discourses 56–72; analyses 70–1; capability approach 64; dialectical analysis 57; entrepreneurship education projects 59–63; ethnographic aspect 63; horizontal analysis 57; international agencies 58–9; longitudinal aspect 63; methods 65–6; participants 66–70; researchers 63–4; transversal analysis 57, 71; vertical analysis 57, 58, 71, 72n1
competencies: NETF objectives 87
competition 5, 13, 83, 102, 115, 116, 154
competitiveness 45, 83, 103, 104
conditionalities (IMF) 26
confidence 27, 50, 101; *see also* self-confidence
Convention on the Rights of the Child (CRC) 24
Cooksey, B. 79
cooperation 13, 77, 88
cooperatives 126, 127, 144, 155
creativity 8, 45, 101, 120, 125, 156
culture: need for wider definition of 27; norms 13, 32; values 83
curricula: *Apprentice* 62, 63, 120–1, 139, 140; ESR policies 78, 79; neo-institutional studies 56; *Parka* 1, 61, 63, 95; VETA 95, 97

De Weerdt, J. 118
decolonization 27, 28, 35, 74, 79
DeJaeghere, J. 4, 50, 51, 64, 92, 104, 161, 162
Democratic African Socialism 28
democratization 28, 134
dependency 30, 48, 116, 122
"dependency of responsible solidarity" 30, 149, 150
development: changing ideas of 81–8; entrepreneurship as poverty alleviation 47; global discourses 60; liberal and neoliberal discourses in 8–12;

Index

neo/liberal governmentality 24–9; *Ujamaa* and 74–6
development accelerators 7, 11
development discourses 5, 8, 34–5, 43, *see also* neoliberalism
developmental mindset 83, 87
discipline 45, 48, 102
discourse analysis 70–1
diverse economies 13, 116, 150, 153, 160, 163
"diversification and vocationalization" 79–80
"doing business reforms" 113–14
donor aid 7, 61, 79
donors: entrepreneurship education and training and implications for 159–61
double meanings: entrepreneurial citizen 114; in entrepreneurship education and training 11–12, 29; of financial responsibility and inclusion 140, 149–50; participation and empowerment 23; rights and responsibilization 29; of self-reliance and inclusion 154
"double movement of capitalism" 154
Duflo, E. 49
Dupas, P. 137

earnings: in the informal sector 119; multiple earnings strategies 125; school enterprises 102
East Africa 6, 50
economic development 155, 156, 163; adoption of entrepreneurship for 41; education and 157; global discourses 88; inclusiveness as separate from 28; in Kagera region 117–19; linking of social, political and 76; private individuals and 30; solidarity and 150; teaching of an entrepreneurial mindset and 87
economic empowerment 11, 35, 155
Economic Empowerment Policy 87
economic equality 9, 30
economic growth: as an international development goal 3; commitment of IMF and World Bank to 26; encounter with unjust political and social practices 12; entrepreneurship education as 5, 8, 43–6; focus of development agenda on 49; national strategy, Tanzania 3, 7; need for twenty-first century skills 31; Nyerere on 76; sub-Saharan Africa 6; sustainable 3, 46
economic inclusion 159
economic inequalities 49, 157, 164
economic justice 157

economic relations 5, 13, 114
economic rights 28, 30, 31, 35, 76, 157
economic wellbeing 10, 33, 35, 77, 130, 150, 154, 158
economically self-sufficient schools (ESS) model 2, 61–2, 79, 88, 93, 94–6; financial management 105–9; frictions between self-reliance and 109–10; learning by doing 100–5; marketization of schools and students 96–100; resistance to 103; utilization of self-reliance discourse 94; *see also* school enterprises
economistic fallacy 153
economy: changing ideas of 81–8
educated citizens 30
educated person 1, 131n7
Educating the Next Wave of Entrepreneurs 44
education: changing ideas of 81–8; citizens engagement 36; dropout from 6, 83, 103; emancipatory approach 81; empowerment 34, 35; encounter with unjust political and social practices 12; future aspirations and engagement with 36; global discourses 60; as inadequate preparation for the global economy 30; initiative analysis 113; liberal and neoliberal discourses in 8–12; liberalization 82; microfinance 137; neo/liberal governmentality 24–9; in the new global agenda 161; NGO alignment with 60; participation 29, 118; postcolonial regimes 76; programs and subjectivities 37; as a public good 25; reforms 56; SDG 4 on 52n5; for self-sufficiency 92–111; Tanzania 1, 2, 5–8, 29; youth monetary contribution to 142; *see also* citizenship education; civic education; entrepreneurship education and training; financial education; quality education; secondary education
Education Act 1978 (Tanzania) 82
Education Act 2016 (Tanzania) 83
Education for All (EFA) 3, 24–5, 28, 83
Education Sector Development Programme 83
Education for Self-Reliance (ESR) 2, 74, 75, 76, 77–81, 93, 94, 95, 100, 104
Education Strategy 2020 (World Bank) 44
Education and Training Policy 82, 83, 86
emotional support 158
employability 7, 46, 49, 50, 51; programs 50; skills 59, 87, 100, 122

Index

employment: education and 25, 85; initiative anylysis 113; migration for 63, 86; NGO alignment with 60; of others 148, 162; *see also* self-employment; informal employment; youth employment
empowerment: financial education 136–7, 155; Gandhi's perspective 52; microfinance 137; neo/liberal governmentality 33–6; social-economic citizens 158; technologies of the self 24; *see also* economic empowerment
Englund, H. 31, 32
enterprise(s): choice associated with 30; development 5, 45, 48, 88, 115, 119, 149; incorporation into global value chain 45; *see also* household enterprises; microenterprises; school enterprises; value-added enterprises
enterprising self 5, 32, 105, 154, 158, 163
entrepreneurial citizens: becoming 113–32; as a social-economic citizen 157–9
entrepreneurial mindset(s) 3, 5, 7, 8, 10, 45, 49, 59, 87, 88, 154, 155, 160
entrepreneurial skills 3, 5, 44, 45, 47, 101, 119, 123, 160–1, 162
entrepreneurs: confidence and motivation 50; factors making/constraining 49; learning-by-doing 100–5; *see also* necessity entrepreneurs; opportunity entrepreneurs; social entrepreneurs
entrepreneurship 13, 27; addressing of high unemployment 7; ambiguity in interpretations and enactment of 87–8; discourses *see* comparative case study; for economic survival 41; economists' definition 41; education as preparation for 82; government role in fostering 46; inclusion in development policies 86; informal/moral economy 5, 86, 88, 115–21, 130–1; multiple goals of 154; *see also* active entrepreneurship
entrepreneurship education and training: definitions 7–8; double meanings in 11–12, 29; effective implementation 87; in formal schooling 44; frictions in 4, 12–13, 109–10, 154–6; goals 3–4, 8; hegemonic discourses 57; for human development and wellbeing 48–51; ILO approach 53n12; importance for youth employment 27; increasing interest in 41; management mechanisms in 11; neo/liberal governmentality 113; outcomes 42–3, 161; as poverty reduction/alleviation 3, 46–8; re-emergence of policies relating to 23; reframing in the global development agenda 161–4; as reframing of link between education and participation 8; and responsibilization *see* responsibilization; sub-Saharan Africa 114; Tanzania *see* Tanzania, entrepreneurship education and training; as a technology of governing/power 3, 10, 23, 113; as a technology of the self 10, 23–4, 113; varying understandings in relation to youth livelihoods 4
Entrepreneurship Education and Training Programs around the World: Dimensions for Success (World Bank) 44
Entrepreneurship Toolkit (USAID) 45, 49
equality: citizenship and 29; contrasted with participation in global economy 28; education and 24, 77; NGOs and fostering of 110; *Ujamaa* and 74–6; using care to fight for 157; youth engagement in fostering 36; *see also* economic equality; inequalities; racial equality; social equality
EQUIP3 47, 48
equity 25, 26, 27, 28, 43
ethical citizenship 157
ethical commitment 114, 163
ethics education 28
Ethiopia 86, 115–16, 128
ethnographic research 56
ethos: business clubs 102; egalitarian 13; of reciprocity and solidarity 150, 155; of sharing and caring 149; social solidarity and economic justice 157; *see also* community ethos
Europe 30
exchange 5, 86, 136, 153
exclusion 29, 31, 36, 48, 57, 93, 113, 114, 125, 127, 130, 146, 154, 156
expertise 10
extrinsic motivation 102

Fairclough, N. 70
family: supporting and contributing to 128, 141, 142, 143, 148, 149, 156, 158; youth responsibility for 105
family social relations 75, 157
family-based microenterprises 2

Farmers' Cooperative Bank (Kagera) 144
fee-paying students 99, 110
Ferguson, J. 3, 5, 8, 9, 12, 13, 116, 117, 122
financial education 130; *Apprentice* 3, 63, 119, 120, 135, 136; in contexts of poverty 136–8; in low income countries 138; *Parka* 3, 94, 95, 101; underlying assumption/premise 135, 137
financial inclusion 134–5, 144–7, 149–50
financial independence 97, 149, 155
financial institutions 24, 137, 140, 144; international financial institutions 24
financial knowledge 105, 115, 138, 139, 141, 143, 147, 150
financial literacy 45, 59, 60, 119, 135, 136, 138, 139–40
financial management 101, 105–6
financial responsibility 140–4, 149–50
financial service providers (FSPs) 134, 144, 147; interest rates 134; fees 134
financial services: connecting youth to 135
financial skills 2, 122
financial support 141, 158
financial wellbeing 11, 108, 136, 137
flexibility 104
flexible skills 42
floating signifiers 60
Foucault, M. 9, 163
freedom: Nyerere on 75; self-employment and 125, *see also* individual freedom
Freedom and Socialism 76
friction metaphor 4, 57
frictions: in entrepreneurship education and training models 4, 12–13, 109–10, 154–6; global encounters 57; in relation to self-reliance 94
Friedman, M. 9
frugality 141, 155
fundi 126, 127, 132n14, 156; *see also* skilled person

Gandhi 52
Garissa youth livelihood project 53n11
gender: and education, Kagera region 118; and employment 7; equality 50; parity 83; *see also* women
Ghana 32, 74–5, 138
Gibson-Graham, J.K. 13, 116, 127, 150, 153, 160
girls boarding school *see* Sasema
global capitalist economy: education for participation in 83; microfinance and integration into 137; national values contrasted with participation in 28; and neoliberalism 5, 11; skill development for 31, 94; state education as inadequate preparation for 30; *see also* capitalist markets
global development agendas 3, 23, 24, 42, 59, 161–4
global discourses 4, 5, 60, 88
global economic growth 43
global economic recession (2008) 6, 41, 42
Global Entrepreneurship Program 44
Global South 12, 60, 94
global value chains 11, 45, 120, 128
global youth unemployment 6
globalization: education reforms 56
government(s): illiberal 12; logics of entrepreneurship education 43; microfinance 144–5; multiplicity of forms, Sub-Saharan Africa 13; need for understanding alternative and local regimes of 52; regimes, Tanzania 74–88; role in fostering entrepreneurship 46; use of management mechanisms 11
government secondary schools 61, *78*, 80, 93
governmentality 9–10; entrepreneurship education as a technique of 3; sub-Saharan Africa 12; *see also* neo/liberal governmentality
Gries, T. 49
group bank accounts 145; group loans 144–5
group enterprises 126–7

Halisi, C.R.D. 28, 31
Hammett, D. 29, 36
Harvey, D. 9
Haya people 117, 118
Hayek, F.A. 9
health care 2, 30, 69, 120, 126, 141, 142, 143, 144, 148, 150, 156
heavily indebted poor country (HIPC) status 82
Heckman, J.J. 162
hegemonic discourses: of development 8, 82; of empowerment 34; of entrepreneurship education 57; of rights and responsibilization, critiques 31
high income countries: entrepreneurship education in 50
Honwana, A.M. 36

household enterprises 8, 47, 88, 115, 122, 125, 156
human capital 8, 25, 43, 51
human development 48–51, 147–9
human dignity 25, 75, 78
human rights approach 9, 25, 29, 31
humanism 25

ILO 42–3, 43, 44, 45, 48, 52n4, 53n12, 87
incentives 61, 108, 109, 110
Incheon Declaration 24–5
inclusion: double meanings of 154; education and 25; friction between enterprising self and 154; hegemonic discourse of empowerment 34; importance for youth, sub-Saharan Africa 36; need for development of relationships 155; Pan-African socialism and 76; *see also* financial inclusion; political inclusion; social inclusion
inclusive citizenship 28
income generation 79, 127–8
independence: from foreign aid 79; select citizens and negotiation of 35; *see also* financial independence; personal independence; political independence
India 52, 137
individual freedom 11, 30, 31, 32, 33, 46, 82
individualism 28, 29, 32, 74, 75, 77
individuals: relationship between state and 27; rights and responsibilization 31; value to society 51
inequalities: addressing, as an international development goal 3; capability approach to human development 49; colonial education and 77; political projects for redressing 159; poverty alleviation discourses 47; social relations and policies 116; *see also* (a)social inequalities
informal economy: as due to lack of social benefits 50; earnings in 119; entrepreneurship in 88; negotiation in 125; participation in 86; preparation for 47; skills training for 42; Tanzania *see* moral economy; urban 113
informal employment 7, 18n12, 50, 53n9, 85, 89n9
innovativeness 41, 45, 60, 88, 103, 104, 125
interest 149, 151n8

international agencies: and entrepreneurship education 8, 41, 43, 47; financial inclusion 134; meaning attributed to empowerment 33; participation of marginalized peoples 33; use of entrepreneurship as a development accelerator 11; use of management mechanisms 11; *see also* ILO; Kauffmann Foundation; USAID; World Bank
international development *see* global development agendas
international foundation 3, 4, 59, 63, 64, 92, 93, 134
International Monetary Fund (IMF) 26, 81, 82
International Youth Foundation's Passport to Success 53n6

job creation 94; donors and the emphasis on 7; entrepreneurship education and 42, 43–6; microfinance and 46, 137, 138; Tanzania 6
Junior Achievement Young Enterprise 94

Kabeer, N. 34
Kagera region 117–19, 144
Kamat, S. 92
Kauffmann Foundation 43, 51
Kenya 28, 32, 74–5
Know Your Business (KAB) program 52n4
knowledge: and access to financial resources 136–7; *Apprentice* and change in 122; and choice 34; liberalism and 10; *see also* financial knowledge; market knowledge; practical knowledge; technical knowledge
Kubow, P.K. 32
kujitegemea 17, 89, 154, 155, 157; *see also* self-reliance

labor market: education as a skill requirement 26; entrepreneurship programs for participation in 3, 47; need for secondary education certification 6; networks and access to 116; Tanzania 85; *see also* employment
Lake Victoria 63, 117, 144
Learning for All (2011) 25
liberal citizenship 28
liberal governmentality 12

Index   175

liberalism 8–12, 37, 82; *see also* neoliberalism
life skills 2, 31, 42, 48, 119, 120–1, 123, 130; *see also* non-cognitive skills
loans: access to 45, 134; collateral 134, 144; repayment of 149; *see also* microfinance
local actors: logics of entrepreneurship education 43
local discourses: development and education 5; entrepreneurship education and training 153; neo/liberalisms and frictions with 4, 12–13
local-global connections 57
local-national connections 57
Locke, J. 8
Logics of Empowerment 34
Lyons, M. 113

McGrath, S. 51
macroeconomic policies 113
Mains, D. 5, 12, 86, 115–16, 128
Malawi 31
Mamdani, M. 27, 35
marginalized youths 3, 33, 46, 60, 94, 105
market(s): access to 45; analysis of 2; efficiency 13; knowledge of 119, 150; scans 60; society 154
market-driven education 7; skills 42
market-led socioeconomic individualism 29
marketization: schools and students 96–100
Marshall, T.H. 157
material conditions: schooling and citizenship 29
material markers: of adulthood 128
mentors/mentoring 44, 60, 121, 124, 130, 139
merry-go-rounds 145–6, 147
microenterprises: *Apprentice* and 62, 125–8, 147–9; family-based 2; in the informal economy 115; job creation 46; as a means to supplement wages 86; non-alleviation of poverty 49; perceived as begging 2; start up after completing ESS model schooling 105; youth livelihood programs 47; *see also* school enterprises
microfinance: access to 45, 50; double promise of 135; empowerment and development discourses 34; ESS model 94; government 144–5; institutions (MFIs) 134, 135, 144; integration into global capital markets 137; percentage of youth population obtaining 139; and profit for investors 137; program outcomes 137–8; as a technology of power and of self 135; Yunus approach to 137
Millennium Development Goals (MDGs) 7, 24, 26, 33
Miller, P. 10, 30
Ministry of Education and Vocational Training (MoEVT) 3
MKUKUTA II 27
mobile money 135, 145, 151n4
monetary contribution: to community and family 129, 141, 142, 143, 147, 148, 149, 156
moral economy(ies) 113; alternative markets 13, 45; community economies 127, 158; entrepreneurship in informal and 5, 86, 88, 115–21, 130–1; Kagera region 118; neo/liberalisms and frictions with 12–13; outcomes of entrepreneurship education 161; wealth sharing 149; relations *see* economic relations; social relations; transactions in 13
moral obligation: responsibilization as 150
moral rights 29, 31, 32
Mosha, H.J. 77
Mosweunyane, D. 32, 35
Motala, E. 113
motivation 50, 87, 101, 102, 108, 120, 122, 125, 130, 150
Msoga, Daniel 101
Msoka, M. 113
Muehlebach, A. 33, 88, 157
Mundy, K. 25, 26
Mushi, P.A.K. 75
mutuality 113, 115
Mwinyi, A.H. 81

Namibia 116
nation-building 27, 74, 79, 88
National Civic Education Programme (Ghana) 32
National Development Vision 2025 (Tanzania) 82–3, 87
National Economic Empowerment Council (NEEC) 86, 87
National Entrepreneurship Training Framework (NETF) 87–8

national identity 28, 32, 33, 78, 156
National Microfinance Bank (NMB) 144
National Strategy for Growth and Reduction of Poverty 3, 7
National Technical Education Policy 82
national unity 27, 28, 76, 78, 81, 83
National Youth Development Policy 7
National Youth Policy 82
Naudé, W. 49
Ndegwa, S.N. 31, 35
necessity entrepreneurs/entrepreneurship 46, 47, 49
NEET 30
neo/liberal governmentality 23–38; discourses of development and education 24–9, 113; and the enterprising self 163; Global south 12; participation and empowerment 33–6; rights and responsibilization 29–33
neo/liberalisms: entrepreneurship education and training 11–12, 153; financial education 136; frictions with local governing and moral economy 12–13
neoliberalism 3, 5, 82, 154; in economic and educational policies 88; education and development 8–12; and empowerment 52; entrepreneurship as poverty alleviation 48; *Ujamaa* as an alternative to 74
networks/networking: access to labor 116; international foundation 59; job creation and economic growth 45; moral economy 13; NGO programs 60; participation in civil society 32; *see also* social networks
NGO programs: hegemonic development discourses 8; neoliberal meaning of empowerment 37; vocational/technical programs 84; *see also Apprentice*; *Parka*
NGOs: adoption of entrepreneurship for economic development 41; as a contested space 92; crucial role in secondary education 92–3; and entrepreneurship education and training 41, 159–61, 162; and financial inclusion 134; global commitment to bottom-up development 92; implementation of human rights initiatives 31; meaning attributed to empowerment 33
Nigeria 74–5
non-cognitive skills 42, 45, 52n3, 120, 162

non-government schools 78, 80, 89n5, 92–3
Nussbaum, M.C. 9
Nyamnjoh, F.B. 31
Nyerere, J.K. 2, 33, 74, 75, 76, 77, 78–9, 81, 126, 154, 158

O-level certification 1, 2, 84, 104, 122
obligation(s) 31, 32, 153
Ong, A. 23
opportunity entrepreneurs 44–5, 46
Organization for Economic Development and Cooperation (OECD): achievement of EFA 25

Pan-African socialism 75–6
Parka 1–2, 2–3; frictions in 154–6; *see also* comparative case study; economically self-sufficient schools (ESS) model
participation 11, 31; active 33; in civil society 32; educational 29, 118; in formal labor market 3, 47; in global economy 28; neo/liberal governmentality 33–6; technologies of the self 24; *see also* youth participation
partnership(s) 43, 60, 69, 86, 137, 162
peer relationships 155, 158
peer support 158
performance measures 11
performance tracking 107
personhood 116, 117
Polanyi, K. 153, 154
political development 75, 76; education 78; inclusion 28, 159; independence 74, 75, 76; instability 47, 48; participation 33, 35, 36, 37, 47; power 27, 31; rights 30, 31, 35; stability 44; subjectives 27, 35
the poor: disempowerment equated with 34; financial institutions and taking advantage of 137; FSPs and higher interest rates for 134; microfinance and 135; *see also* poverty; pro-poor
positive rights 30
postcolonialism: citizenship 159; education 76; political participation 33; relationship between state and individuals 27; rights and obligations 31, 35
poverty: entrepreneurship education and training 159; ESS model as means for overcoming 96–7; financial education in contexts of 136–8; microenterprises and 49; responsibility for getting out of 150; rural areas and vulnerability to 6

poverty alleviation and reduction: as an international development goal 3; education and 3, 8, 24, 25, 43, 46–8; exacerbation of income inequality 49; national strategy, Tanzania 3, 7; need for twenty-first century skills 31; NGO alignment with 60
Poverty Capital 137
Poverty Reduction Strategy Papers (PRSPs) 26, 27, 82, 83
Powell, L. 50–1
power: citizen subjectivities 35; elites 27; *see also* economic power; empowerment; political power; social power; state power; technologies of power
practical knowledge 80
Preece, J. 32, 35
primary education: disadvantage of only 6; emphasis over secondary 80; universalization 77, 83
Primary Education Development Program (PEDP) 83
private sector: investment 45; involvement/influence in education 11, 27, 45–6
private sector education: expansion 26, 80; *Parka* collaboration with 94; school business clubs 101; secondary 61; vocational/technical programs 84
privatization 9, 26, 82
privilege (historically accumulated) 27
pro-poor 3, 13, 47, 48, 49
problem-solving (real-life) 100–1
productionist framework 51
productivity 44, 51, 82, 83
profit 5, 154; cooperation and reduction in 13; financial knowledge and 143; for investors, microfinance and 137; redistribution 103, 105, 110, 156; school enterprises 97, 100, 103, 105–7, 108, 110
program facilitators 119, 120, 121, 125, 130, 139, 140
project management: youth participation 48
propensity score analysis 71, 123, 132n10
protection 25
proven models 60
psychological wellbeing 116

quality education 11, 24, 26
quality of life 30

race 27
racial equality 29
racial privilege 27
reading culture 27
reciprocity 5, 13, 86, 105, 113, 115, 126, 129, 136, 144, 145, 150, 154
Reflections on Africa and Its Future 75
regulation(s) 5, 10, 45
reliance: on one another 13; *see also* self-reliance
repayment of loans 149
resilience 24, 31, 42, 46, 48, 161, 162
resource sharing 126, 130
resources: job creation and economic growth 45
respect 32, 129
responsibility 32, 46; ESS model teachers 106; for getting out of poverty 150; learning 105; neoliberal discourse and 30; *see also* financial responsibility; shared responsibility; social responsibility(ies)
responsibilization 24, 29–33, 48, 114, 120, 130, 141, 150
responsible solidarity 30, 140, 149, 150
rewards (business club) 101–2
"rhetoric of rights": challenge to the 31
rights 10, 11, 12, 27, 29–33, 30, 37; *see also* economic rights; human rights; political rights; social rights
rights-based discourse 3, 8, 32, 47
risk mitigation 125–6, 160
risk-taking 8, 31, 42, 45, 46, 101, 160, 161
Robinsons, J. 137
role models 61, 128
Rose, N. 10, 30, 158
Roy, A. 134–5, 137
rural development 76

safety nets 50
Sasema 61, 95, 96, 97, 98, 101, 102, 103, 105, 106, 107, 109, 110
saving and credit cooperatives (SACCOs) 138, 139, 145
savings 27, 140–1, 143, 145; accounts 138, 140, 144, 147, 150
savings and lendings groups 126, 127, 138–40, 141, 149, 150; coummunity 146–7, 150; community social fund 144; group saving and lending 136, 145; group social funds 138

Index

school enterprises 1; choosing 100; market analysis 2; *see also* Sasema; Usawa
school fees 2, 26, 83, 96, 102, 148
schools: integration into community life 79; self-supporting *see* economically self-sufficient schools (ESS) model; use of management mechanisms 11; *see also* government secondary schools; missionary schools; non-government schools
Schumpeter, J. 41
secondary education: certification 6, 76, 85, 122; colonial 2, 76, 77, 104; crucial role of NGOs in 92–3; diversification and vocationalization 79–80; ILO and UNESCO report on outcomes of entrepreneurship education in 42–3; NGO programs *see Apprentice*; *Parka*; postcolonial 78, 80; progression to 83; teaching of business and non-cognitive skills in 45; universalization 77
Secondary Education Development Program (SEDP) 83
seed money 44, 45
Sekei, L. 139
self-assessment 120
self-confidence 160, 161, 162
self-discipline 24
self-employment 2, 3, 7, 59, 63, 64, 80, 82, 87, 94, 114, 115, 125
self-reliance 5, 27, 87, 88; choice associated with 30; double meanings of 154; entrepreneurial mindset 155; and ESS model *see* economically self-sufficient schools (ESS) model; financial education and economic 142; under Mwinyi regime 82, 83; *see also* Education for Self-Reliance (ESR)
self-sufficiency: entrepreneurship and 116; financial responsibility and 142; *see also* economically self-sufficient schools (ESS) model
sharing: ethos of 149; *see also* resource sharing
Sharma, A. 34, 52, 164
skilled person 131n7
skills: as contested social and political constructions 162, 163; deficit assumption 162; livelihood opportunities 2, 4; in the new global agenda 161; *see also* business skills; entrepreneurial skills; financial skills; technical skills
skills development: *Apprentice* 119–21, 121–6; capability approach 50; donor emphasis on 7; and education 78; ESS model and 94; fostering of 86; neoliberal policies 29; reemergence of 42; (re)emergence of policies related to 23; and responsibilization 30; "skills for the twenty-first century" 30–1
Small Industry and Development Organization (SIDO) 103
Smith, A. 9
social change: contrasted with participation in global economy 28; empowerment linked to 35; entrepreneurship education and ability to anticipate/respond to 43; youth education, Tanzania 5–8; youth engagement in 36
social citizenship 158
social development: cooperatives 155; education and 81, 142, 157, 161; Kagera region 117–19; *Ujamaa* and 75, 76
social equality 28, 29, 30; inequalities 49, 117, 157, 161, 164
social good 94, 105, 109, 110, 134, 148, 154, 156
social inclusion 159; entrepreneurship education and 3, 117, 127; fostering 130; importance 131; Kenya 28
social issues/problems, addressing: liberalism 10; through citizen participation 33; through entrepreneurship education 43, 46, 47–8, 60; through financial inclusion 134–5; through management techniques 11; youth engagement in 36
social justice 8, 25, 43, 163
social networks 85, 119
social policies 50, 110, 116, 117
social protection(s) 30, 50, 86
social relations 161; *Apprentice* and 114, 121–6; entrepreneurialism and 5; exclusion from rights 31; friction between the enterprising self and development of 154; Kagera region 118; learning of non-cognitive skills 162; in a moral economy 5, 13, 115–16; non-markets and alternative markets 13; obligations embedded in 32; *see also* community social relations; family social relations
social responsibility(ies) 28, 31
social rights 28, 30, 31, 35, 76, 157
social solidarity 10, 150, 156, 157

social status 31, 47, 127, 128, 129, 149, 158
social supports 3, 46, 49
social welfare 27, 30, 143, 144, 150, 157
social wellbeing 26, 33, 116, 136, 150, 158, 162
socialism 28, 75–6, 82, 155, 158
social-economic citizen 157–9, 163
"society of the market" 154
socio-emotional skills *see* non-cognitive skills
solidarity 5, 32, 102, 105, 110, 126, 129, 136, 140, 144, 145, 150, 153, 154; *see also* responsible solidarity; social solidarity
South Africa 12, 29, 50–1, 116
Staeheli, L. 29, 36
state(s): affiliation to 31; regulation, political participation 33; relationship between individuals and 27; rights granted by 29
state citizenship 36
Steiner-Khamsi, G. 60
strategic development investment: education as a 26
structure and agency 57
students: character assessments 78; ESS model and marketization of 96–100; quality of pass rates 83–4
sub-Saharan Africa: citizenship and citizenship education 35; dependency 116–17; entrepreneurship education and training 23, 114; governing and economic relations 13; governmentality 12; growth rate 6; informal economy 86; neo/liberal thinking and practices 27; obligations embedded in social relations 32; postcolonial citizenship 159; pressure to education young people 4; rights 37; youth participation 35–6
subsistence agriculture 1, 118, 119
Sustainable Development Goals (SDGs) 24, 25, 52n5, 161, 162
sustainable economic growth 3, 46

tajiri 119
Tanzania: education 1, 2, 5–8, 29–30; empowerment in development discourses 34–5; entrepreneurship 41; failure of technical and vocational training 42; governing regimes 74–88; growth rate 6; job creation 6, 43–6; moral economy 13; need for wider definition of culture 27; neo/liberal discourses in governance 26–7; poverty 6; poverty reduction strategy 3, 7; youth employment 6–7
Tanzania, entrepreneurship education and training: approaches 43–53; convergences and contradictions 5; encounter between neo/liberal and local discourses 5, 153; importance in education and youth policies 7; neo/liberalisms and frictions with local governing and a moral economy 12–13; NGO programs *see Apprentice*; *Parka*; political and social contexts shaping 5; in situ 13–17
teachers (ESS) 98, 103, 105, 106, 108–9
technical knowledge 80, 101
technical skills 30, 42, 59, 78, 119, 123, 160–1
technical trades 62, 120; *see also* carpentry; masonry; mechanics; welding
technologies of power 9, 10, 23, 113, 135, 156
technologies of the self 9, 10, 23–4, 83, 113, 135, 156
Tikly, L. 12, 25
trade experts (*Apprentice*) 121, 122, 125
traditional political structures: participation in 36
trainers (*Apprentice*) 130, 139
training: others 129, 148; *see also* entrepreneurship education and training
transition: from school to work 85–6; to adulthood 128
travelling reforms 60
Tripp, A.M. 13, 41, 86, 113, 115
trust 13, 127, 140, 145, 147
Tsing, A.L. 4, 57, 88

Uganda 63, 81
Ujamaa 5, 18n8, 74–6, 88, 96, 131n7, 157, 158
ujasiriamali 87, 88, 155
uneducated citizens 30, 31
unemployed population 85
unemployment: high 6, 7, 44, 159; *see also* youth unemployment
UNESCO 25, 42–3, 43, 45
United Nations 24–5, 26
United States 9, 30, 43–4, 86
Universal Declaration of Human rights (UDHR) 24
universal literacy 77

universal primary education 83
universal rights 29, 31
USAID 43, 44, 46, 47, 48, 49, 51, 53n11
Usawa 61–2, 95, 96, 97, 98, 104, 105, 106, 107, 108, 109, 110
utu 75

Valerio, A. 7, 42, 46
Vally, S. 113
value chains: support for 86; *see also* global value chains
value-added enterprises 45, 98, 128
value(d): Apprentice and being 127–9
values: African 75; citizenship education 32; communitarian 32, 33; cultural 83; and engagement with education 36; entrepreneurship education 42; ESR attempt to change colonial 77–8; ESS model 105; individual 33; local 27, 64; national 28; neoliberal policies and 29
Van Rooyen, C. 137, 138
Vavrus, F. 34–5, 56–7, 71
village saving and lending associations (VSLAs) 138, 151n6
villagization 76
Vocation and Education Training (VET) institutes 118
Vocational Education and Training Authority (VETA) 3, 104; certificates 84, 120; courses 62; curricula 95, 97
vocational and technical education: capability approach 50–1; deemed a failure 42; entrepreneurship education in *see Apprentice*; *Parka*; participation in 84; preparation for entrepreneurship 82; reemergence in global development agendas 42
vocationalization 79–80, 93, 103
vulnerable groups: entrepreneurship education 46–7

Wainaina, P.K. 28
welfare: capability approach to improving 49; in context of labor surplus 116; demand for education and skills training 119; reform 9; *see also* economic welfare; social welfare
wellbeing: apprentice relationships 122–3; capability approach 156–7; empowerment linked to 35; entrepreneurship for 48–51, 116; reframing of entrepreneurship education and training 160–1; responsibilization and 150; savings and loans and 150; *see also* economic wellbeing; financial wellbeing; social wellbeing
women: *Apprentice* and greater change in skills, knowledge and attitudes 122; employment 7; empowerment 34, 35, 137; enrollment, VET institutes 118; percentage responsible for school fees 148; young women: financial knowledge 141; young women involvement in merry-go-rounds 146; *see also* gender
work membership 114, 116, 129, 156
World Bank: acknowledgement of job creation through microenterprises 46; commitment to equity and economic growth 26; education strategy 25, 26, 44; emphasis on job creation and training 7; entrepreneurship education and training 43, 45–6, 47; on financial literacy 135; funding 80, 83; neoliberal policies 26; recognition of complicated employment environment 48; skills agenda 42; Youth Employment Inventory 53n13
World Economic Forum 44

youth: citizenship 32, 35; common outcomes of financial education, connecting to financial services 135; empowerment 34, 155; engagement in social change 36; entrepreneurial 24, 45; entrepreneurship education *see* entrepreneurship education and training; exclusion from social and economic life 114; FSPs and higher interest rates for 134; informal employment 85; peer support 129; perceived as idle 124, 127, 129; percentage of employable population 85; pressure to educate 4; responsibilization 24, 30, 114, 120, 130, 141; social policies directed at 50; transition from school to work 85–6; UN definition 18n10; *see also* at-risk youth; marginalized youth; students
Youth Development Fund 144
youth employment: entrepreneurship programs as important for 27; initiatives to address 82; Tanzania 6–7
Youth Employment Inventory (World Bank) 53n13

youth livelihood(s): capability approach 49; programs/projects 47, 53n11; varying understandings of entrepreneurship education and training 4
Youth Livelihood Guide (USAID) 48
youth participation 33, 35–6; in business clubs 101–2; community enterprise apprenticeships 119–20; democratic 48; in project management 48; social status and 158; youth organizations 36

youth population: bank credit 139; growth in global 6; and interest in entrepreneurship education 41
youth unemployment: and entrepreneurship education 3, 41–2; global 6; persistence since early 2000s 7; Tanzania 85
Yunus, M. 137

Zambia 116

Helping you to choose the right eBooks for your Library

Add Routledge titles to your library's digital collection today. Taylor and Francis ebooks contains over 50,000 titles in the Humanities, Social Sciences, Behavioural Sciences, Built Environment and Law.

Choose from a range of subject packages or create your own!

Benefits for you

» Free MARC records
» COUNTER-compliant usage statistics
» Flexible purchase and pricing options
» All titles DRM-free.

Benefits for your user

» Off-site, anytime access via Athens or referring URL
» Print or copy pages or chapters
» Full content search
» Bookmark, highlight and annotate text
» Access to thousands of pages of quality research at the click of a button.

 Free Trials Available
We offer free trials to qualifying academic, corporate and government customers.

eCollections – Choose from over 30 subject eCollections, including:

Archaeology	Language Learning
Architecture	Law
Asian Studies	Literature
Business & Management	Media & Communication
Classical Studies	Middle East Studies
Construction	Music
Creative & Media Arts	Philosophy
Criminology & Criminal Justice	Planning
Economics	Politics
Education	Psychology & Mental Health
Energy	Religion
Engineering	Security
English Language & Linguistics	Social Work
Environment & Sustainability	Sociology
Geography	Sport
Health Studies	Theatre & Performance
History	Tourism, Hospitality & Events

For more information, pricing enquiries or to order a free trial, please contact your local sales team: **www.tandfebooks.com/page/sales**

 The home of Routledge books

www.tandfebooks.com